Faye Levy's

SENSATIONAL
CHOCOLATE

HPBooks
a division of
PRICE STERN SLOAN
Los Angeles

Published by HPBooks
a division of Price Stern Sloan, Inc.
11150 Olympic Boulevard
Suite 650
Los Angeles, California 90064

©1986, 1992 HPBooks
Revised Edition
ISBN # 1-55788-049-2

Printed in the United States of America

10 9 8 7 6 5 4 3 2 1

Photography: deGennaro Associates
Food Stylist: Mable Hoffman; Assistant Stylist: Susan Brown Draudt
Cover photo: Chocolate Brazil-Nut Cake, page 9;
Double-Dipped Strawberries, page 150; and assorted chocolate truffles, pages 140-146

Contents

Introduction viii

Light Cakes, Butter Cakes
   & Fudge Cakes x

Layer Cakes, Tortes
   & Mousse Cakes......................19

Pies & Pastries 40

Soufflés, Baked Custards,
   Puddings & Crepes 61

Mousses, Bavarian Creams
   & Charlottes...........................78

Ice Creams, Frozen Desserts
   & Ice Cream Cakes..................97

Cookies, Brownies
   & Petits Fours 117

Truffles, Candies & Drinks.........138

Frostings, Sauces & Basics 157

Mail-Order Sources 179

Index 180

Top: Checkerboard Cake, page 21; Middle: Cold Chocolate-Raspberry Soufflé, page 87; Bottom: Chocolate-Strawberry Bombe, page 108

FAYE LEVY

Award-winning author Faye Levy was born and brought up in Washington, D.C., has lived on three continents and has written cookbooks in three languages—English, French and Hebrew. In 1986 two of Faye's books won distinguished awards: Faye Levy's *Chocolate Sensations* was voted the Best Dessert and Baking Book of the Year by the International Association of Cooking Professionals/Seagram Awards; and *Classic Cooking Techniques* won as the best Basic/General Cookbook. Faye is the author of the best selling *Sensational Pasta* (HPBooks), the *Fresh From France* cookbook series (Dutton) and *Faye Levy's International Cookbook* series (Warner).

Faye is one of this country's top culinary columnists. She wrote The Basics column for *Bon Appétit* magazine for six years and has been a nationally syndicated columnist of the Los Angeles Times for the last two years. Her creative dishes have been featured on the covers of *Bon Appétit* and *Gourmet* and in *Chocolatier*, *Cook's* and *Western Chef* magazines.

Faye holds the Grand Diplôme of the first graduating class of the Parisian cooking school La Varenne, where she spent over five years studying cooking and working as the cookbook editor. She also studied dessert-making at Lenôtre's school for professional chefs near Paris.

Faye specializes in teaching the basics of fine cuisine and dessert making. Her students like her easy-to-follow recipes and emphasis on the pleasure of cooking. She lives in Santa Monica, California, with her husband/associate Yakir Levy.

ACKNOWLEDGEMENTS

I want to express my deep gratitude to Veronica Durie, my editor, for originating the idea of my chocolate book. I am grateful to Jeanette Egan, Laura Gates, Wendy Pratt and Beth Bender for their important contributions to Sensational Chocolate.

For five years my beloved teachers and associates at La Varenne Cooking School in Paris—Anne Willan, Master chefs Fernand Chambrette, Albert Jorant and Claude Vauguet—and Denis Ruffel of the wonderful Parisian Pâtisserie Millet, shared with me their vast knowledge of the art of dessert making, and I am truly thankful to them.

My sincere thanks to Leona Fitzgerald, Annie Horenn, Teri Appleton and Patsy Allen for their help in recipe testing. Thanks also to the photographers of deGennaro Associates—Tommy Miyasaki, Dennis Skinner and David Wong-and to food stylists Mable Hoffman and Susan Brown Draudt. Finally, a big thank-you to Yakir Levy for helping to plan and write the book.

Shown on the following pages is an array of sensational chocolate desserts, beginning with top row: Mocha Petits Pots de Crème, page 67; Bittersweet Belgian Truffles, page 141. Middle row: Triple Chocolate Mousse Parfaits, page 84; Chocolate Symphony, page 36; Chocolate-Coconut Chiffon Cake, page 6; Chocolate-Apricot Terrine, page 86. Front row: Chocolate-Dipped Orange Sections, page 151; Sultan's Cream Puffs, page 50; Meringue Mushrooms, page 128; Rigo Jancsi, page 30; Chocolate-Marble Chiffon Pie, page 48.

Chocolate's popularity is at an all-time high. For many people, dessert means "chocolate." Although chocolate desserts have long played a central part in the celebration of happy events, this role has been greatly expanded. Chocolate cakes star not only at children's parties but also as wedding cakes and on the dessert tables of the most elegant of restaurants.

Across the country cooking teachers are giving more and more classes on the preparation of exquisite chocolate desserts. Chocolate desserts are favorites among readers of national food-oriented magazines. Now a wider variety of brands and types of chocolate is available not only in specialty stores but also in progressive supermarkets. Chocolate exhibitions, chocolate shows, chocolate contests and other chocolate events take place on a regular basis in cities throughout the country. In a major story, "Chocolate, Food of the Gods," *National Geographic* pointed out that it has become a multibillion-dollar industry.

With the abundance of fine chocolates on the market, many of which are imported from Europe, we are developing a taste for top quality chocolate and an appreciation of refined chocolate desserts. We are getting away from frostings containing a large percentage of powdered sugar and favor those that give more emphasis to the flavor of pure chocolate.

A passionate fondness for chocolate has become so pervasive in America that a special word has been coined for chocolate aficionados—"chocoholics." Many people who would not go so far as to identify themselves as "addicted" to chocolate do pride themselves in being chocolate connoisseurs.

Moist brownies, chocolate layer cakes and chocolate chip cookies have been favorite sweet treats in this country for years. Lately we have witnessed a renewed interest in these traditional American delicacies and in new creative versions of them, along with a growing popularity of all types of European chocolate desserts: delicious Italian gelatos and French parfaits, light cakes with luscious frostings, cream puffs, crisp cookies and buttery pastries, rich mousses and charlottes served with smooth custard sauces, Bavarian creams and airy soufflés. The large numbers of Americans who have traveled to Europe have contributed significantly to this phenomenon.

Introduction

In spite of the general enthusiasm for chocolate, in many areas it is difficult to purchase fine chocolate cakes and desserts. Chocolate desserts designed for adults, such as truffles flavored with brandy or liqueur, cannot even be purchased in most states. The best way to enjoy the greatest variety of desserts of excellent quality is to make them at home. Preparing desserts provides pleasure and enables us to control their contents so they are fresh, natural and free of preservatives.

The emphasis of this book is practical. In developing the recipes, taste is my primary concern. Presentation of desserts is simple, quick and attractive.

What is Chocolate

Like coffee and wine, chocolate is complex. Its taste is affected by the quality of the cocoa beans, by how much they are roasted, and by the way in which the various steps in the production of chocolate are carried out. All these factors make possible a great variety of chocolates of different degrees of chocolate flavor and color.

Chocolate is made from beans that grow in pods on the cacao tree in Central and South America and in Africa. The beans are roasted and ground to a thick paste, which is essentially unsweetened chocolate. It contains chocolate solids and cocoa butter. Sugar is added in varying amounts to produce semisweet and bittersweet chocolate. Extra cocoa butter can be added to make extra-rich chocolate. To make cocoa, the chocolate is dried and a portion of the cocoa butter is removed.

Types of Chocolate

Bittersweet, extra-bittersweet and semisweet chocolates are quite similar for the purpose of dessert making and can usually be interchanged in recipes. Generally semisweet is the sweetest of the three, bittersweet is next and extra-bittersweet is the most bitter, as their names suggest. One manufacturer's bittersweet is sometimes sweeter than another's semisweet; however, while some manufacturers have several types of semisweet or bittersweet chocolates which differ from each other in their fluidity or in how much the cocoa bean is roasted. Fine chocolate is often sold in bars as "eating chocolate" and is good for cooking as well. Sometimes it is sold in the candy section of the supermarket instead of in the baking ingredients section. A great variety of brands of fine chocolate can be purchased at gourmet shops and by mail order. (For addresses see page 179.)

Unsweetened chocolate contains no sugar and is used in recipes in combination with sweet ingredients.

Milk chocolate is a sweet chocolate containing milk powder.

White chocolate also contains milk powder and sugar, like milk chocolate. It does not contain chocolate solids and is not officially considered "chocolate" in America (although it is in Europe) and here is labeled "coating." Be sure to use fine quality real white chocolate and not to confuse it with "fake" coatings. You can tell them apart by reading the ingredients on the label; "real" white chocolate should have cocoa butter, not palm oil or vegetable shortening, as an ingredient. Often the white chocolate sold in bulk is "real."

Couverture, sometimes called "coating chocolate," is the finest chocolate, with the highest cocoa butter content. Couverture is available by mail order and in specialty food shops as bittersweet, semisweet, white and milk chocolate. It is ideal for dipping because it is very fluid when melted and can be used to flavor desserts as well, whenever you would like to use the best quality chocolate. Some types of chocolate from Europe are labeled "fondant chocolate" and are good quality chocolates but are not as rich in cocoa butter as couverture. Do not confuse couverture with "confectionary coating," which has been treated so it melts easily and does not have the same good taste as true chocolate.

Chocolate pieces, or chocolate chips, are available as semisweet, bittersweet, milk and white chocolate and as regular-sized, mini or maxi pieces. These started out as semisweet pieces for making chocolate chip cookies but now a greater variety is available. The mini chips are good for garnish because of their tiny size. The maxi are best for cookies. Chocolate pieces can be melted but they are designed to hold their shape and are not quite as rich in cocoa butter as plain chocolate. It is therefore best to reserve them for desserts in which you want them to be in pieces.

Unsweetened cocoa is the best type to use for making fine desserts, rather than sweetened cocoa.

Dutch-process cocoa, or cocoa processed with alkali, is a type of unsweetened cocoa. It is generally darker and a bit less bitter than regular cocoa and is preferred by many cooks. When it is important for a recipe, the ingredients specify "Dutch-process."

As a chocolate treat for brunch or teatime or for a finale to an elegant meal, one of these cakes would be perfect. Tall, tender Chocolate-Coconut Chiffon Cake or rich Chocolate-Brazil Nut Cake is ideal for a party, while the light Chocolate Crown makes an enticing dessert after any dinner.

These chocolate cakes are relatively easy and quick to make since they do not require filling or splitting into layers. Most of the cakes can stand unadorned; others require only a simple frosting or sauce.

Whipped cream, whether plain, as sweetened Chantilly Cream, or flavored with liqueurs or chocolate, is the most wonderful accompaniment for light cakes and fudge cakes. It plays a double role, as a rich complement for light cakes and a light-textured partner for fudge cakes. Use it as a frosting, serve it on the side, or pipe it inside a ring-shaped cake the Chocolate Crown.

Frosted cakes, especially those with whipped cream, are best served cold. If a cake is served plain, it tastes better at room temperature.

Light Cakes,
Butter Cakes
&
Fudge Cakes

Light Cakes

Light cakes include cakes made with little or no butter, such as sponge cakes and chiffon cakes. A relatively high proportion of egg whites makes them light.

Many of these cakes, especially those made in the style of eastern Europe, are nut based. The rich nuts help prevent the nut cakes from drying out. Only a small amount of flour, cornstarch or potato starch is added to give these cakes a little extra body so they won't collapse. A variety of nuts are used, from almonds in Chocolate Cake à l'Orientale to macadamias in Hawaiian Chocolate-Flecked Nut Cake.

Butter Cakes

Loaf cakes and coffeecakes enriched with butter have long been favorites throughout Europe and America. Often they are made from a white batter studded with bits of chocolate so the buttery taste of the cake is noticeable. In some cases melted chocolate is blended with the batter to give a rich result approaching a fudge cake.

Many of these cakes make good gifts because they keep well. What makes them stay moist and fresh-tasting so long is a high proportion of nuts, butter, liqueur or some combination of these. Their richness makes frosting unnecessary and so they are easy to transport.

Fudge Cakes

Fudge cakes are becoming more American than apple pie. They contain generous amounts of chocolate and often of butter as well. This makes them the richest and usually the densest of cakes. They can contain ground nuts, as in the Queen of Sheba Cake and Chocolate-Hazelnut Cake with Fudge Frosting, or they can be made without any flour.

Hawaiian Chocolate-Flecked Macadamia Nut Cake

Hawaii, the world's major supplier of macadamia nuts, inspired the name of this cake. The finely chopped chocolate in the batter harmonizes with the fine flavor of the nuts but does not overpower them. Macadamia nut liqueur, also a product of Hawaii, moistens the cake and flavors the light chocolate frosting.

2-1/3 cups macadamia nuts (about 10 oz.), preferably unsalted

10 whole macadamia nuts, preferably unsalted (for garnish)

5 oz. semisweet chocolate, coarsely chopped

3/4 cup sugar

1/4 cup all-purpose flour

1/2 teaspoon baking powder

5 large eggs, separated

1/4 teaspoon cream of tartar

Chocolate & Macadamia Liqueur Whipped Cream, page 163

2 tablespoons macadamia nut or hazelnut liqueur (for moistening)

Chocolate Leaves, page 177, or Cutouts, page 175, if desired (for garnish)

If using salted nuts, desalt those for cake and for garnish, page 178. Set aside 10 nuts for garnish. Position rack in center of oven and preheat to 325F (165C). Lightly butter a 9-inch springform pan. Line base with parchment paper or foil. Butter paper or foil and flour lined pan.

Finely chop chocolate in a food processor. Transfer to a large bowl. Grind 1 cup nuts with 3 tablespoons sugar in processor to a fine powder. Add to chocolate. Repeat with remaining 1-1/3 cups nuts and 3 more tablespoons sugar. Sift flour and baking powder over nut mixture. Stir with a fork.

Beat egg yolks in a large bowl. Beat in 1/4 cup sugar. Beat at high speed about 5 minutes or until mixture is pale and very thick.

In a large dry bowl, beat egg whites with cream of tartar to soft peaks. Gradually beat in remaining 2 tablespoons sugar. Beat at high speed until whites are stiff and shiny but not dry.

Sprinkle about 1/3 of nut mixture over yolk mixture and fold in gently. Fold in about 1/3 of whites. Lightly but quickly fold in remaining nut mixture and whites in 2 batches, just until batter is blended.

Spread batter in prepared pan. Bake about 55 minutes or until a cake tester inserted in cake's center comes out clean. Cool in pan on a rack 10 minutes. Run a metal spatula carefully around cake. Invert cake onto a rack. Release spring and remove side and base of pan. Carefully peel off paper; cool cake. Turn cake onto another rack, then onto a platter so cake's smooth side faces up. *Cake can be prepared 2 days ahead and kept, wrapped, at room temperature.*

Prepare chocolate whipped cream. With a pastry brush, dab top and side of cake evenly with liqueur. Spread chocolate cream evenly over cake; smooth side and top. Garnish with whole nuts and Chocolate Leaves or Cutouts. Refrigerate at least 1 hour before serving. *Frosted cake can be kept, covered with a cake cover or large bowl, 1 day in refrigerator.*

Makes 10 to 12 servings

Chocolate Cake à l'Orientale

Candied ginger, oranges and almonds give this cake an Oriental touch, in keeping with today's fashion of incorporating the exciting tastes of the Orient into Western desserts. The cake is lighter than a butter cake, yet richer and moister than a sponge cake. For an elegant garnish, set Chocolate-Dipped Orange Sections, page 151, on the whipped cream-frosted cake.

Chocolate-Almond-Ginger Cake:

3 oz. semisweet chocolate, chopped

2 tablespoons strained fresh orange juice

1/4 cup unsalted butter, cut in 4 pieces

1/2 cup whole blanched almonds (about 2-1/4 oz.)

1/2 cup plus 1 tablespoon sugar

1/3 cup very finely chopped crystallized ginger (about 1-1/2 oz.)

2 tablespoons all-purpose flour

2 tablespoons cornstarch

3 large eggs, separated

1 tablespoon grated orange zest

1/4 teaspoon cream of tartar

Whipped Cream:

3/4 cup whipping cream, well-chilled

1-1/2 teaspoons sugar

Cake: Position rack in center of oven and preheat to 350F (175C). Lightly butter a round 9-inch layer cake pan. Line base with parchment paper or foil; lightly butter paper or foil. Melt chocolate with orange juice and butter in a medium bowl over nearly simmering water. Stir until smooth. Remove from pan of water; let cool. Grind almonds with 3 tablespoons sugar in a food processor to a fine powder. Transfer to a medium bowl; add chopped ginger. Sift flour and cornstarch over mixture; mix thoroughly.

Beat egg yolks in a large bowl. Add 1/4 cup sugar and beat at high speed about 5 minutes or until mixture is pale and very thick. Stir in orange zest and chocolate mixture.

In a large dry bowl, beat egg whites with cream of tartar to soft peaks. Gradually beat in remaining 2 tablespoons sugar. Beat at high speed until whites are stiff and shiny but not dry. Gently fold about 1/3 of whites into chocolate mixture until nearly incorporated. Sprinkle about 1/2 of almond mixture over chocolate mixture; fold in gently. Lightly but quickly fold in another 1/3 of whites, then remaining almond mixture, then remaining whites, just until batter is blended.

Transfer batter to prepared pan. Bake about 28 minutes or until a cake tester inserted in center of cake comes out nearly clean. Cool in pan on a rack 5 minutes. Run a metal spatula carefully around cake. Invert cake onto rack. Carefully peel off paper; cool cake completely. Crust is crumbly; some may fall off. Carefully turn cake onto another rack, then onto a platter with crusty side down. Refrigerate cake at least 1 hour before frosting. *Cake can be kept, wrapped, 3 days in refrigerator.*

Whipped Cream: In a large chilled bowl whip cream with sugar until stiff. Using a long metal spatula, spread whipped cream evenly over cake; smooth side and top. Refrigerate at least 1 hour before serving. *Frosted cake can be kept, covered with a cake cover or large bowl, 8 hours in refrigerator.*

Makes 6 to 8 servings

Moist Mocha Squares

Like a soufflé, this dark chocolate- and coffee-flavored cake is light-textured
yet very moist. Although it is good on its own, the easy-to-make coffee sauce of
creamy café-au-lait color dresses it up elegantly.

5 oz. semisweet chocolate, chopped

3 tablespoons water

1 teaspoon instant coffee powder or
freeze-dried coffee granules

1/2 cup plus 2 tablespoons (5 oz.)
unsalted butter, cut in pieces,
room temperature

4 large eggs, separated

1/2 cup plus 2 tablespoons sugar

1/4 teaspoon cream of tartar

5 tablespoons all-purpose flour,
sifted

Quick Coffee Sauce, page 170

Position rack in center of oven and preheat to 325F (165C). Lightly butter an
8-inch-square baking pan. Line base with parchment paper or waxed paper.
Butter paper and flour lined pan. Melt chocolate with water and coffee in small
bowl over nearly simmering water. Stir until smooth. Add butter pieces; stir
until blended. Remove from pan of water; let cool.

Beat egg yolks in a large bowl. Beat in 1/2 cup sugar; whip at high speed about
5 minutes or until mixture is pale and very thick.

In a large dry bowl, beat egg whites with cream of tartar to soft peaks.
Gradually beat in remaining 2 tablespoons sugar. Whip at high speed until
whites are stiff and shiny but not dry.

Gently stir chocolate mixture into yolk mixture with a wooden spoon. Sift
flour over chocolate mixture; fold in gently with a spatula. Gently fold in
whites in 3 batches. Transfer batter to prepared pan. Bake about 40 minutes or
until a cake tester inserted in center of cake comes out clean. Cool cake in pan
on a rack until lukewarm; cake will settle slightly in center. *Cake can be kept,
wrapped, 3 days at room temperature.*

Cut cake in squares while in pan. Serve lukewarm or at room temperature,
with sauce.

Makes 8 to 9 servings

Chocolate-Pecan Gâteau

A variety of cuisines leave their mark on this impressive dessert: Native American pecans add richness to the light-textured, Austrian-style chocolate sponge cake. The cake is topped by a luscious French chocolate buttercream that gains its smoothness from Italian meringue.

---

2 oz. semisweet chocolate, coarsely chopped

2/3 cup pecan halves (about 2 oz.)

3/4 cup plus 2 tablespoons sugar

3/4 cup plus 2 tablespoons cake flour

3 tablespoons unsweetened cocoa powder

1 teaspoon baking powder

6 large eggs, separated

3 tablespoons rum

1/2 teaspoon cream of tartar

1/2 cup (4 oz.) unsalted butter, melted and cooled

Chocolate Meringue Buttercream, page 161

10 to 12 pecan halves (for garnish)

Position rack in center of oven and preheat to 350F (175C). Lightly butter a 9-inch springform pan and line its base with parchment paper or foil. Butter paper or foil and flour lined pan. Grind chocolate in a food processor to a fine powder; transfer to a medium bowl. Grind 2/3 cup pecans with 2 tablespoons sugar in processor to a fine powder; add to chocolate. Sift flour, cocoa and baking powder over nut mixture; stir gently until blended.

Beat egg yolks in a large bowl. Beat in 1/2 cup sugar; whip at high speed about 5 minutes or until mixture is pale and very thick. Beat in 1 tablespoon rum.

In a large dry bowl, beat egg whites with cream of tartar to soft peaks. Gradually beat in remaining 1/4 cup sugar. Beat at high speed until whites are stiff and shiny but not dry.

Sprinkle about 1/3 of nut mixture over yolk mixture; fold gently until nearly incorporated. Lightly fold in 1/3 of whites. Fold in remaining nut mixture and whites in 2 batches. When batter is nearly blended, gradually pour in melted butter while folding. Fold quickly just until batter is blended.

Spread batter evenly in prepared pan. Bake about 40 minutes or until a cake tester inserted in center of cake comes out clean. Cool in pan on a rack 5 minutes. Run a metal spatula carefully around cake. Invert cake onto rack. Release spring and remove side and base of pan. Carefully peel off paper; cool cake completely. Turn cake onto another rack, then onto a platter so smooth side of cake faces up. *Cake can be kept, wrapped, 3 days in refrigerator.*

Prepare buttercream. Set aside 3/4 cup buttercream for garnish. With a pastry brush, dab top and side of cake evenly with remaining rum. Using a long metal spatula, spread remaining buttercream evenly over cake; smooth side and top. Using a pastry bag and medium star tip, pipe a ruffle of reserved buttercream along top edge of cake. Arrange 10 to 12 pecan halves in circle on cake. Refrigerate cake about 2 hours or until buttercream is firm. *Frosted cake can be kept, covered with a cake cover or large bowl, 2 days in refrigerator.* Serve at room temperature.

Makes 10 to 12 servings

Variation

Omit buttercream. Serve slices of unfrosted cake with Vanilla Bean Custard Sauce, page 169.

Chocolate Crown

This beautiful bittersweet ring-shaped cake of deep chocolate color and flavor has a dark shiny glaze, encircling a snowy white mound of Chantilly Cream.

Chocolate Butter Sponge Cake:

5 oz. semisweet chocolate, chopped

3 tablespoons unsalted butter, cut in 3 pieces

5 tablespoons all-purpose flour

1/2 teaspoon baking powder

3 large eggs, separated

1/3 cup sugar

1 teaspoon pure vanilla extract

1/4 teaspoon cream of tartar

Chocolate Glaze:

5 oz. semisweet chocolate, chopped

2 tablespoons unsalted butter, cut in 2 pieces

2 tablespoons water

1 teaspoon pure vanilla extract

Chantilly Cream, page 162

Cake: Position rack in center of oven and preheat to 350F (175C). Generously butter a 5-cup ring mold. Melt chocolate with butter in a small bowl over nearly simmering water. Stir until smooth. Remove from pan of water; let cool. Sift flour and baking powder into a small bowl.

Beat egg yolks in a large bowl. Add 3 tablespoons sugar and beat at high speed about 5 minutes or until mixture is pale and very thick. Beat in vanilla. Stir in chocolate mixture.

In a large dry bowl, beat egg whites with cream of tartar to soft peaks. Gradually beat in remaining 2-1/3 tablespoons sugar. Beat at high speed until whites are stiff and shiny but not dry. Gently fold about 1/3 of whites into chocolate mixture until nearly incorporated. Sprinkle about 1/2 of flour mixture over chocolate mixture; fold in lightly. Fold in another 1/3 of whites, then remaining flour mixture, then remaining whites. Fold just until blended.

Spread batter in prepared mold. Bake about 17 minutes or until a cake tester inserted in cake comes out clean. Cool cake in mold on a rack about 30 minutes; cake will settle slightly. Run a metal spatula carefully around outer edge of cake. Run a thin-bladed flexible knife around center. Invert cake onto a platter; cool completely. *Cake can be kept, covered with plastic wrap or foil, 1 day at room temperature.*

Glaze: Melt chocolate with butter and water in a small bowl over nearly simmering water. Stir until smooth. Remove from water. Stir in vanilla. Spoon glaze slowly over cooled cake, letting it trickle down inner and outer sides of cake. Wipe platter clean.

Serve cake within 30 minutes if soft glaze is desired; cool at room temperature 1-1/2 hours for firmer glaze. In cool weather keep cake at room temperature so glaze will be shiny. Refrigerate cake if weather is hot. *Glazed cake can be kept, covered with a cake cover or large bowl, 8 hours at cool room temperature or 1 day in refrigerator.*

Prepare Chantilly Cream just before serving. Using a pastry bag and medium star tip, pipe cream into center of cake in a dome shape. Pipe decorative lines or swirls of whipped cream on top of dome. Serve as soon as possible.

Makes 8 to 10 servings

Chocolate-Coconut Chiffon Cake

Incredibly tender, moist and rich, this tall, dark dramatic cake topped with generous
swirls of creamy, chocolaty frosting is an ideal party dessert. The cake uses
unsweetened coconut, which can be purchased at specialty markets or health-food stores.
If only coarsely shredded or flaked coconut is available, grind it first in a food processor.

Photo on pages vi-vii.

---

3 oz. semisweet chocolate, chopped

2 oz. unsweetened chocolate, chopped

2 cups cake flour

1 teaspoon salt

1 tablespoon baking powder

1-1/2 cups sugar

6 large egg yolks

1/2 cup vegetable oil

3/4 cup cold tap water

8 large egg whites

1/2 teaspoon cream of tartar

1 cup finely grated dried unsweetened coconut (about 3-1/4 oz.)

Chocolate Velvet Frosting, page 159

2 tablespoons finely grated dried unsweetened coconut (for garnish)

Position rack in center of oven and preheat to 325F (165C). Have ready a 10"
x 4" tube pan with removable tube; do not butter it. *Do not use a nonstick pan.*
Combine chocolates in a medium bowl and melt them over nearly simmering
water. Stir until smooth. Remove from water; let cool. Sift flour, salt and baking
powder into a large bowl. Add 1 cup sugar; stir until blended. In another bowl
combine egg yolks, oil and water; beat until smooth.

Make a large well in bowl of dry ingredients; pour in yolk mixture. Gently stir
dry ingredients into yolk mixture using a wooden spoon. Add melted chocolate, stirring gently just until there are no lumps.

In a large dry bowl, beat egg whites with cream of tartar to soft peaks.
Gradually beat in remaining 1/2 cup sugar. Beat at high speed until whites are
stiff and shiny but not dry. Fold about 1/4 of whites into chocolate mixture
until nearly blended. Gently fold chocolate mixture into remaining whites.
When nearly blended, sprinkle 1 cup coconut over mixture and fold in lightly.

Transfer batter to prepared pan. Bake about 1 hour 10 minutes or until a cake
tester inserted in cake comes out clean. Invert pan on its "feet" or on heatproof
funnel or bottle; let stand until completely cool, about 1-1/2 hours. Run a
metal spatula gently around side of cake. Push up tube to remove side of pan.
Run a thin-bladed knife around tube. Run metal spatula carefully under cake
to free it from base; turn out carefully onto a platter. *Cake can be kept, wrapped,
2 days at room temperature.*

Prepare frosting. Gently brush any crumbs off top of cake. Using a long metal
spatula, spread frosting evenly and generously on side, top and inner surface of
cake. Swirl top. Lightly sprinkle top outer edge of cake with 2 tablespoons
coconut. Refrigerate at least 1 hour before serving. *Frosted cake can be kept, covered with a tall cake cover, 3 days in refrigerator.*

Makes 14 to 16 servings

Marbled Chocolate Coffeecake

Crowned by a shiny chocolate glaze, this Bundt cake is enriched with
sour cream and swirled with chocolate.

1-3/4 cups all-purpose flour

1 teaspoon baking powder

1/2 teaspoon baking soda

1/2 pint dairy sour cream (1 cup)

1 teaspoon pure vanilla extract

1 tablespoon unsweetened
    cocoa powder, sifted

3 oz. semisweet chocolate,
    finely grated

1/2 cup (4 oz.) unsalted butter,
    slightly softened

3/4 cup sugar

3 large eggs

Chocolate Glaze, page 160

Position rack in center of oven and preheat to 350F (175C). Generously butter a 9-1/2" x 4" fluted tube pan or Bundt pan, taking care to butter tube and each fluted section. Sift flour, baking powder and baking soda into a large bowl. In a medium bowl mix sour cream and vanilla. In a small bowl gently mix cocoa and chocolate with a fork.

Cream butter in a medium bowl. Add sugar and beat until smooth and fluffy. Add eggs, 1 at a time, beating well after each addition. Gently stir in about 1/2 of flour mixture, then 1/2 of sour-cream mixture, then remaining flour, last remaining sour-cream mixture, until no trace of flour remains. Do not beat.

Transfer 2 cups batter to a medium bowl. Gently stir in chocolate mixture. Spread 1 cup white batter in prepared pan. Pour chocolate batter into pan, then pour remaining white batter on top. Swirl a knife gently through batter to give a marbled effect.

Bake about 50 to 55 minutes or until a cake tester inserted in cake comes out clean. Cool in pan on a rack 10 minutes. Run a thin-bladed knife around tube but not around side of pan. Invert cake onto rack; cool completely. Transfer to a platter. *Cake can be kept, wrapped, 2 days at room temperature.*

Spoon glaze slowly over cake, letting it trickle down grooves on cake's side. Serve cake within 30 minutes for soft glaze; cool at room temperature 1-1/2 hours for firmer glaze. Keep cake in refrigerator if weather is hot. If weather is cool, keep it at room temperature for shinier glaze. *Glazed cake can be kept, covered with a cake cover or large bowl, 8 hours at cool room temperature or 1 day in refrigerator.* Serve at room temperature.

Makes 8 to 10 servings

Variation

Omit glaze and sprinkle cake with sifted powdered sugar before serving.

Chocolate-Studded Kugelhopf

Travelers to Austria, Germany and Alsace will find the traditional kugelhopf everywhere.
This extra-buttery version of the coffeecake has a new twist—milk chocolate chips
are added to the customary raisins and almonds. The golden cake is made from
an easy, yeast-leavened dough and is baked in a fluted tube pan.
Serve it at teatime or for brunch.

1/2 cup dark raisins

2 tablespoons kirsch

1 cup milk

2 (1/4-oz.) pkgs. active dry yeast (about 2 tablespoons)

2/3 cup sugar

3-1/2 cups all-purpose flour

1-1/2 teaspoons salt

3 large eggs

1 cup (8 oz.) unsalted butter, cut in 16 pieces, room temperature

16 to 18 whole blanched almonds

1 (12-oz.) pkg. milk chocolate pieces (2 cups)

Powdered sugar

Put raisins in a small jar or bowl and add kirsch. Cover tightly; shake to mix. Let soak at least 4 hours or overnight in refrigerator.

Heat milk to warm (110F, 45C) in a small saucepan. Pour 1/2 cup warm milk into a small bowl; sprinkle with yeast and 1/4 teaspoon sugar. Let stand 10 minutes or until foamy. Put 1/2 cup flour in a medium bowl. Add yeast mixture and 1/4 cup milk; stir to combine. A few lumps may remain. Cover with slightly damp towel or plastic wrap; let stand about 15 minutes.

Spoon remaining 3 cups flour into mixer bowl; make a well in center of flour. Add salt, remaining sugar and remaining 1/4 cup milk. Using a wooden spoon, mix ingredients in well briefly. Add eggs and 8 butter pieces to well. Using dough hook mix at low speed, scraping bowl occasionally, until dough is smooth. Gradually beat in remaining butter pieces, followed by yeast mixture. Beat on medium speed until dough is very smooth, 10 to 12 minutes. Cover and set in a warm draft-free place 30 minutes or until dough begins to rise but does not double in bulk.

Generously butter a 9-1/2" x 4" kugelhopf mold, fluted tube pan or Bundt pan, taking care to butter tube and each ridge. Put 1 almond in base of each ridge. Stir chocolate, raisins and kirsch into risen batter. Carefully transfer batter to pan, without moving almonds. Smooth top. Cover and let rise in a warm draft-free place 40 minutes.

Position rack in center of oven and preheat to 400F (205C). Uncover dough and let rise about 20 minutes or until it nearly reaches top of pan. Bake kugelhopf 10 minutes. Reduce oven temperature to 350F (175C); bake about 45 minutes longer or until a cake tester inserted in kugelhopf comes out clean. If kugelhopf browns enough on top before it is done, cover it with foil.

Cool in pan on a rack about 10 minutes. Invert cake onto rack; cool completely. *Cake can be kept, wrapped, 2 days at room temperature.* Sprinkle with powdered sugar just before serving.

Makes 12 to 16 servings

Variation

If a mixer with a dough hook is not available, mix dough with a wooden spoon. With cupped hand under dough, slap dough against bowl to knead it for 5 minutes or until dough is smooth.

Chocolate-Brazil Nut Cake

In this dark, exotic cake, the distinctive taste of Brazil nuts is complemented by
the equally assertive flavor of chocolate. The crunchiness of the nuts
contrasts with the smooth, honey-accented chocolate-ganache frosting.

Photo on cover.

1-1/2 cups Brazil nuts (about 7 oz.),
   toasted and skinned, page 179

6 oz. semisweet chocolate, chopped

3/4 cup sugar

1/4 cup all-purpose flour

1/2 teaspoon baking powder

3/4 cup (6 oz.) unsalted butter,
   slightly softened

6 large eggs, separated

1/4 teaspoon cream of tartar

Chocolate-Honey Frosting, page 158

About 1/4 cup Brazil nuts, chopped
   (for garnish)

Position rack in center of oven and preheat to 350F (175C). Lightly butter a 9-inch springform pan. Line base with parchment paper or foil. Butter paper or foil and flour lined pan. Melt chocolate in a medium bowl over nearly simmering water. Stir until smooth. Remove from pan of water; let cool. In a food processor, grind toasted nuts with 4 tablespoons sugar in 2 batches to a fine powder. Transfer to a large bowl. Sift flour and baking powder over nut mixture; mix thoroughly.

Cream butter in a large bowl. Add 6 tablespoons sugar and beat until smooth and fluffy. Add egg yolks, 1 at a time, beating thoroughly after each addition. Stir in melted chocolate.

In a large dry bowl, beat egg whites with cream of tartar to soft peaks. Gradually beat in remaining 2 tablespoons sugar. Beat at high speed until whites are stiff and shiny but not dry.

Sprinkle about 1/3 of nut mixture over chocolate mixture; fold gently until nearly incorporated. Lightly fold in about 1/3 of whites. Fold in remaining nut mixture and whites in 2 batches, just until batter is blended.

Spread batter in prepared pan. Bake about 43 minutes or until a cake tester inserted in center of cake comes out clean. Cool in pan on a rack 10 minutes; cake will settle slightly in center. Run a metal spatula carefully around cake. Invert cake onto rack. Release spring and remove side and base of pan. Carefully peel off paper. Invert cake onto another rack; cool completely. Turn cake onto a platter so smooth side of cake faces up. *Cake can be kept, wrapped, 2 days in refrigerator.*

Prepare frosting; set aside about 3 tablespoons for garnish. Using a long metal spatula, spread remaining frosting evenly over cake; smooth side and top. Swirl frosting at top, from edge inward, forming small curves. Using a pastry bag fitted with a small star tip, pipe reserved frosting in a ring of rosettes about halfway between edge and center of cake. Fill center of ring with chopped Brazil nuts. Press gently so they adhere to frosting. Refrigerate at least 1 hour before serving. *Frosted cake can be kept, covered, 3 days in refrigerator.* Serve at room temperature.

Makes 12 servings

Chocolate-Wine Cake

When I took a course in marrying wine and food at the Académie du Vin in Paris, we discussed the difficulty of matching wine with chocolate. As ingredients in a dessert, however, they can go together well. Here, for example, red wine flavors both the moist, tender, dark chocolate cake and its shiny cocoa glaze. The tanginess of the wine complements the bittersweet taste of the chocolate and adds an intriguing flavor.

Chocolate-Wine Butter Cake:

1 cup dry red wine (such as California Burgundy)

6 oz. semisweet chocolate, chopped

1-3/4 cups cake flour

1-1/4 teaspoons baking powder

1/2 teaspoon baking soda

1/2 cup plus 2 tablespoons (5 oz.) unsalted butter, slightly softened

1 cup sugar

3 large eggs

Cocoa-Wine Glaze:

6 tablespoons sugar

3 tablespoons unsweetened cocoa powder, preferably Dutch-process, sifted

1/2 cup dry red wine

5 tablespoons unsalted butter, chilled, cut in 5 pieces

Cake: Position rack in center of oven and preheat to 350F (175C). Generously butter a 9-1/2" x 4" fluted tube pan or Bundt pan, taking care to butter tube and each ridge. Bring wine to a boil in a medium, non-aluminum saucepan. Boil about 2-1/2 minutes or until wine is reduced to 3/4 cup; if it reduces too far, add water to obtain 3/4 cup liquid. Pour 1/2 cup reduced wine into a bowl; let cool.

Melt chocolate in remaining 1/4 cup reduced wine in a medium bowl over nearly simmering water. Stir until smooth. Remove from water; let cool. Sift flour, baking powder and baking soda into a bowl.

Cream butter in a large bowl. Add sugar; beat until smooth and fluffy. Beat in eggs 1 at a time. Gradually beat in chocolate. Stir in about 1/3 of flour mixture, followed by 1/2 of wine. When nearly blended, stir in another 1/3 of flour mixture, then remaining wine, and last remaining flour. Stir just until batter is blended.

Spread batter in prepared pan. Bake about 55 minutes or until a cake tester inserted in cake comes out clean. Cool in pan on a rack 15 minutes. Run a thin-bladed knife around tube but not around side of pan. Invert cake carefully onto rack; cool completely. Transfer to a platter. *Cake can be kept, wrapped, 3 days at room temperature.*

Glaze: In a small saucepan whisk sugar with cocoa and wine until blended. Bring to a boil over medium-high heat, whisking. Simmer over low heat 3 minutes, whisking occasionally. Remove from heat. Stir in butter, 1 piece at a time, until blended in. Cool glaze 5 minutes. Refrigerate, stirring occasionally, about 40 minutes or until thick but still pourable. Stir glaze until smooth. Very slowly spoon glaze over cake, moving spoon back and forth to cover top ridges and letting glaze trickle down grooves on side of cake. If necessary, repeat spooning several times. Wipe platter clean.

Serve cake within 30 minutes for soft glaze; for firmer glaze, cool at room temperature 1-1/2 hours. If weather is cool, keep cake at room temperature so glaze will be shinier. Refrigerate cake if weather is warm. *Glazed cake can be kept, covered with a cake cover or large bowl, 8 hours at cool room temperature or 1 day in refrigerator.* Serve at room temperature.

Makes 10 to 12 servings

Queen of Sheba Cake

Imaginative French chefs named this sumptuous chocolate cake, made with generous amounts of butter and almonds, for the biblical Queen of Sheba, who is believed to have been a dark, rich beauty who reigned over the area that is now Yemen or Ethiopia. The cake is moist and therefore needs no filling. If you prefer, omit the frosting and serve the cake with whipped cream or with Vanilla Bean Custard Sauce, page 169.

---

4 oz. semisweet chocolate, chopped

3/4 cup whole blanched almonds (about 3-1/2 oz.)

2/3 cup sugar

1/4 cup all-purpose flour

1/2 cup (4 oz.) unsalted butter, slightly softened

3 large egg yolks

4 large egg whites

1/4 teaspoon cream of tartar

Chocolate Truffle Frosting, page 158

Position rack in center of oven and preheat to 350F (175C). Butter a round 9-inch layer cake pan. Line base with parchment paper or foil. Butter paper or foil and flour lined pan. Melt chocolate in a medium bowl over nearly simmering water. Stir until smooth. Remove from pan of water; let cool. Grind almonds with 2 tablespoons sugar in a food processor to a fine powder. Transfer to a medium bowl. Sift flour over almonds; mix well.

Cream butter in a medium bowl until smooth and fluffy. Beat in cooled chocolate. Beat in egg yolks, 1 at a time, then 1/3 cup sugar.

In a large dry bowl, beat egg whites with cream of tartar until soft peaks form. Gradually beat in remaining 3-1/3 tablespoons sugar. Beat at high speed until whites are stiff and shiny but not dry. Fold about 1/4 of whites into chocolate mixture. Quickly spoon remaining whites on top and begin folding. Sprinkle almond mixture on top and fold lightly and quickly, just until blended.

Transfer batter to prepared pan. Bake 25 to 30 minutes or until a cake tester inserted about halfway between edge and center of cake comes out clean, but cake's center is still slightly soft. Cool cake in pan on a rack 5 minutes. Run a metal spatula carefully around cake. Invert cake onto rack. Carefully peel off paper; cool cake completely. Turn cake onto another rack, then onto a platter so smooth side of cake faces up. *Cake can be kept, wrapped, 2 days in refrigerator.*

Using a long metal spatula, spread frosting on cake. If desired, swirl frosting on top. Refrigerate 2 hours before serving. *Frosted cake can be kept, covered, 2 days in refrigerator.* Serve at room temperature.

Makes 8 servings

Flourless Fudge Cake with Raspberry-Brandy Sauce

The star of the dessert table in fine restaurants is often a flourless chocolate cake made from a soufflé-like mixture. In this version, raspberries and raspberry-brandy sauce add freshness, color and lightness to balance the richness and concentrated flavor of the dense bittersweet cake.

Photo opposite.

---

10 oz. semisweet chocolate,
   chopped

2 oz. unsweetened chocolate,
   chopped

1/3 cup water

1-1/2 cups (12 oz.) unsalted butter,
   cut in 12 pieces

1 cup sugar

6 large eggs, separated

Raspberry-Brandy Sauce, page 168

1-1/2 cups fresh raspberries
   (for garnish)

Position rack in center of oven and preheat to 300F (150C). Butter an 8-inch springform pan. Line base with parchment paper or foil. Butter paper or foil and flour lined pan. Melt chocolates in water in a large heatproof bowl over nearly simmering water. Stir until smooth. Add 4 butter pieces. Stir until blended. Gradually stir in 3/4 cup sugar. Add remaining butter and stir until smooth. Remove chocolate mixture from water. Quickly whisk in egg yolks, 1 at a time.

In a large dry bowl, beat egg whites until very foamy. Gradually beat in remaining 1/4 cup sugar. Beat until soft peaks form. Fold about 1/4 of whites into chocolate mixture. Return mixture to remaining whites; fold gently together. Chocolate mixture tends to sink but fold until batter is blended.

Transfer batter to prepared pan; pan will be quite full. Bake 1 hour. Reduce oven temperature to 250F (120C). Bake 15 minutes longer or until a thick crust forms on top, and center of top does not shake when pan is moved gently. Cake should feel firm all over except in very center. Cake will crack on top; center will rise less than rest of cake.

Cool briefly in pan on a rack; cake will settle slightly in center. When side of pan is just warm, gently release spring but do not remove side of pan. Cool cake to room temperature. Gently remove side of pan. Carefully invert cake onto a plate. Slide a metal spatula gently under base of pan; remove base and paper from cake. Cover and refrigerate 12 hours or overnight before serving. *Cake can be kept, wrapped, 1 week in refrigerator.*

Cut cake very carefully with a sharp knife to avoid crumbling. Serve chilled or at cool room temperature. Set each slice of cake on an individual plate; spoon sauce around, not over cake. Place 4 or 5 raspberries on sauce.

Makes 12 servings

Chocolate-Hazelnut Cake with Fudge Frosting

The unusually moist interior of this very chocolaty cake is due to the generous quantities of chocolate, butter and nuts and the technique of melting the butter into the chocolate. The cake is coated with a not-too-sweet fudge frosting but is also delicious served on its own or accompanied by whipped cream or Spirited Custard Sauce, page 169, flavored with hazelnut liqueur.

1 cup hazelnuts (about 4-1/2 oz.), toasted and skinned, page 179

1/2 cup sugar

5 oz. semisweet chocolate, chopped

2 tablespoons water

1/2 cup (4 oz.) unsalted butter, cut in 8 pieces, room temperature

4 large eggs, separated

1 teaspoon pure vanilla extract

2 tablespoons potato starch

1/4 teaspoon cream of tartar

Fudge Frosting, page 159

Position rack in center of oven and preheat to 325F (165C). Lightly butter an 8-inch springform pan. Line base with parchment paper or foil. Butter paper or foil and flour lined pan. Cool toasted hazelnuts completely. Set aside 8 to 10 attractive nuts for garnish. Grind remaining nuts with 2 tablespoons sugar in a food processor to a fine powder. Transfer to a medium bowl.

Melt chocolate in water in a large bowl over nearly simmering water. Stir until smooth. Add butter; stir until blended in. Remove from water. Whisk egg yolks to blend. Add yolks to chocolate mixture, whisking vigorously. Stir in 1/4 cup sugar, followed by vanilla, ground nuts and potato starch.

In a large dry bowl, beat egg whites with cream of tartar to soft peaks. Gradually beat in remaining 2 tablespoons sugar. Beat at high speed until whites are stiff and shiny but not dry.

Gently fold about 1/3 of whites into chocolate mixture until nearly incorporated. Lightly but quickly fold in remaining whites in 2 batches, just until batter is blended.

Spread batter in prepared pan. Bake about 1 hour or until a cake tester inserted in center of cake comes out clean. Cool in pan on a rack about 10 minutes. Run a metal spatula carefully around cake. Invert cake onto rack. Gently release spring and remove side and base of pan. Carefully peel off paper; cool cake completely. Invert cake onto another rack, then onto a platter so smoothest side of cake faces up. *Cake can be kept, wrapped, 2 days at room temperature or in refrigerator.*

Using a long metal spatula, spread frosting evenly over cake; smooth side and top. Garnish with reserved hazelnuts. Refrigerate 1 hour before serving. *Frosted cake can be kept, covered, 2 days in refrigerator.* Serve at room temperature.

Makes 8 to 10 servings

Self-Frosted Chocolate Cake

This cake is simple and fun to make. Part of the rich, mousse-like mixture is used to make a glossy chocolate frosting which is softer than buttercream and spreads easily. With the addition of flour, the remaining mixture becomes a base for the tender, fudgy cake.

8-1/2 oz. fine-quality bittersweet chocolate, chopped

3/4 cup (6 oz.) unsalted butter, cut in pieces, room temperature

1/2 cup all-purpose flour

1/4 teaspoon baking powder

6 large egg yolks

2/3 cup sugar

1 teaspoon pure vanilla extract

4 large egg whites

Position rack in center of oven and preheat to 350F (175C). Butter an 8-inch springform pan. Line base with parchment paper or foil. Butter paper or foil and flour lined pan. Melt chocolate in a medium bowl over nearly simmering water. Stir until smooth. Add butter; stir until blended in. Remove from water; let cool. Sift flour and baking powder into a small bowl.

Beat egg yolks lightly in a large bowl. Add 6 tablespoons sugar. Beat at high speed about 5 minutes or until mixture is pale and very thick. Stir in chocolate mixture and vanilla.

In a large dry bowl, beat egg whites until soft peaks form. Gradually beat in remaining 4-2/3 tablespoons sugar. Beat at high speed until whites are stiff and shiny but not dry. Gently fold about 1/3 of whites into chocolate mixture until nearly incorporated. Lightly fold in remaining whites in 2 batches, just until blended. Gently spoon 2 cups mixture into a small bowl. Cover and reserve to use as frosting.

Sprinkle flour mixture over remaining chocolate mixture; fold in gently just until batter is blended. Spread in prepared pan. Bake 30 to 35 minutes or until a cake tester inserted in center of cake comes out clean. Meanwhile, refrigerate frosting mixture, or, if you are concerned about the safety of using raw eggs, follow variation below.

Cool cake in pan on a rack 10 minutes. Run a metal spatula around cake. Gently release spring and remove side of pan. Let cake cool to lukewarm; it will settle slightly in center. Invert cake onto another rack; remove base of pan. Carefully peel off paper; cool cake completely.

If frosting is stiff, let it stand at room temperature about 1/2 hour or until easy to spread. Turn cake onto another rack, then onto a platter so smooth side of cake faces up. Using a long metal spatula, frost cake; swirl top. Refrigerate 2 hours before serving. *Cake can be kept, covered with a cake cover or large bowl, 4 days in refrigerator.*

Makes 8 to 10 servings

Variation

To cook egg yolks: Spoon frosting mixture into a medium-size metal bowl. Set it in a pan of nearly simmering water over low heat. Heat, stirring constantly, until mixture reaches 160F (70C) on an instant-read or candy thermometer, about 7 minutes. Remove from water and immediately stir until cool. Refrigerate mixture.

White Chocolate Cheesecake

White chocolate is my favorite type for flavoring cheesecake. Its delicate taste enhances the flavor of the cheese, instead of clashing with it as bittersweet chocolate often does. This cake, based on my mother's sour cream-topped cheesecake, has a creamy texture and a subtle flavor.

Photo on back cover.

Pecan-Cocoa Crumb Crust:

18 squares (about 5 oz.) graham crackers

1/4 cup pecan halves, coarsely chopped

3 tablespoons sugar

2 tablespoons unsweetened cocoa powder

7 tablespoons unsalted butter, melted and cooled

White Chocolate-Cheese Filling:

6 oz. fine-quality white chocolate, finely chopped

3/4 cup whipping cream

1 lb. cream cheese, cut in pieces, room temperature

3/4 cup plus 2 tablespoons sugar

4 large eggs

1 teaspoon pure vanilla extract

Topping & Garnish:

1-1/2 cups dairy sour cream

1/4 cup sugar

1 teaspoon pure vanilla extract

About 1/8 oz. semisweet chocolate, if desired

Quick Chocolate Curls of white and dark chocolate, page 172, if desired

Crust: Position rack in center of oven and preheat to 350F (175C). Lightly butter a 9-inch springform pan. Grind crackers in a food processor to a fine powder, or put them in a plastic bag and crush them with a rolling pin. Measure 1-1/4 cups. Mix crumbs with pecans and sugar in a large bowl. Sift in cocoa; stir until blended. Add melted butter; mix well with a fork. Using a spoon, press mixture in an even layer on base and 1-1/4 inches up side of pan. Bake 10 minutes. Cool completely.

Filling: Melt chocolate in 1/2 cup whipping cream in a medium bowl over nearly simmering water, stirring often. Remove from water; let cool. If necessary, whisk until smooth. Using flat (creaming) beater of mixer, if available, beat cream cheese with remaining 1/4 cup cream at low speed until perfectly smooth. Gradually beat in sugar. Beat in eggs, 1 at a time. Beat until perfectly smooth. Stir in cooled chocolate and vanilla until well blended.

Carefully pour filling into crust. Bake about 1 hour 5 minutes or until center is barely firm and top begins to crack. Remove from oven; cool 15 minutes. Increase oven temperature to 425F (220C).

Topping: Mix sour cream, sugar and vanilla in a medium bowl. Spread topping evenly on cheesecake without letting it drip over crust. Return cake to oven. Bake 7 minutes or until edge of topping sets. Remove from oven; cool completely. Grate semisweet chocolate over cake, if using. Cover and refrigerate at least 1 day before serving. *Cheesecake can be kept 4 days in refrigerator.* Just before serving, carefully run a metal spatula around cake and remove side of pan. Garnish with chocolate curls, if using. When serving, free each slice from underneath to remove crust from pan. For neat slices rinse knife after each cut.

Makes 12 servings

Chef Chambrette's Chocolate Macaroon Cake

Master Chef Fernand Chambrette, my co-author in a cookbook we published in France, gave me the idea for this cake. It is a macaroon-lover's dream—a whole cake made from a chocolate macaroon-type mixture, topped with a white amaretto cream frosting and elegantly garnished with easy-to-make chocolate-dipped almonds. The small, flourless, deep-brown cake has a chewy crust and an incredibly moist center.

4 oz. semisweet chocolate, chopped

2 cups whole blanched almonds (about 9-1/2 oz.)

3/4 cup sugar

8 large egg whites

Amaretto Whipped Cream, page 163

Chocolate-Dipped Almonds, page 151

Position rack in center of oven and preheat to 325F (165C). Lightly butter an 8-inch springform pan. Line base and side of pan with parchment paper or waxed paper; generously butter paper. Melt chocolate in a medium bowl over nearly simmering water. Stir until smooth. Remove from water; let cool.

Grind almonds with 2 tablespoons sugar in a food processor to a fine powder. Add 2 egg whites (about 1/4 cup) and 1/4 cup sugar; process 10 seconds or until smooth. Add 2 more egg whites and 1/4 cup sugar; process again. Transfer to a medium bowl.

In a large dry bowl, beat remaining 4 egg whites to soft peaks. Gradually beat in remaining 2 tablespoons sugar. Beat at high speed until whites are stiff and shiny but not dry.

Gradually stir chocolate into almond mixture. Gently fold about 1/4 of whites into chocolate mixture until nearly incorporated. Fold in remaining whites in 3 batches. Chocolate mixture is dense and not easy to blend with whites but continue folding until batter is blended.

Spread batter in prepared pan. Bake about 40 minutes or until cake springs back when pressed lightly. Cool in pan on a rack 5 minutes. Invert cake onto rack. Gently release spring and remove side and base of pan. Carefully peel off paper; cool cake. Turn cake onto another rack, then onto a platter so smooth side of cake faces up. *Cake can be kept, wrapped, 3 days at room temperature.*

Using a long metal spatula, spread whipped cream evenly over cake; smooth side and top. Refrigerate about 1 hour before serving. *Frosted cake can be kept, covered with a cake cover or a large bowl, 4 hours in refrigerator.* Just before serving, arrange chocolate-dipped almonds on cake with chocolate ends pointing inward.

Makes 8 servings

Shown on the following page is Chocolate Gâteau with Raspberries and Chocolate Leaves, page 27.

A wide selection of cakes, fillings and frostings in exciting combinations make the creations in this chapter the most festive of desserts.

The most frequently used cake bases for layer cakes, tortes and mousse cakes are sponge cakes of two types— those made with separated eggs and those, called *genoises,* in which whole eggs are whipped until very light. For crunchy layers, *dacquoises,* or light nutty meringues, are used. Butter cakes are best for especially rich layers.

Chocolate Layer Cakes

The cake layers of classic French chocolate gâteaux generally are flavored with cocoa so they remain light, while Austrian layer cakes can contain either cocoa or chocolate. In these types of European cakes, chocolate appears in the rich fillings and frostings. Traditional American cakes follow the Austrian custom in flavoring the cake layers with either cocoa or chocolate, but the fillings and frostings are often sweeter and less buttery than the European ones.

Chocolate Tortes

Many elegant layer cakes are referred to as *tortes,* a term which comes from the German word for cake. Often these are nut cakes with lavish fillings and frostings. The famous Sachertorte, however, is not a nut cake and not necessarily a layer cake.

Nuts give many chocolate tortes a distinct flavor and a pleasant crunchiness, making them delicious even when served plain. In many tortes the same nut appears in both the cake and the filling. Austrian and Hungarian tortes in particular often contain generous amounts of walnuts, hazelnuts or almonds. The French prefer to stick chopped toasted nuts on the side of the cake as in Classic Chocolate Gâteau, or to use them in the filling in the form of praline, or caramelized toasted nuts.

Fillings & Frostings for Layer Cakes & Tortes

For chocolate layer cakes and tortes there are four basic fillings and frostings: chocolate ganache, buttercream, flavored whipped cream and powdered sugar icing.

Ganache is the most chocolaty filling of all. It tastes like the inside of a truffle and for good reason—it is the same mixture! Ganache is basically made of only two ingredients,

chocolate and cream, although it can be further enriched with butter or can be mixed with extra flavorings.

Buttercream is used in the greatest array of cakes because it is the most versatile filling and frosting. It can be made in an endless variety of flavors and is very smooth and easy to spread and pipe.

Whipped cream, whether plain, chocolate-flavored or spiked with liqueur, makes a delicious filling and frosting, but it does not keep long.

Powdered sugar icing, long a favorite for topping American cakes, is very sweet and less popular today. It is good on individual cakes or brownies, though, such as Brandied Brownies, page 123.

Cakes in good-quality pastry shops always impressed me when they were elegantly frosted in one color and decorated with another; I thought that this could be done only in a professional kitchen because there must be so many frostings and fillings around. The chefs at La Varenne in Paris showed me that there is actually a very easy technique for doing this. Simply make buttercream, divide it in two, and add a flavoring of a different color to each. I use this technique often now to easily obtain beautiful cakes with two or three buttercreams. Look for these frostings in Biarritz Pistachio-Chocolate Cake and Two-Tone Chocolate-Raspberry Cake.

Chocolate Mousse Cakes

Mousse cakes are a new category of desserts made of cake with mousse filling. In recent years they have become great favorites, partly because of their lavish appearance. The layers of mousse filling are strikingly thick which makes a mousse cake exceptionally attractive when cut. The fillings are lighter because most of them are based on cream instead of butter or are lightened by Italian meringue. These cakes are the most important modern development in the art of dessert-making and have come into being as a result of the revolution in French cooking known as "nouvelle cuisine."

The filling of these cakes is much softer than most standard recipes. Instead of being spread, it is usually layered with the cake in a mold.

Layer Cakes, Tortes & Mousse Cakes

Chocolate Dream

This impressive, not-too-sweet chocolate layer cake is surprisingly easy to make. Layers of moist chocolate genoise are sandwiched with a generous amount of chocolate cream filling. More cream filling coats the sides, while the top is crowned with a dark chocolate glaze.

Rich Chocolate Genoise:

1 oz. unsweetened chocolate, chopped

3 oz. semisweet chocolate, chopped

2 tablespoons unsalted butter

3/4 cup cake flour

1/2 teaspoon baking powder

4 large eggs

3/4 cup sugar

Chocolate Whipped Cream, page 164

Chocolate Glaze:

3 oz. semisweet chocolate, finely chopped

1/4 cup whipping cream

Genoise: Position rack in center of oven and preheat to 350F (175C). Lightly butter an 8-inch springform pan. Line base with parchment paper or foil. Butter paper or foil and flour lined pan. Melt chocolates with butter in a medium bowl over nearly simmering water. Stir until smooth. Remove from water; let cool. Sift flour and baking powder into a medium bowl.

Beat eggs lightly in a large bowl. Whisk in sugar. Set bowl in a pan of hot water over very low heat. Whisk about 3 minutes or until mixture is barely lukewarm. Remove from water. Beat mixture at high speed about 5 minutes or until completely cool and very thick.

Sift about 1/3 of flour over egg mixture; fold in as gently as possible. Repeat with remaining flour in 2 batches. When batter is nearly blended, add 1/2 cup batter to chocolate mixture; fold until blended. Add chocolate batter to remaining batter; fold gently until blended.

Carefully pour batter into prepared pan; spread evenly. Bake about 35 minutes or until cake shrinks slightly from side of pan and top springs back when lightly pressed. Cool in pan on a rack about 5 minutes. Run a metal spatula carefully around edge of cake. Invert cake onto a rack. Carefully peel off paper; cool cake completely.

Assembly: Prepare Chocolate Whipped Cream. Using a long serrated knife, cut cake in 2 layers. Set bottom layer on a platter. Spoon all but about 3/4 cup chocolate cream over it. Spread in a smooth layer. Refrigerate 30 minutes, leaving remaining cream at room temperature. Top with second cake layer. Spread remaining cream around side of cake; smooth with spatula. Refrigerate 1 hour.

Glaze: Put chocolate in a small bowl. Bring cream to a full boil in a small heavy saucepan. Pour over chocolate all at once. Stir with a whisk until mixture is smooth. Cool to approximately body temperature or until thickened. Spoon glaze over top of cake. Spread in a smooth layer just to edge. Do not let glaze mix with frosting on side. Swirl glaze slightly in center. If desired, make lines on side of cake with large side of cake decorating comb. Refrigerate 1 hour or until glaze sets. *Frosted cake can be kept, covered, 2 days in refrigerator.*

Makes 8 to 10 servings

Checkerboard Cake

Guests always try to guess how this "puzzle" was put together. The special technique is easy—you pipe the white and chocolate batters in circles and the cake comes out looking like it is made of squares! Raspberry preserves delicately flavor the chocolate frosting and are spread as a filling between the cake layers.

Photo on page iii.

---

3 cups plus 3 tablespoons cake flour

2-1/2 teaspoons baking powder

1/2 cup plus 1 tablespoon milk

1/2 cup plus 1 tablespoon unsweetened Dutch-process cocoa

1 cup plus 6 tablespoons (11 oz.) unsalted butter, slightly softened

1-1/4 cups plus 2 tablespoons sugar

6 large eggs

2 teaspoons pure vanilla extract

1/2 cup red raspberry preserves (for filling)

Raspberry Chocolate Frosting, page 172

White or dark Chocolate Cutouts, page 175, if desired

Cake: Preheat oven to 350F (175C). Cut 3 8-inch rounds of parchment paper. Using cutters or small pan lids, trace 3 circles on each parchment round: a 2 inch, a 4 inch and a 6 inch. Line base of 3 round 8-inch layer pans with parchment rounds, tracing side down. Butter paper and sides of pans. Prepare 2 large pastry bags fitted with large plain tips. Sift flour and baking powder into a large bowl. In another bowl whisk 1/2 cup milk into cocoa until blended.

Cream butter in a large bowl. Add sugar; beat until smooth. Add eggs, 1 at a time, beating thoroughly after each; batter may appear separated. Beat in 3/4 cup flour mixture. Beat in vanilla. Using a wooden spoon, stir in remaining flour mixture. Stir until no trace of flour remains; do not beat.

Transfer 2-3/4 cups batter to a medium bowl. Add cocoa mixture; stir just until blended. Stir remaining 1 tablespoon milk into white batter. Spoon white batter into 1 pastry bag and chocolate batter into second pastry bag.

Beginning at outside of 1 pan, pipe a white circle, following markings on parchment paper. Pipe a chocolate circle inside it, then a white circle, and fill center circle with chocolate. Repeat with a second pan. When piping batter into third pan, reverse order and begin with a chocolate circle. Fill any spaces with any remaining batter of appropriate color and smooth them gently without mixing batters.

Bake about 16 to 18 minutes or until a cake tester inserted in center of cakes comes out clean. Invert cakes onto racks. Carefully peel off paper; cool cakes completely.

Assembly: Use cake layer that began with a chocolate outer circle for center. Spread preserves on bottom layer. Set center layer on top and spread preserves over it. Top with third cake layer.

Using a long metal spatula, spread frosting on side and top of cake. Swirl frosting at top, forming small curves. Or smooth top and decorate with a zigzag motion using cake decorating comb. If desired, pipe remaining frosting in a ring of small rosettes around edge of cake, using a pastry bag fitted with small star tip. Decorate side or top with a few Chocolate Cutouts. Refrigerate at least 1 hour before serving. *Frosted cake can be kept, covered, 4 days in refrigerator.* Serve at room temperature.

Makes about 12 servings

Tip

One pastry bag can be used instead of two to make this cake. Pipe white batter first, skipping places for chocolate batter. Fill pastry bag with chocolate batter and pipe it into spaces.

Shown on the following page are from top: Chocolate-Cashew-Maple Cake, page 28; Biarritz Pistachio-Chocolate Cake, page 23; Two-Tone Chocolate-Raspberry Cake, page 29.

Biarritz
Pistachio-Chocolate Cake

Named for one of France's most popular resort towns, this colorful classic cake features
three buttercreams—pistachio, vanilla and chocolate—all made from one basic mixture.

Photo opposite.

Chocolate-Pistachio Genoise:

3 oz. fine-quality bittersweet
 chocolate, chopped

3 tablespoons unsalted butter

1/2 cup shelled, unsalted, green
 pistachios (about 2 oz.)

1 cup sugar

3/4 cup plus 2 tablespoons
 cake flour

1/2 teaspoon baking powder

5 large eggs

Kirsch Syrup:

3 tablespoons sugar

3 tablespoons water

1 tablespoon plus 2 teaspoons
 kirsch

Pistachio, Chocolate &
Vanilla Buttercreams:

3 cups Classic Buttercream,
 page 160

2 teaspoons pure vanilla extract

4 oz. fine-quality bittersweet
 chocolate, melted and cooled

1-1/4 cups shelled, unsalted, green
 pistachios (about 5 oz.)

Genoise: Position rack in center of oven and preheat to 350F (175C). Lightly butter a 9-inch springform pan. Line base with parchment paper or foil. Butter paper or foil and flour lined pan. Melt chocolate with butter in a medium bowl over nearly simmering water. Stir until smooth. Remove from water; let cool. Grind pistachios with 2 tablespoons sugar in a food processor to a fine powder. Transfer to a medium bowl. Sift flour and baking powder over pistachios; mix well.

Beat eggs in a large bowl. Whisk in remaining 3/4 cup plus 2 tablespoons sugar. Set bowl in a pan of hot water over very low heat. Whisk about 3 minutes or until batter is barely lukewarm to touch. Remove from water. Beat mixture at high speed 5 minutes or until completely cool and very thick. Sprinkle about 1/3 of nut mixture over batter; fold in as gently as possible. Repeat with remaining nut mixture in 2 batches. When nearly blended, add 1 cup batter to chocolate mixture; fold until blended. Add chocolate batter to remaining batter; fold gently until blended.

Spread batter in prepared pan. Bake about 40 minutes or until cake shrinks slightly from side of pan and a cake tester inserted in center of cake comes out clean. Cool in pan on a rack about 10 minutes. Run a metal spatula carefully around edge of cake. Invert cake onto a rack. If cake remains in pan, release spring to make unmolding easier. Carefully peel off paper; cool cake completely. Crust is crumbly and a little of it will come off.

Syrup: Heat sugar and water in a small heavy saucepan over low heat, stirring until sugar dissolves. Increase heat to medium-high and, without stirring, bring to a boil. Pour into a heatproof bowl; cool completely. Stir in kirsch; cover.

Buttercreams: Prepare buttercream. Beat in vanilla. Spoon 2/3 cup buttercream into a medium bowl. Whisk in melted chocolate; set aside. Grind 1/4 cup pistachios in a food processor until fine. Transfer 1 cup vanilla buttercream to a medium bowl; stir in ground pistachios. Chop remaining pistachios; set aside.

Assembly: Using a long serrated knife, cut cake in 2 layers. Set bottom layer on a cardboard round of same diameter as cake or on base of springform pan. Using a brush, dab bottom cake layer with about 2/3 of Kirsch Syrup. Spoon all of pistachio buttercream onto layer; spread carefully with a long metal spatula. Evenly sprinkle with 1/4 cup chopped pistachios. Press lightly to stick them to buttercream. Dab syrup very lightly on soft side of top cake layer. Turn over and set on cake, crust-side up. Remove any loose crust from side of cake. Spread vanilla buttercream on side and top of cake; smooth side and top.

Using a pastry bag and small or medium star tip, pipe chocolate buttercream in a ruffle near top edge of cake. Lift cake on base and stick finely chopped pistachios onto its side in a thin border near base. Sprinkle remaining pistachios on top of cake. Refrigerate 2 hours. *Frosted cake can be kept, covered, 3 days in refrigerator.* Serve at room temperature.

Makes about 12 servings

Chocolate-Cashew-Maple Cake

Decorated with a feathery chocolate design, this cake is composed of moist thin layers of
dark chocolate cake, subtly flavored with cashews and
topped with golden maple frosting.
Photo on page 22.

Chocolate-Cashew Cake:

5 oz. semisweet chocolate, chopped

1-1/4 cups unsalted cashew nuts
(about 6 oz.)

2/3 cup sugar

1/4 cup all-purpose flour

1/2 teaspoon baking powder

2/3 cup unsalted butter,
slightly softened

5 large eggs, separated

1/4 teaspoon cream of tartar

Maple Frosting, page 162

1 oz. semisweet chocolate, chopped
(for garnish)

Cake: Preheat oven to 350F (175C). Lightly butter 2 round 9-inch layer pans. Line base of each with a round of parchment paper or foil. Butter paper or foil and flour lined pans. Melt chocolate in a medium bowl over nearly simmering water. Stir until smooth. Remove from water; let cool. Grind nuts with 3 tablespoons sugar in a food processor to a fine powder. Transfer to a medium bowl. Sift flour and baking powder over nut mixture; stir until blended.

Cream butter in a large bowl. Add 5 tablespoons sugar; beat until smooth and fluffy. Beat in egg yolks, 1 at a time.

In a large dry bowl, beat egg whites with cream of tartar to soft peaks. Gradually beat in remaining 2-2/3 tablespoons sugar. Beat at high speed until whites are stiff and shiny but not dry.

Stir melted chocolate into yolk mixture, then gently fold in about 1/4 of whites until nearly incorporated. Sprinkle about 1/4 of nut mixture over chocolate mixture; fold in gently. Repeat with remaining whites and nut mixture, each in 3 batches. Fold quickly just until batter is blended.

Divide batter between prepared pans; spread evenly. Bake about 16 to 20 minutes or until a cake tester inserted in center of cakes comes out clean. Cool in pans on racks 5 minutes; cakes will settle. Run a thin-bladed knife around sides of cakes several times. Invert cakes onto racks. Carefully peel off paper or foil; cool cakes completely. *Cake can be kept, wrapped, 2 days in refrigerator.*

Assembly: Have ready a parchment piping cone or a small pastry bag with very fine plain tip. Set bottom cake layer on a platter. Spread a very thin layer of frosting over it. Set second layer on top. Set aside 2 tablespoons frosting in a small bowl. Using a long metal spatula, spread remaining frosting over cake; smooth side and top.

Melt 1 ounce chocolate in a very small bowl over nearly simmering water. Stir until smooth. Remove from water; cool slightly. Whisk into reserved 2 tablespoons frosting. Spoon into paper cone. Beginning in center of cake, pipe chocolate in a spiral design. Using dull side of a thin-bladed knife, draw knife in a line from center of cake to edge. Then draw knife in a line inward from edge to center. Draw knife 8 or 10 times in this way, so that lines formed on chocolate design are spaced equally apart; they will make a feathery design. *Frosted cake can be kept, covered, 2 days in refrigerator.* Serve at room temperature.

Makes 10 to 12 servings

Two-Tone Chocolate-Raspberry Cake

Raspberry-topped pink rosettes of buttercream on a background of chocolate make a dramatic, beautiful garnish on this cake. It is made from light, bittersweet chocolate sponge cake layers sandwiched with raspberry filling and topped with chocolate-raspberry frosting—both from the same basic buttercream. If you like, serve each slice of cake with Raspberry Sauce, page 102.

Photo on page 22.

Bittersweet Chocolate Sponge Cake:

3/4 cup cake flour

1/3 cup unsweetened Dutch-process cocoa powder

6 large eggs, separated

3/4 cup plus 1 tablespoon sugar

1/2 teaspoon cream of tartar

1 oz. bittersweet chocolate, coarsely grated (about 1/2 cup)

1-2/3 cups fresh raspberries (about 8 oz.)

Classic Buttercream, page 160

4 oz. bittersweet chocolate, melted and cooled

Raspberry-Brandy Syrup, page 170

8 to 10 fresh raspberries (for garnish)

Cake: Position rack in center of oven and preheat to 350F (175C). Lightly butter a 9-inch springform pan. Line base of pan with parchment paper or foil. Butter paper or foil and flour lined pan. Sift flour and cocoa into a medium bowl.

Beat egg yolks lightly in a large bowl. Beat in 1/2 cup sugar; continue beating at high speed about 5 minutes or until mixture is pale and very thick.

In a large dry bowl, beat egg whites with cream of tartar to soft peaks. Gradually beat in remaining 5 tablespoons sugar. Beat at high speed until whites are stiff and shiny but not dry. Gently fold about 1/4 of whites into yolk mixture until nearly incorporated. Sprinkle grated chocolate over mixture; fold in. Sprinkle about 1/3 of cocoa mixture over yolk mixture; fold in gently. Fold in another 1/4 of whites. Fold in remaining cocoa mixture and whites in alternate batches, just until blended.

Spread batter in prepared pan. Bake about 35 minutes or until a cake tester inserted in center of cake comes out clean. Cool in pan on a rack 3 minutes. Run a thin-bladed knife around cake. Invert cake onto rack. Carefully peel off paper; cool cake completely.

Assembly: Puree 1-2/3 cups raspberries in a food processor until very smooth. Strain puree into a medium bowl, pressing on pulp in strainer. Use a rubber spatula to scrape mixture from underside of strainer. Measure 1/2 cup puree. Gradually beat it into buttercream.

Set aside 1 cup raspberry buttercream for pink filling. Spoon another 1/3 cup buttercream into pastry bag fitted with medium star tip. Whisk melted chocolate into remaining buttercream.

Using a serrated knife, cut cake in 2 layers. Set one layer on cake plate. Using brush, dab cake with Raspberry-Brandy Syrup. Spread with reserved raspberry buttercream. Dab syrup on soft side of top layer. Turn over and set on cake, crust-side up.

Using a long metal spatula, spread chocolate buttercream evenly over side and top of cake; smooth side and top. Pipe 8 to 10 rosettes of raspberry buttercream for garnish. Refrigerate at least 1 hour. *Frosted cake can be kept, covered, 3 days in refrigerator.* Bring cake to room temperature. Just before serving, top each rosette with a raspberry.

Makes 10 to 12 servings

Rigo Jancsi

During a recent European chocolate research trip, my husband and I revisited some of our favorite dessert cities in Italy, Austria, Germany, Switzerland and France. One of the highlights was a fabulous Hungarian cake that we had in Salzburg, Austria. It was a chocolaty, light-textured cake, with thick layers of two fillings and a dark chocolate glaze. This is a recreation of that cake.

Photo on pages vi-vii.

Rich Chocolate Sponge Cake:

3 oz. bittersweet chocolate, chopped

2 tablespoons unsalted butter

1 tablespoon water

4 large eggs, separated

1/2 cup sugar

1/4 teaspoon cream of tartar

6 tablespoons all-purpose flour, sifted

1/3 cup apricot preserves (for spreading)

Shiny Chocolate Glaze:

2 oz. bittersweet chocolate, chopped

3 tablespoons unsweetened Dutch-process cocoa powder

5 tablespoons sugar

1/4 cup water

Chocolate & Vanilla Cream Fillings:

4 oz. bittersweet chocolate, chopped

1 pint whipping cream (2 cups), well-chilled

3 tablespoons sugar

2 teaspoons pure vanilla extract

Cake: Position rack in center of oven and preheat to 375F (190C). Lightly butter corners of a 17" x 11" rimmed baking sheet. Line with foil or parchment paper; butter foil or paper. Melt chocolate with butter and water in a small bowl over nearly simmering water. Stir until smooth. Let cool.

In a large bowl beat egg yolks with 6 tablespoons sugar at high speed 5 minutes or until very thick. Quickly stir chocolate mixture into yolk mixture.

In a large dry bowl, beat egg whites with cream of tartar to soft peaks. Beat in remaining 2 tablespoons sugar. Beat at high speed until whites are stiff. Gently fold about 1/3 of whites into chocolate mixture until nearly blended. Sprinkle with 1/2 of flour; fold in gently. Fold in another 1/3 of whites, then remaining flour, last remaining whites. Fold just until blended.

Spread batter evenly on prepared baking sheet. Layer will be very thin. Bake 10 minutes or just until firm. Carefully transfer cake with paper or foil to a rack. Let cool. Slide a cutting board under cake without removing paper or foil. Using a sharp knife, cut cake crosswise in 2 equal pieces, about 8 inches wide. Carefully lift 1 piece from paper or foil onto rack. Set second layer on platter.

Heat preserves in a small saucepan over low heat until hot. Strain into a small bowl. Brush preserves lightly over cake layer on platter. Let stand 30 minutes to dry slightly.

Glaze: Set rack with second cake piece above a tray. Melt chocolate in a medium bowl over nearly simmering water. Stir until smooth. Remove from water. Mix cocoa, sugar and water in a bowl. Add to chocolate; mix well. Set above hot water over low heat. Heat about 5 minutes or until sugar dissolves. Cool to 94F to 98F (34C to 35C). Pour glaze over cake layer on rack. Spread very lightly until evenly covered; touch it as little as possible. Refrigerate about 30 minutes or until set.

Fillings: Melt chocolate in a small bowl over a pan of hot water over low heat. Stir until smooth. Turn off heat but leave chocolate above water. In a large chilled bowl whip cream with sugar and vanilla until stiff. Set aside 1 cup whipped cream for top of cake. Remove chocolate from above water; cool 30 seconds. Quickly stir 2/3 cup whipped cream into chocolate, then fold mixture quickly into remaining whipped cream in bowl until smooth.

Assembly: Spread chocolate cream over apricot-glazed cake. Spoon white cream in small dabs over top. Smooth top lightly. Refrigerate 30 minutes.

Cut chocolate-glazed cake layer in 2-inch squares by cutting it in 4ths lengthwise and in 5ths crosswise; use a large knife and cut with heel of knife. With a metal spatula, set squares side by side on top of cake, touching each other. Refrigerate cake 45 minutes. *Cake can be kept, covered, 3 days in refrigerator.*

To serve, follow edges of top squares of cake and cut carefully through layers. Use a large knife to cut each row and a smaller knife to cut into individual squares. Rinse knife between each cut.

Makes 20 small servings

Black Forest Cherry Torte

A classic favorite throughout Europe, this version of the cake is more in the Austrian and French style than in the original German tradition. It combines a dark chocolate-colored, light-textured cake, kirsch and plenty of whipped cream. Tart cherries are customary but sweet ones are used here because they are easier to find. If fresh cherries are not in season, use frozen or canned.

Poached Cherries:

14 oz. fresh sweet cherries

Zest of 1 lemon

1/2 cup sugar

1 vanilla bean, if desired

2 cups water

2 teaspoons fresh strained
   lemon juice

Rich Cocoa Sponge Cake:

2/3 cup all-purpose flour

1/3 cup unsweetened Dutch-process
   cocoa powder

1/2 teaspoon baking powder

5 large eggs, separated

3/4 cup plus 2 tablespoons sugar

1/4 teaspoon cream of tartar

5 tablespoons butter, melted
   and cooled

3 tablespoons kirsch
   (for moistening)

Kirsch Whipped Cream, page 163

Quick Chocolate Curls, page 172,
   if desired

12 long Chocolate Scrolls, page 176,
   or grated chocolate

Cherries: Pit cherries with cherry pitter or point of vegetable peeler, reserving any juice. Using a vegetable peeler, peel wide strips of yellow part of lemon peel, without white pith. In a medium saucepan stir sugar with vanilla bean, lemon strips and water over low heat until sugar dissolves. Bring to a boil over high heat without stirring. Add lemon juice and cherries with their juice. Cover and cook over low heat about 8 minutes or until tender. Let cool. Cover and refrigerate 2 hours or overnight. Remove vanilla bean.

Cake: Preheat oven to 350F (175C). Butter an 8-inch springform pan. Line base of pan with parchment paper or foil. Butter paper or foil and flour lined pan. Sift flour, cocoa and baking powder into a medium bowl.

Beat egg yolks in a large bowl. Beat in 3/4 cup sugar; whip at high speed about 5 minutes or until mixture is pale and very thick.

In a large dry bowl, beat egg whites with cream of tartar to soft peaks. Gradually beat in remaining 2 tablespoons sugar. Beat at high speed until whites are stiff and shiny but not dry. Gently fold about 1/3 of whites into yolk mixture until nearly incorporated. Sprinkle with about 1/2 of cocoa mixture; fold in gently. Fold in another 1/3 of whites, then remaining cocoa mixture, last remaining whites. Gradually pour in melted butter while folding. Fold just until blended.

Spread batter in prepared pan. Bake about 35 minutes or until a cake tester inserted in center of cake comes out clean. Cool in pan on a rack 5 minutes. Run a thin-bladed knife carefully around cake. Invert cake onto rack. Carefully remove base of pan and peel off paper. Cool cake completely. *Cake can be kept, wrapped, 1 day in refrigerator.*

Assembly: Measure 1/3 cup syrup from cherries. Add 3 tablespoons kirsch; cover. Thoroughly drain 1-3/4 cups cherries on paper towels. Set aside 10 attractive cherries for top of cake.

Using a long serrated knife, cut cake in 3 layers. Set bottom layer on a serving plate. Brush with kirsch syrup. Spread with 1 cup whipped cream. Arrange about 3/4 cup cherries evenly on top. Press them gently into cream. Set second cake layer on top, brush with syrup and spread with 1 cup whipped cream. Scatter another 3/4 cup cherries over cream. Brush soft side of third layer with syrup. Turn over and set on cake crust-side up. Reserve about 1/3 cup whipped cream for garnish. Spread remaining cream on side and top of cake.

Garnish: Use a long metal spatula or pie server to stick chocolate curls, if using, on side of cake a few at a time. Set Chocolate Scrolls in center of cake or sprinkle with grated chocolate. Using a pastry bag and large star tip, pipe reserved whipped cream in 10 rosettes on top edge of cake. Refrigerate until ready to serve. *Frosted cake can be kept, covered, 6 hours in refrigerator.* A short time before serving, thoroughly drain reserved cherries on paper towels. Pat dry. Set each cherry on a rosette of whipped cream.

Makes 10 servings

Sachertorte

Sachertorte, the most famous culinary creation of Austria, was made prominent during a lengthy trial in which two Viennese institutions, the Sacher Hotel and the celebrated pastry shop Demel's, claimed to own the original, authentic recipe. It is a not-too-sweet chocolate cake with apricot glaze and a sweet chocolate icing and is served with generous amounts of whipped cream.

Photo opposite.

Bittersweet Chocolate Cake:

4-1/2 oz. fine quality bittersweet chocolate, chopped

1/2 cup (4 oz.) unsalted butter, slightly softened

2/3 cup sugar

5 large eggs, separated

1 teaspoon pure vanilla extract

2/3 cup cake flour, sifted

1/3 cup plus 1 tablespoon apricot preserves (for brushing)

Sweet Chocolate Glaze:

1-1/4 cups sugar

1/2 cup water

6 oz. fine-quality bittersweet chocolate, chopped

1/2 teaspoon vegetable oil

1-1/2 cups whipping cream, well-chilled (for accompaniment)

Cake: Position rack in center of oven and preheat to 350F (175C). Lightly butter a 9-inch springform pan. Line base of pan with parchment paper or foil. Butter paper or foil and flour lined pan. Melt chocolate in a medium bowl over nearly simmering water. Stir until smooth. Remove from water; let cool.

Cream butter in a large bowl. Add 1/2 cup sugar; beat until smooth and fluffy. Beat in egg yolks, 1 at a time. Beat 3 minutes until fluffy. Stir in chocolate and vanilla.

In a large dry bowl, beat egg whites to soft peaks. Gradually beat in remaining 2-2/3 tablespoons sugar. Beat at high speed until whites are stiff and shiny but not dry. Gently fold about 1/3 of whites into chocolate mixture until nearly incorporated. Sprinkle with about 1/3 of flour; fold in gently. Lightly fold in remaining whites and flour, each in 2 batches, until batter is blended.

Spread batter in prepared pan. Bake about 35 to 40 minutes or until a cake tester inserted in center of cake comes out clean. Cool in pan on a rack 5 minutes. Run a thin-bladed knife around cake. Invert cake onto a rack. Carefully peel off paper; cool cake completely. Turn cake smoothest side up. Set on a cardboard round or base of springform pan the same diameter as cake, then on a rack.

Heat preserves in a small saucepan over low heat until hot but not boiling. Strain into a small bowl, pressing on apricot pieces. Using a pastry brush, brush preserves over side and top of cake. Let stand 2 hours to dry.

Glaze: Stir sugar and water in a heavy medium saucepan over low heat until sugar dissolves. Bring to a boil. Pour into a heatproof bowl; cool syrup to body temperature.

When syrup is cool, melt chocolate in a medium bowl over nearly simmering water. Stir until smooth. Remove from water; cool slightly. Using a whisk, gently stir chocolate into syrup in 3 batches. Set bowl of chocolate-syrup mixture above hot water over low heat. Heat, stirring, 5 minutes. Stir in oil. Remove glaze from water and cool, stirring gently with spatula, until just warm (105 to 110F, 40 to 45C).

Pour glaze over center of cake. Spread with 1 motion of spatula so glaze flows down side. Do not touch top any more. Quickly spread glaze smooth on side. Transfer cake carefully with wide spatulas to platter. Cake can be served immediately. *Frosted cake can be kept, covered with a cake cover or large bowl, 1 day at room temperature.*

In a large chilled bowl whip cream to soft peaks. Serve a generous spoonful of whipped cream alongside each cake slice; or whip cream until stiff and pipe next to each cake slice using a pastry bag and medium star tip.

Makes 8 servings

Chocolate Symphony

Fine pâtisseries in France proudly display cakes of this type, made of a soft creamy mousse layered with delicately crisp chocolate-nut meringues. I learned how to make them from my friend Denis Ruffel, one of the most talented pastry chefs in France and head pastry chef of the excellent Parisian pâtisserie Millet. Three chocolate preparations make this harmonious dessert: a chocolate dacquoise cake, Chocolate Grand Marnier Bavarian Cream and a garnish of chocolate-ganache rosettes.

Photo on pages vi-vii.

Chocolate Dacquoise:

Scant 1 cup whole blanched almonds (about 5 oz.)

3/4 cup plus 3 tablespoons sugar

1/4 cup unsweetened Dutch-process cocoa powder

2 tablespoons plus 1-1/2 teaspoons all-purpose flour

5 large egg whites

1/4 teaspoon cream of tartar

Chocolate Grand Marnier Bavarian Cream, page 88

Ganache:

7-1/2 oz. semisweet chocolate, finely chopped

3/4 cup whipping cream

Dacquoise: Preheat oven to 300F (150C). Butter corners of 2 baking sheets and line bases with parchment paper or foil. Butter and lightly flour paper or foil. Using inside of an 8-inch springform pan rim as guide, trace a circle onto each baking sheet. Have ready a rubber spatula for folding and a pastry bag fitted with a 1/2-inch plain tip. Grind almonds with 1/2 cup sugar in a food processor to a fine powder. Transfer to a medium bowl. Sift cocoa and flour into a small bowl.

In a large dry bowl, beat egg whites with cream of tartar to soft peaks. Gradually beat in remaining 7 tablespoons sugar at high speed; beat until whites are stiff and shiny. Gently but quickly fold in cocoa mixture in 2 batches until blended. Gently fold in nut mixture in 2 batches.

Immediately spoon mixture into pastry bag. Beginning at center of a circle marked on baking sheet, pipe mixture in a tight spiral until circle is covered. Repeat with second circle. If any mixture remains, pipe it in small mounds onto baking sheets.

Bake in center of oven 45 minutes or until rounds are firm to touch. If baking on 2 oven shelves, switch their positions halfway through baking time. Gently release layers from paper or foil, using a large metal spatula. Gently peel off any remaining paper or foil if necessary. Cool layers completely on a rack. *Layers can be kept 5 days in an airtight container in dry weather.* Save small mounds for accompanying ice cream.

Filling: Prepare Bavarian cream. Put bottom cake layer in a 9-inch springform pan. Pour 3 cups Bavarian cream over cake. Tap pan on work surface to remove bubbles. Freeze 10 minutes, leaving remaining mixture at room temperature. Set top cake layer in place. Pour remaining Bavarian cream over it; spread evenly. Refrigerate 12 hours or overnight; cover when top sets. Run spatula around cake. Carefully release spring and remove side of pan. *Cake can be kept, covered, 2 days in refrigerator.*

Ganache: Put chocolate in a medium bowl. Bring cream to a full boil in a small heavy saucepan. Pour over chocolate all at once. Stir with a whisk until mixture is smooth. Cool to room temperature. Refrigerate, stirring often, about 15 minutes or until thick enough to pipe but not set. If ganache becomes too stiff to pipe, set bowl of mixture above a saucepan of hot water and stir until softened.

Using a pastry bag and medium star tip, pipe rosettes of ganache on top of cake in lines radiating from center like spokes of a wheel. Pipe a ruffle of ganache around base of cake. Refrigerate 30 minutes or until set. Use a heavy knife to cut cake; be sure to cut through bottom cake layer.

Makes 10 to 12 servings

Chocolate Swiss Roll with Berries & Cream

This festive cake is ideal for summer—it is rich but light, chocolaty, quick to prepare and full of berries. Do not worry if it cracks a little during rolling; the raspberry-brandy whipped cream and fruit garnish will cover the entire cake.

Chocolate Sponge Cake:

3 oz. semisweet chocolate, chopped

2 tablespoons unsalted butter

1 tablespoon water

6 tablespoons all-purpose flour

3 tablespoons cornstarch

6 large egg yolks

1/2 cup sugar

4 large egg whites

1/4 teaspoon cream of tartar

Berry & Cream Filling:

1-1/4 cups crosswise slices of strawberries

2-1/2 cups whipping cream, well-chilled

3 tablespoons plus 1 teaspoon sugar

4-1/2 teaspoons clear raspberry brandy

3/4 cup raspberries

3/4 cup blackberries

A few blackberries, raspberries and small strawberries

Small Chocolate Cutouts, such as crescents, page 175, if desired

Cake: Position rack in center of oven and preheat to 375F (190C). Lightly butter corners of a 17" x 11" rimmed baking sheet. Line base and sides with foil or parchment paper. If necessary, use 2 overlapping pieces of foil so sides are lined completely. Butter foil or paper. Melt chocolate with butter and water in a medium bowl over nearly simmering water. Stir until smooth. Remove from water; let cool. Sift flour and cornstarch into a medium bowl.

Beat egg yolks in large bowl. Add 6 tablespoons sugar. Beat at high speed about 5 minutes or until mixture is pale and very thick. Fold chocolate mixture quickly into yolk mixture.

In a large dry bowl, beat egg whites with cream of tartar to soft peaks. Beat in remaining 2 tablespoons sugar; beat at high speed until whites are stiff but not dry. Gently fold about 1/3 of whites into chocolate mixture until nearly incorporated. Sprinkle with about 1/2 of flour mixture; fold in gently. Fold in another 1/3 of whites, then remaining flour mixture, then remaining whites, just until blended.

Transfer batter to prepared baking sheet; spread evenly but lightly. Bake about 6 minutes or until cake is just firm and springs slightly back from edges. Cake will be very thin. Transfer cake with foil or paper to rack. Cool cake to room temperature.

Filling: Halve any large strawberry slices. In a large chilled bowl, whip cream with sugar until stiff. Add raspberry brandy; beat at low speed until just blended. Reserve 3 cups cream for filling in a medium bowl and fold in strawberries, raspberries and blackberries.

Move cake, still on its foil or paper, to a large board or tray. Spread gently with filling, using a metal spatula. Avoid squashing berries.

With the aid of the foil or paper, gently roll up cake, beginning at long side, and turn cake over onto platter. Gently turn over again so seam side is down. Spread cake with remaining cream. Refrigerate at least 30 minutes before serving. *Cake can be kept 8 hours in refrigerator.* Decorate with a row of berries alternating with small Chocolate Cutouts, if using. Cut with a serrated knife.

Makes 8 to 10 servings

Zuccotto

This hemispherical-shaped dessert is made by lining a bowl with sponge cake, then adding layers of chocolate cream and chocolate chip whipped cream with candied fruit.
In Italy Zuccotto is decorated with powdered sugar and cocoa
but here whipped cream and cocoa are used.

Sponge Cake:

6 tablespoons all-purpose flour

7 tablespoons potato starch

4 large eggs, separated

1/2 cup sugar

1/2 teaspoon pure vanilla extract

1/4 teaspoon cream of tartar

Double Chocolate Cream Filling:

1 pint whipping cream (2 cups), well-chilled

1/4 cup sugar

1/2 cup hazelnuts, toasted, skinned and chopped, page 179

1/4 cup diced candied fruit, finely chopped

1/3 cup mini, semisweet, real chocolate pieces

3 oz. semisweet chocolate, chopped

3 tablespoons brandy (for moistening)

4 teaspoons water (for moistening)

3/4 cup whipping cream, well-chilled (for frosting)

About 2 teaspoons unsweetened cocoa powder, preferably Dutch-process (for sprinkling)

Cake: Position rack in center of oven and preheat to 400F (205C). Lightly butter corners of a 17" x 11" rimmed baking sheet. Line base with foil or parchment paper; butter foil or paper. Sift flour and potato starch into a bowl.

Beat egg yolks in a large bowl. Beat in 1/4 cup sugar; whip at high speed 5 minutes or until mixture is pale and very thick. Beat in vanilla. In a large dry bowl, beat egg whites with cream of tartar to soft peaks. Gradually beat in remaining 1/4 cup sugar. Beat at high speed until whites are stiff but not dry.

Sprinkle about 1/3 of flour mixture over egg yolk mixture; fold gently until nearly incorporated. Gently fold in about 1/3 of whites. Fold remaining flour and whites, each in 2 batches, adding each when previous one is nearly blended in. Transfer batter to prepared baking sheet and spread evenly but lightly. Bake about 6 minutes or until cake is just firm and springy to touch; its color will remain pale. Transfer cake with foil or paper to a rack. Cool to room temperature. Cover with towel if not using immediately.

Filling: Cut an 18" x 12" sheet of waxed paper in half lengthwise. Fold each piece in half lengthwise. Line a 6-cup smooth glass bowl with the 2 folded strips of waxed paper so that they meet in an X on bottom of bowl.

Turn cake over onto another rack or tray. Carefully peel off paper or foil. Turn over again onto a board or tray. Cut 3 crosswise strips of cake, about 3-1/4 inches wide. Use 1 strip to line center of bowl. Using other 2 strips, line bowl completely with a layer of cake, cutting them as necessary so that bowl is lined up to rim. Fill in any holes with small pieces of cake. Reserve remaining cake.

In a large chilled bowl, whip cream to soft peaks. Beat in sugar; whip until stiff. Fold in hazelnuts, candied fruit and mini chocolate pieces. Set aside 2-1/2 cups cream mixture to flavor with chocolate. Melt chocolate in a small bowl over nearly simmering water. Stir until smooth. Remove from water; cool 30 seconds. Quickly stir about 1/2 cup reserved cream mixture into chocolate. Return to reserved 2 cups cream mixture; fold quickly until blended. Mix brandy with water in a small bowl. Brush on cake in bowl. Pour chocolate mixture into cake-lined bowl. Top gently with white mixture. Cut remaining cake to fit top of bowl. Set it in place; brush with remaining brandy. Cover and refrigerate at least 10 hours. *Cake can be kept, covered, 2 days in refrigerator.*

To serve: Cut 4 strips of waxed paper 1-1/2 inches wide and about 12 inches long. Fold each in half lengthwise. Lightly butter 1 side of each strip. In a large chilled bowl, whip cream until very stiff. Unmold cake onto a platter; remove paper. Spread whipped cream over cake. Drape strips of paper across cake, buttered side up, so all cross in center. Using a small sieve, sift cocoa over areas of cake between strips of paper. Beginning with top strip, lift each strip straight up; it will leave a design. Carefully smooth cream with metal spatula if necessary. *Cake can be kept, covered with a large overturned bowl, 4 hours in refrigerator.* Serve cold.

Makes 10 servings

White Chocolate Mousse Cake with Dark Chocolate Chips

Layers of a tender chocolate cake are filled with a white chocolate mousse dotted with dark chocolate chips. A chocolate glaze on top and a ruffle of whipped cream complete this delight.

Moist Chocolate Cake:

4 oz. semisweet chocolate

1-1/2 cups cake flour

1-1/2 teaspoons baking powder

1/2 cup plus 2 tablespoons (5 oz.) unsalted butter, slightly softened

1/2 cup firmly packed light-brown sugar

2/3 cup granulated sugar

2 large eggs

3/4 cup milk

White Chocolate Mousse:

1-2/3 cups whipping cream

1-1/2 teaspoons unflavored gelatin

3 tablespoons water

4 oz. fine-quality white chocolate, chopped

5 tablespoons unsalted butter, room temperature

2 tablespoons sugar

1/4 cup mini, semisweet, real chocolate pieces

Chocolate Glaze, page 160

1-1/2 cups whipping cream, well-chilled (for garnish)

1 tablespoon mini, semisweet, real chocolate pieces (for garnish)

Cake: Position rack in center of oven and preheat to 350F (175C). Lightly butter 2 round 9-inch layer pans. Line base of each pan with parchment paper or foil; butter paper or foil and flour lined pans. Melt chocolate in a medium bowl over nearly simmering water. Stir until smooth. Remove from water; let cool. Sift flour and baking powder into a medium bowl.

Cream butter in a large bowl. Add sugars; beat until smooth and fluffy. Add eggs, 1 at a time, beating thoroughly after each addition. Beat in melted chocolate at low speed. Blend in about 1/4 of flour mixture at low speed, then about 1/3 of milk. Blend in remaining flour mixture in 3 batches alternating with remaining milk in 2 batches. Mix just until batter is blended.

Spread evenly in prepared pans. Bake about 25 minutes or until a cake tester inserted in centers of cakes comes out clean. Cool in pans on racks 5 minutes. Invert cakes onto racks. Carefully peel off paper or foil; cool cakes completely.

Mousse: Oil inner side of a 9-inch springform pan. Put 1 cake layer in pan. Refrigerate all but 1/4 cup cream. Sprinkle gelatin over water in a small cup.

Combine white chocolate and remaining 1/4 cup cream in a small bowl over nearly simmering water. Leave until partially melted, stirring occasionally. Remove from water. Whisk until smooth. Whisk in butter by tablespoons. Set cup with gelatin in a shallow pan of hot water over low heat. Melt gelatin, stirring often, about 3 minutes. Stir into chocolate mixture.

In a large chilled bowl, whip chilled cream with sugar until nearly stiff. Gently fold into chocolate mixture, blending thoroughly. Fold in chocolate pieces.

Assembly: Pour 2 cups mousse over cake in pan. Spread so mousse flows between cake and pan. Freeze 15 minutes, keeping remaining mousse at room temperature.

Put second cake layer on top. Pour remaining mousse over it. Spread so mousse flows between side of cake and side of pan. Smooth top. Refrigerate about 4 hours or until set.

Make glaze and cool until thickened. Pour over center of chilled cake. Using a long metal spatula, slowly spread glaze towards edge, turning cake. Spread nearly to edge but leave about 1/4 inch border unglazed. Refrigerate at least 30 minutes or until set. *Cake can be kept, covered, 2 days in refrigerator.*

Put damp towel around sides of pan. Run a metal spatula carefully around edge of dessert. Release spring and remove side of pan carefully. If necessary, smooth mousse on side with spatula.

For garnish, whip cream in a large chilled bowl until stiff. Using a pastry bag and large star tip, pipe a ruffle of whipped cream at top outer edge of cake. Set chocolate pieces on cream. Pipe ruffle of cream around base of cake.

Makes about 12 servings

Pies and pastries play the role of crisp containers to contrast with soft chocolate fillings such as chocolate mousse, Bavarian cream and pastry cream. Even the pastry itself is sometimes flavored with chocolate, like the chocolate dough used in Chocolate-Mint Cream Puffs.

Chocolate Pies & Tarts

Both American flaky pie pastry and French sweet pie pastry are excellent with chocolate fillings. Instead of pastry, quick crusts made from chocolate wafers, amaretti cookies or other packaged cookies can make delicious cases for creamy chocolate mousses and other soft mixtures. Crusts can also be made entirely of chocolate and nuts, as in Chocolate-Marbled Chiffon Pie.

Traditional American treats, like pecan pie and custard pie, become even better when enriched with chocolate. Nuts are a wonderful addition to many chocolate pies and tarts, such as Chocolate-Almond Fudge Tart with its topping of whipped cream and toasted sliced almonds, or fudgy Double-Chocolate Pecan Pie.

Pies & Pastries

Other Chocolate Pastries

Cream puffs made of choux pastry are the easiest pastries to make and are well-loved companions for chocolate. Profiteroles topped with hot chocolate sauce are one of the most popular desserts in fine restaurants but are simple to prepare. Chocolate Gâteau Paris Brest is a spectacular ring-shaped cake made of choux pastry topped with toasted almonds and filled with a creamy chocolate-praline cream.

Although puff pastry is time-consuming to make at home, now it can be purchased not only from bakeries but also at fine supermarkets. It is layered with a creamy chocolate filling and frosted with a quick glaze to make Chocolate Napoleon.

Yeast-risen doughs can also be matched with chocolate fillings and toppings. Chocolate-Pear Pizza, for example, has a base of yeast dough covered with chocolate sauce and sliced pears. To make a rich type of cinnamon rolls, easy brioche dough is used. It is spread with a cinnamon-flavored pastry-cream filling and is liberally studded with dark chocolate chips and white raisins.

Berries, Chocolate & Cream Tart

The German technique of brushing the pastry base with melted chocolate provides flavor and helps keep the pastry crisp in this light, summery tart. It is filled with a generous mound of fluffy whipped cream, dotted with colorful berries and chocolate chips.

8-inch Sweet Pastry Shell, page 59

Berry & Chocolate Cream Filling:

2 oz. semisweet chocolate, chopped

1/2 pint whipping cream (1 cup), well-chilled

2 tablespoons sugar

1/2 cup blueberries

1/2 cup raspberries

1/4 cup mini, semisweet, real chocolate pieces

Pastry: Position rack in lower third of oven and preheat to 425F (220C). Line tart shell with parchment paper or foil; fill with dried beans or pie weights. Set tart shell on a baking sheet. Bake 10 minutes or until side is firm and beginning to brown. Reduce oven temperature to 375F (190C). Carefully remove paper with beans. Bake shell 14 minutes or until base is firm and just beginning to brown.

Set tart shell on a flat-bottomed upside-down bowl. Remove side of pan. Transfer shell to a rack; cool to lukewarm. Gently remove base of pan. Cool shell completely. Transfer to a platter. *Tart shell can be kept, covered, 1 day at room temperature.*

Filling: Melt chocolate in a small bowl over nearly simmering water. Stir until smooth. Remove from water; let cool. Brush chocolate on base and side of baked tart shell. Refrigerate about 30 minutes or until set.

In a large chilled bowl, whip cream with sugar until stiff. Set aside 3 or 4 of each type of berry for garnish. Fold chocolate pieces and remaining berries into cream. Spoon mixture into tart. Spread evenly, mounding in center. Refrigerate about 30 minutes. *Tart can be kept 1 day in refrigerator.*

Up to 30 minutes before serving, garnish tart with reserved berries. To serve, cut with a sharp heavy knife. Use a little extra pressure to cut pastry base with its firm chocolate coating.

Makes 6 to 8 servings

Double-Chocolate Pecan Pie

A fudgy version of America's traditional favorite. If desired, accompany each wedge of pie with whipped cream or a scoop of vanilla ice cream.

3/4 cup light corn syrup

1/2 cup sugar

1 tablespoon unsweetened cocoa powder

1/4 cup unsalted butter, cut in 4 pieces

3 large eggs

1 teaspoon pure vanilla extract

1 cup pecans, coarsely chopped (about 3-1/2 oz.)

1 cup semisweet real chocolate pieces (6 oz.)

9-inch unbaked Pie Shell, page 58, or packaged shell

1/2 cup pecan halves

Position rack in lower third of oven and preheat to 425F (220C). Mix corn syrup, sugar, cocoa and butter in a heavy medium saucepan. Bring to a boil over medium heat, stirring constantly. Reduce heat to low; cook without stirring 5 minutes. Remove from heat; cool 10 minutes.

Lightly beat eggs in a large bowl. Stirring constantly with a whisk, slowly but steadily pour syrup mixture into eggs. Whisk until well-blended; mixtures will not blend at first but will do so after continued whisking. Cool 5 minutes. Stir in vanilla, chopped pecans and chocolate pieces. Pour into pie shell. Arrange pecan halves on top in an attractive pattern.

Bake 15 minutes. Reduce oven temperature to 350F (175C). Bake 20 minutes or until a thin-bladed knife inserted halfway between center and edge of filling comes out nearly clean, with only a bit of batter sticking to it; if it comes out chocolaty because it hit a chocolate piece, test again. Cool on a rack. Serve pie slightly warm or at room temperature.

Makes 8 to 10 servings

Chocolate-Almond Fudge Tart

The dark fudgy filling of this tart is baked in sweet almond pastry, then topped with whipped cream and sprinkled with a generous amount of toasted sliced almonds.

Almond Pastry Shell:

1/2 cup whole blanched almonds (about 2-1/2 oz.)

1/4 cup sugar

1/4 teaspoon salt

1-1/2 cups all-purpose flour

7 tablespoons unsalted butter, well-chilled, cut in 14 pieces

1 large egg, beaten

1/2 to 1 teaspoon iced water, if needed

Chocolate-Almond Filling:

4 oz. bittersweet chocolate, chopped

7 tablespoons unsalted butter

1/2 cup whole blanched almonds (about 2-1/2 oz.)

1/2 cup sugar

2 large eggs

1 tablespoon all-purpose flour

Almond & Cream Topping:

1/4 cup sliced almonds

1/2 pint whipping cream (1 cup), well-chilled

1-1/4 teaspoons sugar

3/4 teaspoon pure vanilla extract

Grind almonds with 2 tablespoons sugar in a food processor to a fine powder. Add salt, flour and remaining 2 tablespoons sugar. Process briefly to blend. Scatter butter pieces over mixture. Process using quick on/off pulses until mixture resembles coarse meal. Pour egg evenly over mixture. Process using on/off pulses, scraping down occasionally, until dough forms sticky crumbs that can easily be pressed together but does not come together in a ball. If crumbs are dry, sprinkle with 1/2 teaspoon water and process using on/off pulses until dough forms sticky crumbs. Add more water in same way, 1/2 teaspoon at a time, if crumbs are still dry.

Continue as directed in paragraphs 3 to 5 under Sweet Pastry Shell, page 59.

Position rack in lower third of oven and preheat to 425F (220C). Line pastry shell with parchment paper or foil; fill with dried beans or pie weights. Set shell on a baking sheet. Bake 10 minutes or until side is firm and beginning to brown. Reduce oven temperature to 375F (190C). Carefully remove paper with beans. Bake shell 10 minutes or until base is firm.

Transfer tart pan to a rack; cool while preparing filling. Reduce oven temperature to 350F (175C).

Filling: Melt chocolate with butter in a medium bowl over nearly simmering water. Stir until smooth. Remove from water; cool slightly. Grind almonds with 2 tablespoons sugar in a food processor to a fine powder.

Whisk eggs in a medium bowl. Whisk in remaining 6 tablespoons sugar. Still using whisk, stir in chocolate mixture, almonds and flour. Pour into partially baked tart shell. Bake about 25 minutes or until a cake tester inserted in center of filling comes out clean. Set tart on a flat-bottomed upside-down bowl; remove side of pan. Transfer tart to a rack.

Topping: Toast sliced almonds in a shallow baking pan in oven, stirring often, about 6 minutes or until lightly browned. Transfer to a plate.

When tart is lukewarm, gently remove base of pan. Cool completely. Transfer to a platter. Refrigerate 30 minutes. *Tart can be kept, covered, 2 days in refrigerator.*

In a large chilled bowl, whip cream with sugar and vanilla until stiff. Spread cream over top of tart, covering it completely. Swirl top. Sprinkle toasted almonds over top.

Makes 8 servings

Chocolate-Cashew Custard Pie

The contrast of three textures—flaky pie crust, crunchy cashews and creamy dark chocolate filling—makes this a delightful treat. This pie is much richer than traditional custard pies.

9-inch unbaked Pie Shell, page 58, or packaged shell

10 oz. semisweet chocolate, chopped

6 large egg yolks

1-1/2 cups whipping cream

1/2 cup unsalted cashews (about 2-1/4 oz.)

Position rack in center of oven and preheat to 425F (220C). Line pie shell with buttered parchment paper or foil, buttered-side down. Fill with dried beans or pie weights. Bake 10 minutes or until side is firm. Carefully remove paper with beans. Bake pie shell 7 minutes or until base is firm. Transfer to a rack; cool. Reduce oven temperature to 325F (165C).

Melt chocolate in a medium bowl over nearly simmering water. Stir until smooth. Remove from water; let cool.

Whisk egg yolks with cream in a large bowl until blended. Gradually stir in chocolate, using a whisk. Pour into pie shell. Arrange cashews on top in 3 circles, with all cashews facing same direction and lined up so baked pie can be cut in pieces between rows of cashews and not through them. Leave center of pie uncovered by cashews.

Return pie to center of oven. Bake about 30 minutes or until top looks just set and does not move or stick to your finger when lightly touched (touch it quickly because it is hot). Cool to room temperature. Refrigerate at least 1 hour. *Pie can be kept, covered, 2 days in refrigerator.* Serve at room temperature.

Makes about 10 servings

Chocolate Bavarian Pie

Bavarian cream is one of the most luscious of desserts on its own but it is even more interesting as a pie because of the contrast with the texture of the crust. In this pie, the creamy chocolate filling is served in an easy-to-make crisp dark chocolate crust.

Chocolate-Wafer Crust:

6-1/2 oz. chocolate wafers
(about 29 wafers)

6 tablespoons unsalted butter,
melted and cooled

Chocolate Bavarian Cream:

3 oz. fine-quality semisweet
chocolate, chopped

1-3/4 teaspoons unflavored gelatin

3 tablespoons water

3/4 cup milk

3 large egg yolks

1/4 cup sugar

1/2 pint whipping cream (1 cup),
well-chilled

Quick Chocolate Curls, page 172, or
Chocolate Leaves, page 177, if
desired

Crust: Preheat oven to 350F (175C). Grind cookies in a food processor to fairly fine crumbs; measure 1-1/2 cups. Transfer measured crumbs to a medium bowl. Add melted butter; mix lightly with a fork. Lightly pat mixture in an even layer in a 9-inch pie pan, using a fork, up to rim of pan. Bake about 10 minutes or until crisp. Cool completely.

Bavarian cream: Melt chocolate in a medium bowl over nearly simmering water. Sprinkle gelatin over 3 tablespoons water in a small cup.

Bring milk to a boil in a small heavy saucepan. Whisk egg yolks in a large bowl. Add sugar; whisk until smooth. Gradually whisk in hot milk. Return mixture to saucepan, whisking. Cook over medium-low heat, stirring and scraping bottom of pan constantly with a wooden spoon, until mixture reaches 165F to 170F (75C) on an instant-read or candy thermometer, about 5 minutes. To check without thermometer, see page 169. Remove from heat and immediately add softened gelatin; whisk until it completely dissolves. Pour into a large bowl; stir about 30 seconds to cool.

Remove chocolate from pan of water. Stir until smooth. Using a whisk, stir custard mixture, about 1/2 cup at a time, into chocolate. Return mixture to large bowl. Cool to room temperature, stirring occasionally.

Chill bowl of chocolate mixture, stirring often, in refrigerator about 20 minutes or in a larger bowl of iced water about 10 minutes, or until mixture is cold and beginning to thicken but is not set. In a large chilled bowl, whip cream until nearly stiff. Fold into chocolate mixture. Pour into pie crust. Refrigerate about 2 hours or until set. *Pie can be kept, covered, 2 days in refrigerator.* Garnish with chocolate curls or leaves just before serving.

Makes 8 servings

Strawberry-White Chocolate Tart

This dessert looks like a classic strawberry tart but holds a surprise—a white-chocolate filling, which provides a sweet, creamy complement to the berries.

Photo opposite.

9- to 9-1/2-inch Sweet Pastry Shell, page 59

White Chocolate Pastry Cream:

3 large egg yolks

3 tablespoons sugar

1 tablespoon cornstarch

1/2 cup whipping cream

1/2 cup milk

Butter

4 oz. fine-quality white chocolate, chopped

Strawberry Topping:

5 cups small strawberries (about 1-1/4 lbs.)

1/2 cup strawberry preserves

Position rack in lower third of oven and preheat to 425F (220C). Line tart shell with parchment paper or foil; fill with dried beans or pie weights. Set tart shell on a baking sheet. Bake 10 minutes or until side is firm and beginning to brown. Reduce oven temperature to 375F (190C). Carefully remove paper with beans. Bake shell 14 minutes or until base is firm and just beginning to brown.

Set tart shell on a flat-bottomed upside-down bowl. Remove side of pan. Transfer shell to a rack; cool to lukewarm. Gently remove base of pan. Cool shell completely. Transfer to a platter. *Tart shell can be kept, covered, 1 day at room temperature.*

Pastry cream: Whisk egg yolks in a heatproof medium bowl. Add sugar and whisk until blended. Lightly whisk in cornstarch.

Bring cream and milk to a boil in a heavy medium saucepan over medium-high heat. Gradually whisk hot cream mixture into yolk mixture. Return to saucepan. Cook over medium heat, whisking constantly, until mixture is very thick and nearly comes to a boil. Remove from heat. Transfer to a shallow bowl; dab with a small piece of butter to prevent a skin from forming. Cool to room temperature.

Melt white chocolate in a medium bowl over nearly simmering water, stirring occasionally. Stir until smooth. Remove from water; let cool. Whisk into pastry cream. Cover and refrigerate at least 2 hours. *Pastry cream can be kept, covered, 2 days in refrigerator.*

Topping: Up to a few hours before serving, spread pastry cream in baked tart shell. Top with strawberries, pointing upward, arranged close together.

Heat preserves in a small saucepan over low heat until hot but not boiling. Strain into a small bowl, pressing on pieces. Using a pastry brush, gently brush preserves on strawberries, brushing each berry individually. Refrigerate until ready to serve. Serve tart within 4 hours so pastry remains crisp.

Makes 8 servings

Chocolate-Marbled Chiffon Pie

Creamy white and dark chocolate fillings are swirled together inside a rich chocolate-nut crust.

Photo on pages vi-vii.

Chocolate-Walnut Crust:

3 oz. bittersweet chocolate, chopped

3 tablespoons unsalted butter

1-1/2 cups walnuts (about 5 oz.), toasted, page 179, and cooled

3 tablespoons sugar

White & Dark Chocolate Chiffon Filling:

1 (1/4-oz.) envelope unflavored gelatin (scant 1 tablespoon)

1/4 cup cold water

3 oz. fine-quality white chocolate, chopped

3/4 cup milk

3 large eggs, separated (see variation)

5 tablespoons sugar

4 oz. bittersweet chocolate, chopped

1/2 pint whipping cream (1 cup), well-chilled

Crust: Melt chocolate and butter in a medium bowl over nearly simmering water. Stir until smooth. Remove from water; cool slightly.

Grind nuts with sugar in a food processor to a fine powder. Transfer to a medium bowl. Add chocolate mixture; mix well with a fork. Spread evenly in a 9-inch pie pan, using the back of a spoon. Push mixture evenly up side of pan so it forms a border about 1/4 inch above rim of pan. Refrigerate 30 minutes or until firm.

Filling: Sprinkle gelatin over 1/4 cup water in a small cup. Melt white chocolate in a small bowl over nearly simmering water. Whisk until smooth. Remove from water; let cool.

Bring milk to a boil in a very small heavy saucepan. Whisk egg yolks in a large bowl. Add 3 tablespoons sugar; whisk until smooth. Gradually whisk in hot milk. Return mixture to saucepan, whisking. Cook over medium-low heat, stirring and scraping bottom of pan constantly with a wooden spoon, until mixture reaches 165F to 170F (75C) on an instant-read or candy thermometer, about 4 minutes. To check without thermometer, see page 169. Remove from heat and immediately add softened gelatin; whisk until it completely dissolves. Pour into a large bowl; stir about 30 seconds to cool. Whisk in white chocolate.

Chill mixture by setting bowl in a larger bowl of iced water about 10 minutes, stirring very often, or until mixture is cold and barely beginning to thicken but is not set. If mixture becomes too firm, it will be difficult to marble.

Melt bittersweet chocolate in a small bowl over nearly simmering water. Remove from heat but leave chocolate above water. In a large chilled bowl, whip cream until nearly stiff.

When custard begins to thicken, remove from bowl of iced water. In a small bowl, whip egg whites to soft peaks. Gradually beat in remaining 2 tablespoons sugar; beat at high speed until whites are stiff and shiny but not dry.

Gently fold cream into custard mixture. Fold in whites, blending thoroughly. Transfer 2 cups custard to a small bowl. Remove dark chocolate from above water. Whisk 3/4 cup custard from bowl into chocolate. Return chocolate mixture to remaining custard in small bowl; fold quickly until blended.

Spoon about half of dark chocolate mixture into pie shell. Spoon white chocolate mixture over it. Quickly spoon remaining dark chocolate in 4 large spoonfuls on top of white mixture, spacing them evenly apart. Gently swirl a thin knife through mixtures to marble them. Refrigerate about 2 hours or until set. *Pie can be kept, covered, 2 days in refrigerator.*

Makes 8 servings

Variation

If you are concerned about the safety of using raw eggs, omit egg whites and increase amount of whipping cream to 1-1/2 cups. Whip cream with 2 tablespoons sugar.

Chocolate-Mint Cream Puffs

Light puffs of chocolate dough coated with a dark chocolate glaze hold a refreshing mint filling.

Chocolate Choux Pastry, page 60

Mint Pastry Cream:

1 large bunch fresh mint
(about 4-3/4 oz.)

2 cups milk

5 egg yolks, room temperature

7 tablespoons sugar

3 tablespoons cornstarch

1/4 cup butter, room temperature

Additional butter

Chocolate Glaze, page 160

**Fresh mint sprigs, if desired
(garnish)**

Pastry: Position rack in lower third of oven and preheat to 400F (205C). Lightly butter 2 baking sheets. Using a pastry bag and 1/2-inch plain tip, shape mounds of Chocolate Choux Pastry dough about 1-1/2 inches in diameter, spacing them about 2 inches apart on buttered baking sheets. Brush with extra beaten egg remaining from making dough, gently pushing down any points.

Bake about 30 minutes or until dough is puffed and firm. Using a serrated knife, carefully cut off top third of each puff; set aside as a "hat." Cool puffs on a rack. *Puffs can be kept 1 day in an airtight container but taste best on day they are baked.*

Pastry cream: Remove mint leaves from stems; you should have about 4 cups leaves. Coarsely chop leaves. Bring milk to a boil in a heavy medium saucepan. Add mint; remove from heat and stir. Cover and let stand 1 hour. Strain milk into a heavy medium saucepan, pressing on mint in strainer.

Whisk egg yolks lightly in a medium bowl. Add sugar; whisk until blended. Lightly stir in cornstarch, using whisk. Bring mint-flavored milk to a boil in a heavy medium saucepan. Gradually whisk hot milk into yolk mixture. Return to saucepan. Cook over medium-low heat, whisking constantly, until mixture is very thick and barely comes to a boil. Do not overcook or yolks will curdle. Remove from heat. Whisk in butter. Transfer to a bowl; dab with a small piece of additional butter to prevent a skin from forming. Refrigerate until completely cool.

Whisk pastry cream until smooth. Using a pastry bag and medium star tip, pipe pastry cream generously into cream puffs. Set reserved "hats" on top. Refrigerate 1 hour. *Filled puffs can be kept 1 day in refrigerator.*

Make glaze and cool until thickened. Using a teaspoon, spoon glaze over each filled puff, covering top third and letting glaze run down side. Cool about 15 minutes; on a hot day, refrigerate. To serve, garnish each plate with a fresh mint sprig.

Makes about 16 puffs

Sultan's Cream Puffs

In classic cuisine, desserts containing almonds, citrus fruits or other ingredients that were associated with the Near East were sometimes called *à la sultane*. These almond-topped cream puffs filled with a creamy chocolate-orange mixture are rich enough to please any sultan!

Photo on pages vi-vii.

Choux Pastry, page 60

2 tablespoons sliced almonds

Chocolate-Orange Mousseline Filling:

2 large navel oranges

1 cup milk

3 oz. semisweet chocolate, chopped

3 large egg yolks

1/4 cup sugar

1 tablespoon plus 2 teaspoons cornstarch

Butter

1/2 cup whipping cream, well-chilled

Powdered sugar (for sprinkling)

Pastry: Position rack in lower third of oven and preheat to 400F (205C). Lightly butter 2 baking sheets. Using a pastry bag and 1/2-inch plain tip, shape mounds of Choux Pastry dough about 1-1/2 inches in diameter, spacing them about 2 inches apart on buttered baking sheets. Brush them with beaten egg reserved from making dough, gently pushing down any points. Sprinkle a few almond slices on each.

Bake 20 minutes. Reduce oven temperature to 350F (175C). Continue baking about 15 minutes or until dough is puffed and browned; cracks that form during baking should also be brown. Using a serrated knife, carefully cut off top half of each puff; set aside as a "hat." Cool puffs on a rack. *Puffs can be kept 1 day in an airtight container but taste best on day they are baked.*

Filling: Using a vegetable peeler, pare colored part of orange peel, without white pith, in long strips. Heat milk and orange zest strips in a heavy medium saucepan over medium heat until bubbles form around edge of pan. Remove from heat. Cover and let stand 20 minutes. Strain milk into another heavy medium saucepan. Melt chocolate in a small bowl over nearly simmering water. Stir until smooth. Remove from water.

Whisk egg yolks in a medium bowl. Add sugar; whisk until blended. Lightly whisk in cornstarch. Bring milk to a boil. Gradually whisk hot milk into yolk mixture. Return to saucepan. Cook over medium-low heat, whisking constantly, until mixture is very thick and just begins to bubble. Do not overcook or yolks will curdle. Remove from heat. Whisk in chocolate. Transfer to a bowl; dab with a small piece of butter to prevent a skin from forming. Refrigerate until completely cool.

Whisk chocolate mixture until smooth. In a chilled medium bowl, whip cream until stiff. Fold into chocolate mixture. A short time before serving, pipe filling into cream puffs using a pastry bag and medium star tip. Set reserved "hats" on top at an angle to show filling. Sift powdered sugar over cream puffs. *Filled puffs can be kept 1 day in refrigerator.*

Makes about 15 puffs

Chocolate Napoleon

Napoleon is a classic that remains popular because of the contrast between the generous amount of creamy filling and the thin layers of crisp flaky puff pastry. Now it is easy to make with purchased puff pastry.

1/2 (1-lb.) pkg. frozen puff pastry sheets or 14 oz. fresh puff pastry

Chocolate Mousseline Filling:

2 large egg yolks

3 tablespoons sugar

1 tablespoon plus 2 teaspoons cornstarch

3/4 cup milk

6 oz. semisweet chocolate, chopped

Butter

3/4 cup whipping cream, well-chilled

Powdered Sugar Glaze:

1 oz. semisweet chocolate, chopped (for garnish)

2 tablespoons plus 2 teaspoons whipping cream

3/4 cup powdered sugar, sifted

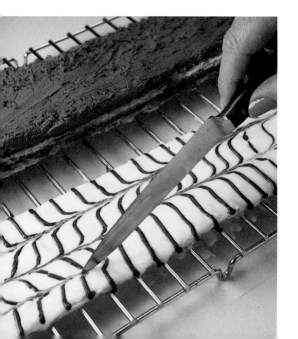

Pastry: If using a sheet of frozen dough, defrost dough 20 minutes and unfold.

Sprinkle water lightly on a 17" x 11" baking sheet. On a cold lightly floured surface, quickly roll fresh pastry to a 17" x 11" rectangle; if using a packaged sheet, roll it to enlarge mainly in lengthwise direction. Keep dough straight and flour often. Roll dough around rolling pin; unroll onto prepared baking sheet. Trim edges if necessary. Prick dough all over with fork at close intervals. Refrigerate 30 minutes. Position rack in center of oven and preheat to 400F (205C). Bake dough 12 minutes or until it begins to brown. Reduce oven temperature to 350F (175C); bake 5 minutes or until golden-brown. Set a large rack over baking sheet; turn pastry over onto rack. Sheet will be very thin. Cool on rack. Slide pastry sheet onto a large cutting board. Using a small sharp knife and cutting with its point, trim edges of pastry straight. Cut it lengthwise in 3 equal strips; each will be about 3-1/8 inches wide.

Filling: Whisk egg yolks in a small heatproof bowl. Add sugar and whisk until blended. Lightly whisk in cornstarch. Bring milk to a boil in a small heavy saucepan. Gradually whisk hot milk into yolk mixture. Return to saucepan. Cook over medium-low heat, whisking constantly, until very thick and comes to a boil. Do not overcook or yolks will curdle. Remove from heat.

Melt chocolate in a medium bowl over nearly simmering water. Stir until smooth. Remove from water; cool slightly. Whisk chocolate into filling mixture. Transfer to a bowl; dab with a small piece of butter to prevent a skin from forming. Cool to room temperature. Cover and refrigerate 20 minutes. In a large chilled bowl, whip cream until stiff. Whisk chocolate mixture until smooth and fold in cream. Refrigerate about 10 minutes.

Assembly: Spread 1-1/2 cups chocolate filling on each of 2 pastry strips. Set 1 filling-topped strip on a platter. Top with second filling-topped strip. Refrigerate while making frosting. Have ready a parchment paper piping cone or a small pastry bag with very fine plain tip. Melt chocolate in a small bowl over nearly simmering water. Stir until smooth. Remove from water; cool slightly. Spoon into paper cone or pastry bag.

Stir cream into powdered sugar in a small bowl. Beat with a wooden spoon until smooth. Spread on third pastry strip. Quickly smooth icing with a metal spatula.

Using paper cone or pastry bag, pipe crosswise parallel lines of chocolate on icing, 1/2 inch apart. Beginning at 1 short end of cake about 1/2 inch from long edge, draw dull side of a thin-bladed knife across chocolate lines, pulling it lengthwise over cake. Alternating end of cake from which you begin, draw knife across lines 2 or 3 more times at equal distances. Set frosted pastry strip on top of cake; press lightly. Refrigerate 30 minutes. *Napoleon can be kept, covered, 1 day in refrigerator but tastes best on day it was baked.* To serve, cut carefully into 1-1/2 inch slices using a serrated knife.

Makes 8 to 10 servings

Profiteroles with Hazelnut Cream

Profiteroles are small cream puffs served with a shiny hot chocolate sauce. As an alternative to whipped cream, the puffs can be filled with ice cream. Good choices are vanilla, coffee, French-Italian Chocolate, page 98, or Chocolate-Mint, page 99.

Photo opposite.

Choux Pastry, page 60

Hazelnut Whipped Cream:

1 cup hazelnuts

2 tablespoons plus 1 teaspoon sugar

1/2 pint whipping cream (1 cup), well-chilled

1/4 cup hazelnut liqueur (Frangelico)

Rich Chocolate Sauce:

5 oz. bittersweet or semisweet chocolate, chopped

4 large egg yolks

1 tablespoon sugar

1/4 cup whipping cream

1/4 cup milk

Pastry: Position rack in lower third of oven and preheat to 400F (205C). Lightly butter 2 baking sheets. Using a pastry bag and medium plain tip, shape mounds of Choux Pastry dough about 1-1/4 inches in diameter, spacing them about 2 inches apart on buttered baking sheets. Brush them with beaten egg left from making dough, gently pushing down any points.

Bake about 28 minutes or until dough is puffed and browned; cracks that form during baking should also be brown. Using a serrated knife, carefully cut off top third of each puff; set aside as a "hat." Cool puffs on a rack. *Puffs can be kept 1 day in an airtight container but taste best on day they are baked.*

Hazelnut cream: Preheat oven to 350F (175C). Toast hazelnuts and remove skins, page 178; cool nuts completely. Grind nuts with 1 tablespoon sugar in a food processor to a fine powder. Transfer to a medium bowl. In a large chilled bowl, whip cream with remaining 4 teaspoons sugar until stiff. Fold in ground nuts in 2 batches. Gradually fold in liqueur. Spoon into cream puffs. Set reserved "hats" on top.

Sauce: Melt chocolate in a medium bowl over nearly simmering water. Stir until smooth. Remove from water.

Whisk yolks with sugar and cream in a small metal bowl. Set in a pan of nearly simmering water. Heat, whisking, until mixture reaches 160F (70C) on an instant-read or candy thermometer, about 1 minute. Immediately remove from water and whisk 1 minute to cool. Whisk in chocolate. Gradually whisk in milk. Return to pan of water and heat, stirring, 3 minutes or until warm. *Sauce can be kept, covered, 1 week in refrigerator; reheat in pan above hot water, stirring constantly, until warm.* Spoon sauce over profiteroles when serving.

Makes about 20 profiteroles

Variation

Profiteroles with Ice Cream: Fill each cream puff generously with ice cream. Set reserved "hat" on top. Freeze while preparing sauce.

Chocolate Gâteau Paris Brest

Praline cream is the traditional filling for this elegant, ring-shaped cream puff cake, but here it has a new chocolate twist. This elegant, light dessert is a perfect finale for a dinner party.

Choux Pastry, page 60

2 tablespoons sliced almonds

Praline Chocolate Whipped Cream:

3 oz. semisweet chocolate, coarsely chopped

1-1/2 cups whipping cream, well-chilled

Almond Praline, page 171

Powdered sugar (for sprinkling)

Pastry: Position rack in lower third of oven and preheat to 400F (205C). Lightly butter a baking sheet. Using an 8-inch cake pan, draw an 8-inch circle on baking sheet; it will be only barely visible.

Using a pastry bag and large plain tip about 5/8-inch in diameter, evenly pipe Choux Pastry dough in an 8-inch ring onto baking sheet, following marked circle. Pipe another ring inside first, touching it. Pipe a third ring on top of crack joining first 2 rings. Brush dough with beaten egg reserved from making dough. Gently mark lines on dough by pressing with bottom of a fork dipped in water. Sprinkle almonds on top.

Bake 20 minutes. Reduce oven temperature to 350F (175C). Continue baking about 20 minutes or until dough is puffed and browned; cracks that form during baking should also brown. Using a serrated knife, carefully split cake in half horizontally. Cool both halves separately on a rack. *Cake can be kept, covered, 1 day at room temperature but tastes best on day it is baked.*

Praline Chocolate Whipped Cream: Melt chocolate in a small heatproof bowl over nearly simmering water. Stir until smooth. Remove from heat but leave chocolate above hot water.

In a large chilled bowl, whip cream until stiff. Remove chocolate from above water; cool 30 seconds. Quickly stir about 1/2 cup whipped cream into chocolate. Quickly fold mixture into remaining whipped cream until smooth. Fold quickly so chocolate does not harden upon contact with cold whipped cream. Fold in praline.

Using a pastry bag and large star tip, pipe all of Praline Chocolate Whipped Cream onto lower half of cake in a ruffle so it shows at edge. Cover with top half of cake. Refrigerate 30 minutes. *Filled cake can be kept, covered, 8 hours in refrigerator.* Sprinkle with powdered sugar before serving.

Makes 6 to 8 servings

Chocolate-Cinnamon Raisin Rolls

These rolls are made of a rich simple-to-make brioche dough spread with cinnamon cream and sprinkled with chocolate pieces and raisins. They are perfect for brunch or teatime.

Photo on page 154.

Easy Brioche Dough:

1 (1/4-oz.) pkg. active dry yeast (about 1 tablespoon)

2 tablespoons warm water (110F, 45C)

1 tablespoon sugar

2 cups all-purpose flour

1-1/4 teaspoons salt

3 large eggs

1 large egg yolk

1/2 cup (4 oz.) unsalted butter, cut in 16 pieces, room temperature

Cinnamon Pastry Cream:

5 large egg yolks

6 tablespoons sugar

3/4 teaspoon ground cinnamon

2 tablespoons plus 2 teaspoons cornstarch

1-1/2 cups milk

Butter

3/4 cup semisweet real chocolate pieces

1/2 cup light raisins

1 egg, beaten with a pinch of salt (for glaze)

Dough: In a small bowl sprinkle yeast over water; add 1/4 teaspoon sugar. Let stand 10 minutes or until foamy. Stir yeast mixture.

Put flour into bowl of mixer; make a well in center. Add salt, remaining 2-3/4 teaspoons sugar and whole eggs. Mix briefly with dough hook of mixer. Add yeast mixture. Mix at low speed until mixture comes together to a dough, pushing in flour occasionally. Scrape down mixture. Add egg yolk; beat until blended. Continue beating on medium speed about 12 minutes or until dough is very smooth. Add butter pieces. Beat on low speed, scraping down dough often, just until butter is blended in. Dough will be soft.

Lightly oil a medium bowl. Place dough in oiled bowl; turn dough over to oil surface. Cover with damp towel or plastic wrap; let dough rise in a warm draft-free place about 1-1/2 hours or until nearly doubled in bulk. Gently turn dough over several times to knock out air. Return to bowl. Cover and refrigerate at least 4 hours or overnight.

Pastry cream: Whisk egg yolks in a medium bowl. Add sugar and cinnamon; whisk until blended. Lightly whisk in cornstarch. Bring milk to a boil in a heavy medium saucepan. Gradually whisk hot milk into yolk mixture. Return to saucepan. Cook over medium-low heat, whisking constantly, until mixture is very thick and barely comes to a boil; it will be too thick to bubble. Cook over low heat, whisking constantly, 1 minute. Do not overcook or yolks will curdle. Remove from heat. Transfer to a bowl; dab with a small piece of butter to prevent a skin from forming. Refrigerate 1-1/2 hours to overnight.

Assembly: Lightly butter 2 baking sheets. On a cool floured surface, roll out dough to a 15" x 10" rectangle, flouring often. Whisk pastry cream. Spread over dough, leaving a 1-inch border on 1 long side. Sprinkle pastry cream evenly with chocolate pieces and raisins. Brush plain border with egg glaze. Roll up dough from opposite long side like a jelly roll. Press roll of dough along egg-brushed border to seal.

Trim ends. Cut a 1-inch slice of rolled dough. Using rubber spatula, set slice on buttered baking sheet, with its more narrow side (side that was pressed with knife) facing down. Slice remaining dough; space slices about 2 inches apart on sheet. Work quickly so dough will not become too soft. Press any uneven slices to an even round shape. Let rise uncovered in a draft-free area about 30 minutes. Meanwhile, position rack in center of oven and preheat to 400F (205C).

Bake rolls 12 minutes. If there is room for only 1 baking sheet on center rack, bake in 2 batches. Reduce oven temperature to 350F (175C). Bake 10 to 12 minutes or until rolls are golden-brown. Transfer to a rack; cool slightly. *Pastries can be kept 1 day in an airtight container but are best freshly baked.* Serve warm or at room temperature.

Makes 15 sweet rolls

Chocolate-Pear Pizza

Do not worry—there is no tomato sauce or cheese here! This pastry is related to pizza only in its form. Its base is made of a rich, sweet, yeast dough, which is spread with chocolate sauce and topped with pear slices.

Sweet Yeast Dough:

1 (1/4-oz.) pkg. active dry yeast (about 1 tablespoon)

3/4 cup warm water (110F, 45C)

1 tablespoon sugar

3 cups all-purpose flour

1 teaspoon salt

2 large eggs

6 tablespoons unsalted butter, cut in 6 pieces, room temperature

Chocolate-Pear Topping:

5 tablespoons unsalted butter, chilled

4 oz. semisweet chocolate, finely chopped

2 ripe medium pears (about 14 oz.)

2 teaspoons grated lemon zest

1/3 cup sugar

Dough: In a small bowl sprinkle yeast over 1/4 cup warm water; add 1 teaspoon sugar. Let stand 10 minutes or until foamy. Combine flour, salt and remaining 2 teaspoons sugar in a food processor fitted with a plastic or metal blade. Process briefly to blend. Add eggs. With blades of processor turning, quickly pour in yeast mixture and remaining water. Process 1 minute to knead dough. Add butter; process just until absorbed. Dough will be soft and sticky.

Lightly oil a medium bowl. Place dough in oiled bowl; turn dough over to oil surface. Cover with damp towel or plastic wrap. Let dough rise in a warm draft-free place about 1 hour or until doubled in bulk. Lightly butter 2 baking sheets. Divide dough in 2 equal parts. Place each on a baking sheet. Pat with lightly floured hands to a 10-inch circle.

Topping: Refrigerate 3 tablespoons butter. Melt chocolate with remaining 2 tablespoons butter in a medium bowl over nearly simmering water. Stir until smooth. Remove from water.

Peel pears; halve and core. Cut in lengthwise slices, about 1/8 inch thick. Using a rubber spatula, spread warm chocolate evenly over each round of dough, leaving a 3/4-inch border. Arrange pear slices pointing inward in a ring on chocolate, leaving center of chocolate uncovered. Sprinkle grated lemon zest evenly over pears. Cut chilled butter in very thin slices, about 1/8 inch thick. Halve butter slices and scatter over pears. Sprinkle pears with sugar. Let rise 15 minutes. Meanwhile, position rack in center of oven and preheat to 425F (220C).

Bake 20 minutes or until dough browns and pears are tender. Serve pizza warm or at room temperature. Serve pizza on day it was baked; or freeze and reheat before serving.

Makes 2 pizzas, each 6 servings

Variation

To make dough by hand: Sift flour into a bowl; make a well in center. Add yeast mixture, remaining water, eggs, remaining sugar and salt to well. Mix ingredients in middle of well. Stir in flour; mix well. Knead dough vigorously, slapping it on a work surface, until it is smooth and elastic. Pound butter with your fist to soften thoroughly. Set butter on top of dough; knead until blended in. If dough is very sticky, flour it occasionally while kneading.

Chocolate Marzipan Filo Triangles

These crisp flaky pastries encase a rich chocolate-almond filling and are easy to prepare using packaged sheets of filo dough.

---

1 lb. filo sheets (about 20 sheets)

1 oz. semisweet chocolate, chopped

1 oz. unsweetened chocolate, chopped

1 cup whole blanched almonds (about 5 oz.)

1/2 cup sugar

1 large egg, beaten

2 tablespoons plus 2 teaspoons brandy

1-1/2 cups (12 oz.) unsalted butter or margarine, melted and cooled

About 2 teaspoons sesame seeds

If filo dough is frozen, thaw in refrigerator 8 hours or overnight. Melt chocolates in a medium bowl over nearly simmering water. Stir until smooth. Remove from water; let cool. Grind almonds with 2 tablespoons sugar in a food processor to a fine powder. Add remaining 6 tablespoons sugar and egg; process until blended. Add chocolate; process until blended. Add brandy; process until blended. Transfer to a bowl.

Position rack in center of oven and preheat to 350F (175C). Butter 2 baking sheets. Remove filo sheets from their package; spread out on a dry towel. Using a sharp knife, cut stack in half lengthwise to form 2 stacks of sheets, about 16" x 7". Immediately cover filo with a piece of waxed paper, then with a damp towel. Work with only 1 sheet at a time; keep remaining sheets covered with paper and towel so they do not dry out.

Carefully remove 1 filo sheet from pile. Brush with melted butter; fold in half lengthwise so dimensions are about 16" x 3-1/2". Place about 1-1/2 teaspoons filling at 1 end of strip. Fold end of strip diagonally over filling to form a triangle. Fold it over and over, keeping it in a triangular shape after each fold, until end of strip is reached. Brush sheet with butter before last fold to stick triangle together. Set pastry on a buttered baking sheet and brush with butter. Cover with plastic wrap. Make pastries with remaining filo sheets and filling. *Pastries can be kept, covered tightly, 1 day in refrigerator.*

Brush pastries again with melted butter. Sprinkle with sesame seeds. Bake about 25 minutes or until golden brown. If baking on 2 racks, switch their positions halfway through baking time. Serve warm or at room temperature.

Makes about 36 pastries

Pie Shell

Homemade pie dough is easy to make in a food processor. Use this pie shell for Double-Chocolate Pecan Pie, page 42, and Chocolate-Cashew Custard Pie, page 44.

1-1/4 cups all-purpose flour

1/4 teaspoon salt

5 tablespoons unsalted butter, well-chilled, cut in 10 pieces

2 tablespoons vegetable shortening, well-chilled, cut in 4 pieces

About 1 tablespoon plus 2-1/2 teaspoons iced water

Process flour with salt in a food processor briefly to blend. Scatter butter and shortening pieces over mixture. Process using quick on/off pulses until mixture resembles coarse meal. Sprinkle evenly with 1 tablespoon water. Process with on/off pulses until it is absorbed. Sprinkle with 1 teaspoon water. Process with on/off pulses, scraping down occasionally, until dough forms sticky crumbs that can easily be pressed together but does not come together in a ball. If crumbs are dry, sprinkle with more water as needed, 1/2 teaspoon at a time. Process using on/off pulses until dough forms sticky crumbs.

Transfer dough to a sheet of plastic wrap. Wrap dough and push together. Shape dough in a flat disc. Refrigerate at least 2 hours. *Dough can be kept 2 days in refrigerator.*

Let dough soften 1 minute at room temperature. Set on a cold lightly floured surface. Knock dough firmly with a heavy rolling pin several times to flatten it. Roll out dough, flouring often and working quickly, to a round about 1/8 inch thick and about 11-1/2 inches in diameter. Roll dough loosely around rolling pin; unroll over a 9-inch pie pan. Gently ease dough into pan, letting excess dough hang over edge of pan.

Trim dough about 1/2 inch from edge of pan with scissors. Fold edge of dough under so it comes just to rim of pan and covers rim. Crimp edge of dough, forming a high border. Prick dough lightly with a fork. Cover with plastic wrap; refrigerate 1 hour. *Pie shell can be kept, covered, 1 day in refrigerator; or it can be frozen.*

Makes 1 9-inch pie shell

Variation

To make dough by hand: Sift flour and salt into a bowl. Cut butter and shortening into flour with a pastry blender or 2 knives until mixture resembles coarse meal. Gradually sprinkle water over mixture, mixing and tossing lightly with a fork, until dough holds together.

Sweet Pastry Shell

Bake this buttery, cookie-like shell for Strawberry-White Chocolate Tart, page 48.
Use the smaller tart shell in the variation for Berries, Chocolate & Cream Tart, page 41.

6 tablespoons sugar

1/4 teaspoon salt

1-1/2 cups all-purpose flour

1/2 cup (4 oz.) unsalted butter, well-chilled, cut in 16 pieces

3 large egg yolks, beaten

1 to 2 teaspoons iced water, if needed

Process sugar with salt and flour in a food processor briefly to blend. Scatter butter pieces over mixture. Process using quick on/off pulses until mixture resembles coarse meal. Pour egg yolks evenly over mixture. Process using on/off pulses, scraping down occasionally, until dough forms sticky crumbs that can easily be pressed together but does not come together in a ball. If crumbs are dry, sprinkle with 1/2 teaspoon water and process using on/off pulses until dough forms sticky crumbs. Add more water in same way, 1/2 teaspoon at a time, if crumbs are still dry.

Transfer dough to a work surface. Blend dough further by pushing about 1/4 of it away from you and smearing it with the heel of your hand against work surface. Continue with remaining dough in 3 batches. Repeat if dough is not yet well-blended. Using a rubber spatula, transfer dough to a sheet of plastic wrap. Wrap dough and push together. Shape dough in a flat disc. Refrigerate at least 6 hours. *Dough can be kept 2 days in refrigerator.*

Butter a 9- to 9-1/2-inch tart pan with removable base. Let dough soften 1 minute at room temperature. Set it on a cold lightly floured surface. Knock dough firmly with a heavy rolling pin several times to flatten it. Roll out dough, flouring often and working as quickly as possible, to a round about 1/4 inch thick and about 11-1/2 inches in diameter. Roll dough loosely around rolling pin; unroll over pan. Gently ease dough into pan. If dough tears, use a piece of dough hanging over rim to patch it.

Using your thumb, gently push down dough slightly at top edge of pan, making top edge of shell thicker than rest of shell. Roll rolling pin across pan to cut off dough at edges. With your finger and thumb, press to push up top edge of dough all around pan so it is about 1/4 inch higher than rim of pan. Refrigerate about 10 minutes. Prick dough all over with a fork. Cover with plastic wrap; refrigerate 1 hour. *Tart shell can be kept, covered, 1 day in refrigerator; or it can be frozen.*

Makes 1 9- to 9-1/2-inch tart shell

Variations

To make dough by hand: Sift flour into a large bowl; make a well in center. Put yolks, salt and sugar in well; mix briefly, using your fingers. Pound butter pieces with rolling pin or your fist to soften them slightly. Separate butter again in pieces; add to well. Using your fingers, mix and crush ingredients in center of well until mixed but still not smooth. Draw in flour and crumble ingredients through your fingers, raising mixture in the air, until dough begins to come together. Add a little water, 1/2 teaspoon at a time, if dough is too dry.

Eight-Inch Sweet Pastry Shell: Prepare dough using 5 tablespoons sugar, pinch of salt, 1-1/4 cups all-purpose flour, 6 tablespoons unsalted butter, 2 large egg yolks, and 1 to 2 teaspoons iced water, if needed. Roll dough to a round about 9-1/2-inches in diameter and fit it into a buttered 8-inch tart pan with removable base.

Choux Pastry

Use to make Profiteroles with Hazelnut Cream, page 53, and
Sultan's Cream Puffs, page 50.

1/2 cup plus 1 tablespoon
   all-purpose flour

1/2 cup water

1/4 teaspoon salt

1/4 cup unsalted butter,
   cut in pieces

3 large eggs

Sift flour onto a piece of waxed paper. In a small heavy saucepan combine water, salt and butter. Cook over low heat, stirring constantly, until butter melts. Bring to a boil; remove from heat. Immediately add flour all at once; stir quickly with a wooden spoon until mixture is smooth. Set pan over low heat; beat mixture about 30 seconds.

Remove from heat; cool about 3 minutes. Add 1 egg; beat thoroughly into mixture. Add second egg; beat mixture until smooth. Beat third egg in a small bowl. Gradually beat 1 or 2 tablespoons of this egg into dough, adding enough so dough becomes very shiny and is soft enough so it just falls from the wooden spoon.

Add a pinch of salt to remaining egg; beat until blended. Reserve as glaze. *Dough is easiest to shape while warm but can be kept, wrapped, 4 hours in refrigerator. Refrigerate glaze until ready to use.*

Makes dough for 15 to 20 cream puffs

Variation

Chocolate Choux Pastry: Prepare as above, using 1/2 cup flour sifted with 1 tablespoon unsweetened Dutch-process cocoa powder. Add 2 teaspoons sugar to ingredients in saucepan before cooking.

Hot desserts like chocolate soufflés, puddings and crepes are preferred by many people as winter treats. Baked custards and puddings that are served cold are loved all year round.

These groups include some of the most spectacular of desserts, from Dark Chocolate-Bourbon Soufflé to Chocolate-Orange Boule de Neige to Chocolate Crepe Gâteau with Brazil Nuts.

Chocolate Soufflés

The most impressive and airy of hot chocolate desserts, soufflés are favorite desserts for ordering at restaurants and are the pride of good home cooks. In spite of their sophisticated appearance and the mystique surrounding them, they are actually easy to prepare. They are often made from a thick base of chocolate pastry cream, similar to the filling of cream puffs, lightened with whipped egg whites. Much of the preparation can be done ahead; only the whipping of the whites, the final blending of the mixture and the brief baking must be done at the last minute.

To the French taste, a soufflé should be very soft in the center and therefore does not usually need a sauce. Many Americans prefer their soufflés firmer and like to accompany them with a sauce, such as the hazelnut liqueur sauce served with Hazelnut-Praline-Chocolate Soufflé.

Chocolate Puddings

The category *chocolate pudding* actually covers a wide variety of desserts. The simplest, bread puddings, the most homey of desserts, bring back memories of family suppers.

Steamed Chocolate-Macadamia Nut Pudding cooks on top of the stove in a water bath and is amazingly light for such a rich mixture. Although it is called *pudding,* it is surely one of the most elegant of desserts. Black Forest Trifle is another luxurious chocolate pudding.

Chocolate Baked Custards

Baked custards are among the most exquisite finales to any meal. Yet these smooth, creamy desserts are quick and easy to prepare. An added bonus is that the required ingredients—milk, eggs, sugar and chocolate—are usually at hand.

The creamiest type of baked custards, known as "petits pots de crème," are baked and served in individual containers.

It is no coincidence that the French call silky smooth custards "crèmes." Smoothness is their main characteristic and everything possible is done to ensure this quality. For this reason, many of these desserts are baked in a water bath: the dishes of custard mixture are set in a large shallow pan in the oven, and the pan is filled with hot water. The water provides moisture and moderates the oven temperature so the custards bake slowly and evenly and do not dry or separate as a result of direct oven heat.

Chocolate Crepes

Golden crepes with a rich chocolate filling are an easy and convenient dessert because they can be prepared ahead and reheated. A favorite French snack is a crepe filled with melted chocolate. Parisians have the choice of having it served to them at a crêperie or by a street vendor, who folds the filled crepe in four and wraps it in paper so it can be eaten during a stroll along the avenues.

Chocolate fillings for crepes are as easy as melting chocolate in cream and stirring in sliced fruit, as in Chocolate-Banana Crepes. Even the crepes themselves can be chocolate-flavored, with the addition of cocoa to the batter. In Crêpes Belle Hélène, the chocolate crepes are filled with sautéed pears and coated with dark chocolate sauce.

Dark Chocolate-Bourbon Soufflé

Accompany this rich, chocolaty soufflé with Bourbon Sauce, page 164, if you like your soufflé relatively firm. If you like a soft soufflé in the French tradition, serve it with or without sauce.

1/2 cup whipping cream

1/2 cup milk

3 large egg yolks

5 tablespoons sugar

1/4 cup all-purpose flour

**4 oz. semisweet chocolate,
   finely chopped**

2 tablespoons bourbon whiskey

5 large egg whites

Pinch of cream of tartar

Bring cream and milk to a boil in a small heavy saucepan over medium-high heat. Whisk egg yolks with 4 tablespoons sugar in a medium bowl until blended. Lightly stir in flour, using a whisk. Gradually whisk hot cream mixture into yolk mixture. Return to saucepan. Cook over medium heat, whisking constantly, until mixture is very thick and comes nearly to a boil. Remove from heat. Add chocolate; whisk until melted. If not using immediately, dab this soufflé base with a small piece of butter to prevent a skin from forming. *Mixture can be kept, covered, 1 day in refrigerator.*

To bake soufflé, position rack in lower third of oven and preheat to 400F (205C). Butter a 5-cup soufflé dish; butter rim of dish generously. Have a round heatproof platter ready near oven. If chocolate mixture is cold, heat in a small saucepan over low heat, whisking, until just warm. Remove from heat. Stir in bourbon.

In a large dry bowl, whip egg whites with cream of tartar to soft peaks. Beat in remaining 1 tablespoon sugar. Whip at high speed until whites are stiff and shiny but not dry. Quickly fold about 1/4 of whites into chocolate mixture. Spoon mixture over remaining whites; fold in lightly but quickly, just until blended.

Transfer mixture to prepared soufflé dish; smooth top. For a soft soufflé with a very moist center, bake about 22 minutes or until puffed and browned; when you gently move oven rack, soufflé should shake very slightly in center. For a firmer soufflé, reduce oven temperature to 375F (190C) and bake about 5 minutes longer; when you carefully move dish, soufflé should not shake. Do not overbake or soufflé may burn and shrink. Set soufflé dish on platter and serve immediately.

Makes 4 servings

Individual Chocolate-Grand Marnier Soufflés in Orange Cups

A dark chocolate soufflé baked and served in an orange makes an exquisite dessert.
The moist, light soufflé is made with fresh orange juice and is delicately flavored with Grand Marnier.

Photo on back cover.

---

8 large oranges, preferably navel oranges

3 large egg yolks

1/4 cup granulated sugar

3 tablespoons all-purpose flour

4 oz. semisweet chocolate, finely chopped

2 tablespoons plus 1 teaspoon Grand Marnier

4 large egg whites

Pinch of cream of tartar

Powdered sugar, if desired (for sprinkling)

Cut a very thin slice from 1 end of each orange so it stands up without rolling; leave some pith on bottom of orange or soufflé will leak out. Cut top third off other end of orange. Using a sharp knife or serrated knife, cut from center to edge of orange several times. Cut around pulp of orange, as if preparing grapefruit. Using a grapefruit knife or serrated knife, scoop out flesh and juice into a strainer set over a bowl. Do not pierce rind; rind should be clean of pulp. Press on flesh and strain juice. Set aside 1 cup juice for soufflé.

Heat 1 cup juice in a small heavy saucepan until lukewarm. Whisk egg yolks with 3 tablespoons granulated sugar in a medium bowl until blended. Lightly stir in flour, using whisk. Gradually whisk juice into yolk mixture. Return to saucepan. Cook over medium-low heat, whisking constantly, about 5 minutes or until mixture is very thick and comes nearly to a boil. Remove from heat. Add chocolate; whisk until melted. If not using immediately, dab this soufflé base with a small piece of butter to prevent a skin from forming. *Mixture can be kept, covered, 1 day in refrigerator.*

To bake soufflés, position rack in lower third of oven and preheat to 425F (220C). Butter a large gratin dish or other shallow baking dish and set oranges in it. Butter 2 (2/3-cup) ramekins. If chocolate mixture is cold, heat it in a small saucepan over low heat, whisking, just until warm. Remove from heat. Stir in Grand Marnier.

In a large dry bowl, whip egg whites with cream of tartar to soft peaks. Beat in remaining 1 tablespoon granulated sugar. Whip at high speed until whites are stiff and shiny but not dry. Quickly fold about 1/4 of whites into chocolate mixture. Spoon mixture over remaining whites; fold in lightly but quickly, just until blended.

Spoon mixture into orange shells, filling them about 3/4 full. Spoon any remaining mixture into buttered ramekins, filling them nearly to top. Bake ramekins about 10 minutes and oranges about 17 minutes or until soufflés are puffed and tops are firm and do not shake when oven shelf is gently moved. Sprinkle with powdered sugar, if using, and serve immediately.

Makes 4 generous or 8 light servings

Tips

The extra soufflé mixture in the two ramekins can be refrigerated and baked the next day. All of soufflé mixture can be baked in ramekins.

Hazelnut Praline-Chocolate Soufflé

Praline made from toasted hazelnuts and caramel is a wonderful partner for chocolate.
Although there are several steps involved in making the praline, this moist, high soufflé is worth it!
Besides, the praline can be made ahead. If you like, serve the soufflé with
Hazelnut Liqueur Sauce, page 170.

1 cup milk

3 large egg yolks

1/4 cup granulated sugar

1/4 cup all-purpose flour

2 oz. semisweet chocolate, finely chopped

Hazelnut Praline, page 171

5 large egg whites

Pinch of cream of tartar

Powdered sugar, if desired (for sprinkling)

Bring milk to a boil in a heavy small saucepan. Whisk egg yolks with 2 tablespoons granulated sugar in a medium bowl until blended. Lightly stir in flour, using a whisk. Gradually whisk in hot milk. Return mixture to saucepan. Cook over low heat, whisking constantly, about 2 minutes or until mixture is very thick and comes nearly to a boil. Remove from heat. Add chocolate; whisk until melted. If not using immediately, dab this soufflé base with a small piece of butter to prevent a skin from forming. *Soufflé base can be kept, covered, 1 day in refrigerator.*

To bake soufflé, position rack in lower third of oven and preheat to 400F (205C). Butter a 5-cup soufflé dish; butter rim of dish generously. Have a round heatproof platter ready near oven. If soufflé base is cold, heat it in a small saucepan over low heat, whisking, until just warm. Remove from heat. Stir in praline powder.

In a large dry bowl, whip egg whites with cream of tartar to soft peaks. Gradually beat in remaining 2 tablespoons granulated sugar. Whip at high speed until whites are stiff and shiny but not dry. Quickly fold about 1/4 of whites into chocolate mixture. Spoon mixture over remaining whites; fold in lightly but quickly, just until blended. Be careful not to deflate mixture; a few streaks of white may remain.

Transfer mixture to prepared soufflé dish; smooth top. For a soft soufflé with a very moist center, bake about 22 minutes or until puffed and browned; when you gently move rack, soufflé should shake very slightly in center. For a firmer soufflé, reduce oven temperature to 375F (190C) and bake about 5 minutes longer; when you carefully move dish, soufflé should not shake. Do not overbake or soufflé may burn and shrink. Set soufflé dish on prepared platter. Sprinkle with powdered sugar, if using, and serve immediately.

Makes 4 servings

Bittersweet Chocolate-Chestnut Soufflé

In this soufflé, the sweet chestnut puree complements the bittersweet chocolate. The soufflé can be prepared quickly because the puree binds the mixture and there is no need to make a flour-thickened soufflé base. Canned sweetened chestnut puree is often labeled chestnut spread or creme de marrons.

---

4 oz. bittersweet chocolate, chopped

1/3 cup whipping cream

1 (8-3/4-oz.) can sweetened chestnut puree (3/4 cup)

3 large egg yolks

6 large egg whites

Pinch of cream of tartar

Powdered sugar, if desired (for sprinkling)

Melt chocolate in cream in a small bowl over nearly simmering water. Stir until smooth. Remove from water. Stir chestnut puree into chocolate mixture. Beat in egg yolks, 1 at a time. *Mixture can be kept, covered, 1 day in refrigerator.*

To bake soufflé, position rack in lower third of oven and preheat to 400F (205C). Butter a 5-cup soufflé dish; butter rim of dish generously. Have ready a round heatproof platter near oven. If chocolate mixture is cold, heat it in a small saucepan over low heat, whisking, until just warm. Remove from heat.

In a large dry bowl, whip egg whites with cream of tartar until whites are stiff but not dry. Quickly fold about 1/4 of whites into chocolate mixture. Spoon mixture over remaining whites; fold in quickly, just until blended.

Transfer mixture to prepared soufflé dish; smooth top. For a soft soufflé with a very moist center, bake about 25 minutes or until puffed; when you gently move rack, soufflé should shake very slightly in center. For a firmer soufflé, reduce oven temperature to 375F (190C) and bake about 5 minutes longer; when you carefully move dish, soufflé should not shake. Do not overbake or soufflé may burn and shrink. Set soufflé dish on platter. Sprinkle with powdered sugar, if using, and serve immediately.

Makes 4 servings

Gingered Chocolate Custards

A powerful punch of fresh ginger essence imparts a refreshing zip to these exceptionally creamy custards, which are favorites in my chocolate cooking classes. The chopped ginger is strained out of the custard so only the exotic flavor remains.

3/4 cup plus 2 tablespoons minced peeled gingerroot (about 6 oz. gingerroot)

1/2 cup water

3/4 cup sugar

1/2 pint whipping cream (1 cup)

3-1/2 oz. semisweet chocolate, chopped

1/2 cup milk

4 large egg yolks

1/2 cup whipping cream, well-chilled (for garnish)

About 2 teaspoons chopped crystallized ginger, if desired (for garnish)

Position rack in center of oven and preheat to 350F (175C). In a small heavy saucepan cook gingerroot with water and 1/2 cup sugar over low heat, stirring, until sugar dissolves. Bring to a boil over high heat. Cover and simmer over low heat about 10 minutes or until ginger is tender. Uncover and cook over medium heat, stirring constantly, about 5 minutes or until liquid is absorbed. Stir in 1 cup cream; bring nearly to a simmer. Cook over low heat 4 minutes. Cool 3 minutes.

Melt chocolate in milk in a medium bowl over nearly simmering water. Remove from water; stir gently until smooth with a whisk. Gradually whisk hot ginger mixture into chocolate.

Whisk egg yolks lightly in a large bowl. Add remaining 1/4 cup sugar; whisk until blended. Gradually pour in about 3/4 cup chocolate mixture in a thin stream, stirring constantly with whisk. Using a wooden spoon, gradually stir in remaining chocolate mixture. Strain mixture into a large measuring cup, pressing on ginger. Skim foam from surface of mixture.

Set 4 (2/3-cup) ramekins in a roasting pan or large shallow baking dish. Pour chocolate mixture into ramekins, dividing it evenly. Place pan with ramekins in oven. Add enough nearly boiling water to pan to come halfway up sides of ramekins. Set a sheet of foil gently on top to cover ramekins loosely, without folding it around edges of pan. Bake about 35 minutes or until top is nearly set and moves only slightly when pan is moved gently. During baking, if water in pan comes close to a boil, add a few tablespoons cold water to pan.

Carefully remove ramekins from pan of water; cool on a rack. Cover and refrigerate 3 hours. *Custards can be kept 2 days in refrigerator.*

In a chilled medium bowl, whip cream until very stiff. Using a pastry bag and large star tip, pipe a rosette of whipped cream on center of each dessert. Sprinkle each rosette with crystallized ginger. Serve dessert cold in ramekins.

Makes 4 servings

Mocha Petits Pots de Crème

During baking, the chocolate forms a dark, glossy topping on these coffee-accented custards. The garnish of whipped cream is not traditional but it adds color and a pleasant lightness.

Photo on pages vi-vii.

Baked Mocha Custards:

4 oz. bittersweet chocolate, chopped

1-1/2 cups milk

2 tablespoons instant coffee granules

4 large egg yolks

5 tablespoons sugar

Kahlua Whipped Cream:

1/3 cup whipping cream, well-chilled

1/2 teaspoon sugar

2 teaspoons coffee liqueur, such as Kahlua

4 chocolate coffee beans, if desired (for garnish)

Custards: Position rack in center of oven and preheat to 350F (175C). Combine chocolate and 1/2 cup milk in a medium bowl over nearly simmering water. When chocolate is nearly melted, remove from water and stir with a whisk until smooth. Bring remaining 1 cup milk to a boil in a small saucepan. Remove from heat; whisk in coffee. Cool 3 minutes. Gradually whisk milk into chocolate mixture.

Whisk egg yolks lightly in a large bowl. Add sugar; whisk until blended. Gradually pour in about 3/4 cup chocolate mixture in a thin stream, stirring constantly with whisk. Using a wooden spoon, gradually stir in remaining chocolate mixture. Strain into a large measuring cup. Skim foam from surface.

Set 4 (2/3-cup) ramekins in a roasting pan or large shallow baking dish. Pour custard mixture into ramekins, dividing it evenly. Place pan with ramekins in oven. Add enough nearly boiling water to pan to come halfway up sides of ramekins. Set a sheet of foil gently on top to cover ramekins loosely, without folding foil around edges of pan. Bake about 25 minutes or until top is nearly set and moves only very slightly when pan is moved gently, or until a cake tester inserted very gently in mixture about 1/2 inch from edge of each ramekin comes out clean. During baking, if water in pan comes close to a boil, add a few tablespoons cold water to pan.

Carefully remove ramekins from pan of water; cool on a rack. Cover and refrigerate 3 hours. *Custards can be kept 1 day in refrigerator.*

Kahlua cream: In a small chilled bowl, whip cream with sugar until soft peaks form. Add liqueur; whip until cream is very stiff. Using a pastry bag and large star tip, pipe a rosette of cream on each serving and top each rosette with a chocolate coffee bean. Serve dessert cold, in ramekins.

Makes 4 servings

Chocolate Crème Brûlée with Raspberries

A crunchy crust of caramelized sugar and a satiny chocolate custard hide a surprise of fresh raspberries.
As a base for the crème brûlée, this modern version makes use of a cooked custard,
which is creamier than a baked custard. In restaurants, the top is caramelized with a blow-torch,
but this home version is done in the broiler and works easily with brown sugar.

Rich Chocolate Custard:

6 oz. fine-quality bittersweet chocolate, chopped

1-1/3 cups whipping cream

5 large egg yolks

3 tablespoons sugar

Fruit & Topping:

1-1/2 cups raspberries, well-chilled

1/2 cup plus 1 tablespoon packed dark-brown sugar

1/2 cup whipping cream, well-chilled

18 raspberries (for garnish)

Custard: Melt chocolate in a medium bowl over nearly simmering water. Stir until smooth. Remove from water; let cool.

Heat cream in a small heavy saucepan until bubbles form around edge of pan. Whisk egg yolks lightly in a medium bowl. Add sugar; whisk until blended. Gradually whisk in hot cream. Return mixture to saucepan. Cook over low heat, stirring mixture and scraping bottom of pan constantly with a wooden spoon, until mixture reaches 160F (70C) on an instant-read or candy thermometer, about 5 minutes. To check without thermometer, see page 169. Immediately pour into a bowl; stir about 30 seconds to cool. Cool 5 minutes.

Pour 1 cup custard over melted chocolate; whisk until blended. Gradually whisk remaining custard into chocolate. Pour into a large bowl; let cool, stirring occasionally. Cover and refrigerate 4 to 6 hours.

Fruit & Topping: Put 1/4 cup berries in 1 layer in each of 6 (2/3-cup) ramekins. Stir custard. Carefully spoon about 1/3 cup custard over berries in each ramekin. Spread with a rubber spatula to cover berries.

Set broiler rack about 4-1/2 inches from heat source. Preheat broiler. Sift 1-1/2 tablespoons brown sugar evenly over each custard, covering it completely. Brush any sugar off rim of dish. Position 2 ramekins so broiler element can heat them evenly. Broil custards, 2 at a time, keeping door open, about 1 minute or until brown sugar turns slightly darker and forms a slightly firm crust. Check crust by tapping very gently with a spoon, not with your fingers. Watch carefully; sugar burns easily. Refrigerate custards 1 hour. *Custards can be kept, uncovered, 1 day in refrigerator.*

In a chilled medium bowl, whip cream until very stiff. Using a pastry bag and medium star tip, pipe a few rosettes of whipped cream onto each custard. Garnish with raspberries.

Makes 6 servings

Chocolate-Orange Boule de Neige

This elegant chocolate dessert is an orange-flavored version of an all-time favorite at
La Varenne Cooking School in Paris, where I studied and worked for over five years.
It consists of a very rich baked custard covered completely with rosettes of whipped cream.
The custard should be baked ahead so it sets completely and the flavors meld.

Chocolate-Orange Custard:

8 oz. semisweet chocolate, chopped

1/2 cup strained fresh orange juice

3/4 cup sugar

1 cup (8 oz.) unsalted butter,
    cut in 8 pieces

4 large eggs, beaten

1 tablespoon plus 2 teaspoons
    grated orange zest

Grand Marnier Whipped Cream:

1-1/2 cups whipping cream,
    well-chilled

2 tablespoons sugar

2 tablespoons Grand Marnier

Custard: Position rack in center of oven and preheat to 350F (175C). Line a 1-quart charlotte mold with 2 layers of foil so they fit tightly.

Melt chocolate in orange juice in a heavy, medium saucepan set in a shallow pan of hot water over low heat. Stir until smooth. Stir in sugar and butter. Leave saucepan in water over low heat until sugar dissolves and butter melts, stirring often. Remove saucepan from water; set over low heat. Cook mixture, stirring, until hot (about 150F, 65C on an instant-read or candy thermometer); do not boil. Remove from heat; very gradually whisk in eggs. Strain into a large bowl. Stir in grated zest.

Pour into lined mold. Bake 40 to 45 minutes or until a thick crust forms on top and center still moves when mold is moved gently. Cool in mold on a rack. Mixture will sink in center as it cools. To counteract this tendency, press on edges of dessert to flatten them slightly. Let cool, pressing again on edges a few times. Cover and refrigerate 6 hours. *Dessert can be kept 2 weeks in refrigerator.*

A short time before serving, run a thin-bladed knife around outer layer of foil in mold; turn out dessert onto a round platter. Carefully peel off foil. Dessert will be quite soft. Return to refrigerator.

Whipped cream: In a large chilled bowl, whip cream with sugar until soft peaks form. Add Grand Marnier; beat until cream is very stiff. Using a pastry bag and medium star tip, pipe rosettes of whipped cream over dessert, beginning in center and piping circles of rosettes until chocolate is completely covered. Refrigerate until ready to serve.

Makes 8 to 10 servings

Steamed Chocolate-Macadamia Nut Pudding

Steaming makes this superb, unusual pudding incredibly light, yet very moist. The hemispherical, elegant dessert of Austrian-German inspiration has an intense chocolate flavor. Macadamia Cream is a delicious accompaniment, but plain whipped cream can be substituted.

Chocolate-Macadamia Pudding:

1 cup macadamia nuts (about 4-1/4 oz.), unsalted or desalted, page 178

4 oz. fine-quality semisweet chocolate, chopped

2/3 cup sugar

1/2 cup (4 oz.) unsalted butter, slightly softened

5 large eggs, separated

Macadamia Cream:

1/2 pint whipping cream, well-chilled (1 cup)

2 tablespoons macadamia nut liqueur or hazelnut liqueur

Pudding: Preheat oven to 350F (175C). Generously butter a 6-cup heatproof bowl; sprinkle with sugar. Choose a heavy pot or stew pan large enough to hold bowl with about 1-1/2 inches of space on all sides. Toast nuts in a shallow baking pan in oven 3 minutes. Transfer to a plate; cool completely.

Melt chocolate in a medium bowl over nearly simmering water. Stir until smooth. Remove from water; let cool. Grind nuts with 2 tablespoons sugar in a food processor to a fine powder. Transfer to a medium bowl. Set aside 2 tablespoons sugar for beating into egg whites.

Cream butter in a medium bowl. Add remaining sugar; beat until fluffy. Beat in egg yolks, 1 at a time. Stir in melted chocolate and macadamia nuts. Prepare a kettle of boiling water for steaming pudding.

In a large dry bowl, whip egg whites to soft peaks. Gradually beat in reserved 2 tablespoons sugar; whip at high speed until whites are stiff and shiny but not dry. Fold about 1/4 of whites into chocolate mixture. Spoon mixture over remaining whites; fold in lightly but quickly, just until blended.

Transfer mixture to prepared bowl. Cover tightly with 2 layers of foil. Tie string around side of bowl so foil is tightly secured. Set in pot. Pour in enough boiling water to come halfway up side of bowl. Cover pot. Set pot over low heat so water just simmers; cook 1 hour and 45 minutes. Check water occasionally; it should simmer but not boil hard. If it boils, add a few tablespoons cold water. If much of water evaporates, add more water. To check if pudding is done, uncover and insert a cake tester; it should come out dry. Otherwise cover again and steam a few minutes longer. *Pudding can be kept warm, covered, 1 hour in its pot of water off heat.*

Macadamia Cream: Just before serving, whip cream in a chilled medium bowl at medium-high speed until soft peaks form. Add liqueur; beat until blended.

Remove pudding from water; discard foil. Set platter on top. Holding firmly together, quickly flip so pudding is right-side up and slips from mold onto platter. Serve hot, cut in wedges. Spoon Macadamia Cream over each piece. *Pudding can be kept, covered, 4 days in refrigerator.* Serve any leftovers cold.

Makes 6 to 8 servings

Chocolate Bread Pudding

For informal family gatherings, especially in the winter, this moist, light bread pudding is an ideal dessert.
It is easy to prepare yet smoother and more elegant than most bread puddings.
Serve it on its own or accompanied by Vanilla Bean or Coffee Custard Sauce, page 169.

5 (3-1/2" x 5" x 1/2") slices French bread (4 oz.)

3 oz. semisweet chocolate, chopped

1/2 cup (4 oz.) unsalted butter, slightly softened

1/4 cup sugar

4 large eggs, separated

Pinch of cream of tartar

Position rack in center of oven and preheat to 250F (120C). Bake bread slices on baking sheet 10 minutes. Turn slices over; bake 5 minutes or until dry. Cool completely. Break into pieces. Grind bread in food processor to fine crumbs.

Increase oven temperature to 350F (175C). Butter a 1-quart charlotte mold or soufflé dish. Coat side and bottom with sugar. Melt chocolate in a small bowl over nearly simmering water. Stir until smooth. Remove from water; let cool.

Cream butter in a large bowl. Add 3 tablespoons sugar; beat until smooth and fluffy. Add egg yolks, 1 at a time, and beat thoroughly after each. Stir in bread crumbs and melted chocolate.

In a large dry bowl, whip egg whites with cream of tartar to soft peaks. Beat in remaining tablespoon sugar; whip at high speed until whites are stiff but not dry. Stir 1/4 of whites into chocolate mixture until blended. Fold in remaining whites in 3 batches; mixture will be thick and seem difficult to blend but continue folding until blended.

Transfer mixture to prepared mold. Set mold in a roasting pan or large baking dish; put in oven. Add enough nearly boiling water to larger pan to come halfway up side of mold. Cover gently with foil without folding it around edges of mold. Bake about 55 minutes or until a cake tester inserted in center of pudding comes out clean. Remove from pan of water; cool on rack. Pudding settles as it cools. Run a thin-bladed knife or metal spatula around pudding and invert onto a platter. Serve lukewarm or cold. *Pudding can be kept, covered, 2 days in refrigerator.*

Makes 4 to 6 servings

Black Forest Trifle

The English originated the famous trifle, a pudding made of pieces of cake layered with custard, whipped cream and fruit. The lovely combination of chocolate and cherries was popularized by the German Black Forest cake. Here is a marriage of both.
Traditionally leftover sponge cake is used for trifle but you can use other light-textured cakes.
This version utilizes ladyfingers.

Cooked Chocolate Custard:

8 oz. semisweet chocolate, chopped

1 cup milk

1 tablespoon cornstarch

1-1/2 cups whipping cream

2 large eggs

2 large egg yolks

3 tablespoons sugar

Ladyfinger & Fruit Layers:

About 3-1/2 oz. ladyfingers
(about 3 inches long)

1/4 cup kirsch

1/2 cup red-cherry preserves

2 cups fresh, dark, sweet cherries,
(8 oz.), halved and pitted

Kirsch Whipped Cream for Trifle,
page 163

Grated semisweet chocolate
(for garnish)

6 whole, dark, sweet cherries, stems
trimmed to 1 inch (for garnish)

Custard: Melt chocolate in 1/2 cup milk in a medium bowl over nearly simmering water. Stir until smooth. Remove from water; let cool.

Mix cornstarch with 1 tablespoon of milk in a small cup until dissolved. Heat cream with remaining milk in a heavy medium saucepan until bubbles form around edge of pan. Whisk eggs and yolks in a medium bowl. Add sugar; whisk until blended. Whisk in dissolved cornstarch. Gradually whisk in hot cream mixture. Return mixture to saucepan. Cook over medium-low heat, whisking constantly, about 5 minutes or until mixture thickens slightly and reaches 160F (70C) on an instant-read or candy thermometer. Do not boil. Remove from heat. Stir 1 minute. Let cool, stirring occasionally. Whisk in chocolate mixture. Cover and refrigerate 4 hours.

Ladyfinger & Fruit Layers: If using packaged ladyfingers, which are usually split in half horizontally and joined in a row, there is no need to separate them into individual ones. Put enough ladyfinger halves in a 1-1/2-quart glass bowl or deep baking dish to make 1 layer. If using homemade ladyfingers, leave them whole. Brush 2 tablespoons kirsch evenly over them. Stir custard; pour 1-3/4 cups custard over ladyfingers in bowl. Cover and refrigerate 1 to 2 hours to firm custard slightly.

Heat preserves until melted in a small saucepan over low heat, stirring occasionally and mashing cherries that are in preserves. Arrange remaining ladyfinger halves in 1 layer on custard in bowl. Brush with remaining kirsch. Spoon preserves evenly over them. Scatter fresh cherries on top. Carefully spoon remaining custard over cherries. Cover and refrigerate 8 hours or overnight. *Dessert can be kept, covered, 2 days in refrigerator.*

Carefully spoon Kirsch Whipped Cream on top of dessert; spread in an even layer. Grate chocolate onto center of dessert. Set whole cherries around edge.

Makes 8 servings

Chocolate-Banana Crepes

Chocolate cream and bananas make a rich,
very easy-to-prepare filling for these lacy crepes.

---

8 Crepes, page 77, room
temperature

Chocolate-Banana Filling:

4 oz. fine-quality semisweet
chocolate, chopped

1/4 cup whipping cream

2 large bananas (about 14 oz.)

2 tablespoons rum

1 tablespoon butter, melted

1/2 cup whipping cream, well-
chilled, if desired (for garnish)

1 banana, if desired (for garnish)

Prepare crepes. Position rack in center of oven and preheat to 400F (205C). Butter a large shallow baking dish.

Filling: Combine chocolate and 1/4 cup cream in a small bowl over nearly simmering water. Leave until melted, stirring occasionally. Meanwhile, cut bananas in small dice; you will have 2 cups. Stir chocolate mixture until smooth. Remove from pan of water. Gradually stir in rum. Gently stir in bananas.

Assembly: Spoon 3 tablespoons filling onto less attractive side of each crepe; spread gently to within about 1/2 inch of edge. Roll up crepes tightly like cigars. Arrange, seam-side down, in buttered baking dish in 1 layer. Brush crepes with melted butter.

Bake crepes 5 to 7 minutes or until hot. Meanwhile, whip 1/2 cup cream, if using, in a chilled medium bowl until soft peaks form. Slice banana. Serve crepes hot. Spoon a little whipped cream onto or next to each crepe; top cream with a few banana slices, if using.

Makes 8 small or 4 generous servings

Chocolate Crepe Gâteau with Brazil Nuts

An impressive "cake" made of layers of crepes baked with Brazil-nut-chocolate filling, then topped with a shiny chocolate sauce.

Photo opposite.

Crepe Gâteau:

3 oz. semisweet chocolate, chopped

1 cup Brazil nuts (about 5 1/4 oz.)

1/2 cup sugar

5 tablespoons unsalted butter, slightly softened

2 large eggs, beaten

2 tablespoons all-purpose flour

10 Crepes, page 77, room temperature

1 tablespoon unsalted butter, melted

Chocolate Sauce:

4 oz. semisweet chocolate, chopped

1/2 cup whipping cream

2 tablespoons coarsely chopped Brazil nuts (for sprinkling)

Crepe Gâteau: Position rack in center of oven and preheat to 350F (175C). Melt chocolate in a small bowl over nearly simmering water. Stir until smooth. Remove from water; let cool. Grind nuts with 2 tablespoons sugar in a food processor to a fine powder. Transfer to a medium bowl.

Cream butter in a medium bowl. Add remaining 6 tablespoons sugar; beat until fluffy. Beat in chocolate. Gradually beat in eggs. Using a wooden spoon, stir in nut mixture and flour.

Lightly butter an 8-inch springform pan. Put 1 crepe flat on base. Spread with 1/4 cup chocolate mixture. Set second crepe on top, smoothing it over filling. Spread with 1/4 cup chocolate mixture. Continue with remaining crepes and chocolate mixture until only 3 crepes are left. If crepes are slightly larger than pan, fold their edges upward slightly or trim them to fit. Spread eighth and ninth crepe with only 3 tablespoons filling each. Set last crepe on top; brush with melted butter.

Set pan on a baking sheet. Bake about 40 minutes or until filling is firm and heated through.

Sauce: Combine chocolate and cream in a medium bowl over nearly simmering water. Leave until nearly melted, stirring occasionally. Stir until smooth. *Sauce can be kept, covered, 1 week in refrigerator. Reheat sauce in a bowl in a pan of hot water before serving.*

When gâteau is baked, let stand 5 minutes. Release spring of pan and unmold dessert. Spoon a little sauce on top of gâteau; spread over top, letting it run down side. Sprinkle chopped Brazil nuts on center of sauce. Serve gâteau in wedges. Serve remaining sauce separately.

Makes 6 to 8 servings

Crêpes Belle Hélène

These chocolate crepes made from a cocoa batter are filled with sautéed fresh pears and served with dark chocolate sauce. Like the classic pears Belle Hélène, combining poached pears and chocolate sauce, they are accompanied by vanilla ice cream.

Pear Filling:

1-1/2 lbs. ripe pears

1 lemon, halved

3 tablespoons unsalted butter

5 to 6 tablespoons sugar

Chocolate Crepes, page 77,
   room temperature

1 tablespoon unsalted butter,
   melted

Dark Chocolate Sauce, page 167

2 tablespoons chopped pistachios,
   walnuts, pecans or almonds, if
   desired (for garnish)

Vanilla ice cream
   (for accompaniment)

Filling: Peel pears; rub with cut side of halved lemon. Halve, core and thinly slice pears. Melt butter in a large skillet. Add pears; turn slices to coat both sides with butter. Cook, uncovered, over medium-low heat, stirring often, about 20 minutes or until very tender. Continue cooking over medium heat about 5 minutes to evaporate some of liquid. Add 5 tablespoons sugar. Cook over medium-high heat, stirring, until mixture thickens. Remove from heat. Taste and add more sugar if desired. *Filling can be kept, covered, 1 day in refrigerator; reheat before filling crepes.*

Assembly: Preheat oven to 400F (205C). Butter a shallow baking dish. Spoon about 2 tablespoons filling onto less attractive side of each crepe near 1 edge; roll up like cigars. Arrange, seam-side down, in buttered baking dish in 1 layer. Brush crepes with melted butter. Bake about 7 minutes or until very hot.

Heat chocolate sauce above hot water. To serve, set 2 hot crepes onto each plate. Spoon sauce over crepes; sprinkle with nuts. Serve with vanilla ice cream.

Makes 4 servings

Crepes

Fill crepes with a chocolate and banana or pear filling, or use them to prepare an impressive Chocolate Crepe Gâteau with Brazil Nuts, page 75. Crepes are easiest to make in a nonstick crepe pan.

2/3 cup milk

1/2 cup water

3 large eggs

3 tablespoons unsalted butter, melted and cooled

3/4 cup all-purpose flour, sifted

1/2 teaspoon salt

1 to 2 tablespoons vegetable oil (for brushing pan)

Combine milk, water, eggs and melted butter in a food processor or blender. Sift in flour and salt; process 5 seconds. Scrape down batter. Process 20 seconds. Transfer to a bowl. Cover and refrigerate 1 hour.

Heat an 8-inch crepe pan or skillet over medium-high heat. Brush pan lightly with oil. Heat until hot enough so a drop of batter added to pan sizzles immediately. Remove drop of batter; remove pan from heat. Stir batter. Fill a 1/4-cup measure about 3/4 full with batter; pour into hot pan. Tilt and rotate pan quickly so batter covers bottom in a thin layer. Return any excess batter to bowl. Return pan to medium-high heat. Loosen edge of crepe from pan with a pancake turner or metal spatula. Cook crepe until underside browns lightly. Turn over and briefly brown other side. Transfer crepe to a plate.

Continue with remaining batter, stirring batter before preparing each crepe. Brush pan lightly with oil as necessary; if using a nonstick crepe pan, no further oil will be needed. Stack crepes on plate. *Crepes can be kept, covered, 2 days in refrigerator, or can be frozen for several weeks.*

Makes about 12 crepes

Variations

To make 8 or 9 crepes: Omit water from batter. Follow recipe, making batter from 3/4 cup plus 1 tablespoon milk, 2 eggs, 2 tablespoons butter, 1/2 cup all-purpose flour and 1/4 teaspoon salt. Use 1 to 2 tablespoons oil for brushing pan.

Chocolate Crepes: Make batter from 3/4 cup milk, 2 eggs, 2 tablespoons butter, 1 teaspoon sugar, pinch of salt, 7 tablespoons all-purpose flour, and 1 tablespoon unsweetened Dutch-process cocoa powder. Cook as above, using 1 to 2 tablespoons oil for brushing pan.

Chocolate mousses, Bavarian creams and charlottes are the dessert-lover's dream. Many of these fabulous cold chocolate desserts are light and creamy and are the perfect finale for a sumptuous dinner. Others are dense in texture and very rich in chocolate taste and color, making them favorites with dedicated chocolate fans. Mousses, Bavarians creams and most charlottes do not require baking and can easily fit into meal- or party-planning because they can be made ahead and served at leisure.

Chocolate Mousses

Chocolate mousse is perhaps the most popular of all elegant desserts. It has the advantage of being one of the quickest and easiest to make as well. It can vary in texture from soft and creamy to firm. Light mousses have an airy texture from the addition of whipped cream, beaten egg whites, or both. A mousse's flavor can be pure chocolate or can be accented by liqueurs or nuts.

Soft chocolate mousses are served in individual cups, ramekins or meringue baskets, while the firmer ones can be unmolded and even cut into slices. Chocolate mousses make luscious fillings for cakes and pies.

For years the traditional way to make chocolate mousse has involved adding egg yolks to melted chocolate, then folding in whipped egg whites. With the current concern about the safety of eating raw eggs, I have developed new versions of many of the chocolate mousses. Still the classic way is the simplest, and I have included a few examples of this method too, in the hope that the "egg situation" will improve.

Chocolate Bavarian Creams

Bavarian creams are among the creamiest of all chocolate desserts, whether they are flavored with dark or white chocolate. They are made from custard sauce, *crème anglaise,* bound with a little gelatin and lightened by whipped cream. Bavarian creams can be molded in a variety of attractive shapes, as in ring-shaped Chocolate-Rum Bavarian Cream, or can be simply prepared in a serving dish and cut into pieces, as in White Chocolate Bavarian Squares.

Chocolate Charlottes

The chocolate charlotte, another light dessert, is one of the most festive endings to a meal. Charlottes are made of a frame of plain or chocolate ladyfingers, holding one or more fillings of mousse or Bavarian cream.

Mousses, Bavarian Creams & Charlottes

The charlottes in this book are of the modern type. They are simpler to prepare than traditional versions because they are assembled in a springform pan rather than in a charlotte mold. There is no need to spend a long time cutting ladyfingers to make a pattern; they just stand against the sides of the mold. Instead of turning the charlotte out, the charlotte is unmolded simply by removing the sides of the pan.

By contrast to these light charlottes, there are dense chocolate desserts combining ladyfingers and mousse-like fillings that have a high proportion of chocolate. Perhaps the most lavish is Chocolate-Cognac Marquise, a rectangular loaf which resembles an extraordinary chocolate bar. The richness of Chocolate-Apricot Terrine, another luxurious chocolate dessert, is balanced by the tartness of the fruit. Whipped cream or custard sauce are the ideal accompaniments for these desserts because they provide a light contrast and refresh the palate so the chocolate can be enjoyed to its fullest!

Chocolate Mousse Supreme

Cream is not used in classic recipes for chocolate mousse, but it contributes richness and a velvety texture to this one. If you like, accompany the mousse with crunchy cookies, such as Crisp Chocolate Chip-Macadamia Nut Cookies, page 121.

---

8 oz. fine-quality bittersweet
    chocolate, chopped

2 tablespoons brandy or Cognac

6 tablespoons water

2 tablespoons unsalted butter, room
    temperature, cut in 4 pieces

3 large egg yolks

2 tablespoons sugar

1-1/4 cups whipping cream,
    well-chilled

Melt chocolate with brandy and 2 tablespoons water in a medium bowl over nearly simmering water. Stir until smooth. Remove from water; stir in butter until blended. Let cool.

Whisk yolks with sugar and 4 tablespoons water in a small metal bowl. Set bowl in a pan of nearly simmering water. Heat, whisking constantly, until mixture reaches 160F (70C) on an instant-read or candy thermometer, about 1 minute. Immediately remove from water and whisk until cool. Stir into chocolate mixture.

In a large chilled bowl, whip cream until nearly stiff. Gently fold into chocolate mixture. Divide mousse among 6 or 7 small ramekins or dessert glasses. Refrigerate at least 3 hours before serving. *Mousse can be kept, covered, 2 days in refrigerator.*

Makes 6 or 7 servings

TO COOK EGG YOLKS FOR FOOD SAFETY

The USDA recommends cooking eggs rather than using them raw, due to the presence of salmonella bacteria in some eggs. For many chocolate mousses, the easiest way to make sure the yolks are thoroughly cooked is to heat them by the "sabayon" method, named for an Italian dessert sauce, zabaglione, made by the same technique.

For this method, the yolks are whisked with sugar and liquid and the bowl of mixture is set in a pan of simmering water. Heat until mixture reaches 160F (70C) on an instant-read or candy thermometer. Whisk constantly while the mixture is over the water and for about two minutes after removing it from the hot water to cool it. This must be done quickly and carefully, as the eggs can quickly go from smooth to scrambled!

White Chocolate Mousse with Strawberry Sauce

Strawberry Sauce provides a contrast of a bright-red color to show off the white mousse, as well as tartness and freshness to balance its sweetness.

Photo on page 85.

White Chocolate Mousse:

1 cup whipping cream

3 large egg yolks

2 teaspoons sugar

6 oz. fine-quality white chocolate, very finely chopped

4 tablespoons unsalted butter, room temperature, cut in 8 pieces

1-1/4 teaspoons finely grated or chopped lemon zest

1 teaspoon pure vanilla extract

Strawberry Sauce:

3 cups strawberries (about 12 oz.)

About 1/2 cup powdered sugar, sifted

1 teaspoon fresh strained lemon juice

4 small strawberries or 8 thin, round, strawberry slices (for garnish)

Mousse: Refrigerate 3/4 cup cream. Whisk yolks with sugar and remaining 1/4 cup cream in a small metal bowl. Set in a pan of nearly simmering water. Heat, whisking constantly, until mixture reaches 160F (70C) on an instant-read or candy thermometer, about 4 minutes. Remove from heat and immediately whip with electric mixer until cool.

Melt white chocolate in a small bowl above a pan of hot water. Remove from water. Add butter and stir to blend. Add yolk mixture and stir until blended. Stir in zest and vanilla.

In a chilled medium bowl, whip remaining 3/4 cup cream until stiff. Fold into white chocolate mixture. Pour into a bowl. Cover and refrigerate 4 hours or until firm enough to spoon into ovals. *Mousse can be kept, covered, 2 days in refrigerator.*

Sauce: Puree strawberries in a food processor or blender. Add 1/2 cup powdered sugar. Process until blended. Transfer to a bowl. Whisk in lemon juice. Taste and whisk in 1 tablespoon powdered sugar, if needed. Cover and refrigerate 30 minutes. *Sauce can be kept, covered, 1 day in refrigerator.*

Carefully spoon 2 oval-shaped tablespoons of mousse onto each serving plate. Stir Strawberry Sauce. Spoon sauce around, not over, mousse. Set a strawberry on each plate or a strawberry slice on each oval.

Makes 4 servings

Creamy Chocolate Mousse with Grand Marnier

For a light texture, only the whites of the eggs are used in this soft, creamy, easy-to-make mousse.
Orange zest adds freshness and Grand Marnier adds spirit
to complement the richness of the chocolate.

---

7 oz. fine-quality semisweet chocolate, chopped

1/2 cup whipping cream

5 large egg whites (see Variation)

2 tablespoons sugar

1 tablespoon Grand Marnier

2 teaspoons grated orange zest

1/3 cup whipping cream, well-chilled, if desired (for garnish)

4 small pieces candied orange peel or candied violet or 4 small Chocolate Leaves, page 177, if desired (for garnish)

Melt chocolate in 1/2 cup cream in a medium bowl over hot water. Stir until smooth. Remove from water; cool 3 minutes.

In a large dry bowl, whip egg whites to soft peaks. Gradually beat in sugar; whip at high speed until whites are stiff and shiny but not dry.

Stir Grand Marnier and orange zest into chocolate. Fold in about 1/4 of whites until blended. Spoon mixture over remaining whites; fold gently just until blended. Divide among 4 or 5 small ramekins. Refrigerate 3 hours. *Mousse can be kept, covered, 1 day in refrigerator.*

In a small chilled bowl, whip 1/3 cup cream, if using, until very stiff. Using a pastry bag and medium star tip, pipe a large rosette of whipped cream on center of each portion. Garnish each rosette with a piece of candied orange peel, violet or a Chocolate Leaf.

Makes 4 or 5 servings

Variation

If you are concerned about the safety of using raw eggs, or if you would like an extra-creamy mousse, omit the egg whites and add 1 cup whipping cream. Chill the cream and whip it in a chilled bowl with the sugar until just stiff. Continue with the recipe, folding the whipped cream into the chocolate-Grand Marnier mixture instead of the whites.

Dark Chocolate Mousse in Meringue Cups

These elegant, pure white, mini-vacherins are filled with a traditional bittersweet mousse, which complements the crunchy sweet meringue. The classic chocolate mousse is quick and easy to prepare and can also be served alone. The cooked meringue from which the cases are shaped is a pleasure to use; it pipes easily and beautifully and keeps well.

Meringue Cups:

4 large egg whites

1-1/4 cups sugar

Dark Chocolate Mousse:

6 oz. fine-quality bittersweet chocolate, chopped

2 tablespoons unsalted butter

4 large eggs, separated

1 tablespoon rum

1 tablespoon sugar

Meringue Cups: Position rack in center of oven and preheat to 200F (95C). Lightly butter corners of 2 baking sheets; line with foil. Butter and flour foil. Using a 3-inch cookie cutter as a guide, mark 8 circles 1-1/2 inches apart onto baking sheets.

Combine egg whites and sugar in a large bowl. Set bowl in a pan of hot water over low heat. Beat with a hand mixer at low speed 4 minutes, then at medium speed about 3 minutes or until mixture is warm to touch. Remove from water. Beat at high speed until completely cooled. Meringue will be very shiny and sticky.

Spoon meringue into a pastry bag fitted with small or medium star tip. Pipe in a tight spiral, beginning in center of 1 marked circle on baking sheet, until circle is completely covered with meringue. Without stopping, continue piping a second layer of meringue on rim of circle, then a third layer so rim is higher than base and forms a case. Pipe 7 more Meringue Cups.

Bake about 1 hour or until meringue feels firm and dry to touch and is not sticky at bottom. Carefully transfer meringues to a rack, using a slotted metal spatula; cool. *Meringues can be kept in an airtight container 1 week in dry weather.*

Mousse: Melt chocolate in a medium bowl over nearly simmering water. Stir until smooth. Remove from water. Stir in butter. Whisk egg yolks to blend. Add all at once to chocolate; whisk vigorously. Whisk in rum.

In a dry medium bowl, whip egg whites to soft peaks. Add sugar; whip at high speed until whites are stiff and shiny but not dry. Quickly stir about 1/4 of whites into chocolate mixture, using whisk. Gently fold in remaining whites. Spoon mousse into a shallow bowl. Refrigerate 1 hour.

Spoon enough mousse into each Meringue Cup to fill it to the top, using about 2 tablespoons mousse for each. Spoon remaining mousse into a serving dish. Refrigerate filled Meringue Cups, uncovered, 1-1/2 hours or until mousse sets. *Dessert can be kept, covered, 1 day in refrigerator.* Serve cold; serve mousse in bowl separately.

Makes 8 servings

Variation

If you are concerned about the safety of using raw eggs, fill the meringue cups with Chocolate Mousse Supreme, page 79, instead of Dark Chocolate Mousse.

Molded Chocolate Mousse

The raisin-studded mousse is prepared in paper baking cups and
is extremely easy to unmold—just peel off the paper.
It is surrounded by creamy Brandy Custard Sauce and garnished with raisins.

Photo on page 84.

1/2 cup dark raisins

1/4 cup brandy

Chocolate Mousse:

8 oz. fine-quality semisweet
 chocolate, chopped

3 large egg yolks

3 tablespoons powdered sugar

5 tablespoons water

1/2 cup (4 oz.) unsalted butter,
 slightly softened

2/3 cup whipping cream, well
 chilled

Spirited Custard Sauce, page 169,
 using 1-1/2 tablespoons brandy
 (from raisins above)

Put raisins in a small jar or bowl; pour brandy over them. Cover tightly; shake to mix. Cover and leave to macerate at least 30 minutes or up to 2 hours at room temperature.

Mousse: Melt chocolate in a medium bowl over nearly simmering water. Stir until smooth. Remove from water; let cool. Set 8 paper baking cups in muffin pans. Drain raisins, reserving brandy.

Whisk yolks with sugar and 5 tablespoons water in a small metal bowl. Set bowl in a pan of nearly simmering water. Heat, whisking constantly, until mixture reaches 160F (70C) on an instant-read or candy thermometer, about 1 minute. Immediately transfer to another bowl and whisk until cool.

Cream butter in a medium or large bowl until smooth. Beat in egg mixture in 2 batches. Beat in chocolate in 2 batches.

Stir in 1/4 cup raisins and 2 tablespoons of their brandy. Combine remaining raisins and remaining brandy; cover and set aside.

In a chilled medium bowl, whip cream until stiff. Fold cream, in 3 batches, into chocolate mixture. Spoon into paper baking cups, using about 1/3 cup mousse for each cup. Tap molds to even top surface. Refrigerate about 5 hours or until firm. *Mousse can be kept, covered, 1 week in refrigerator.*

Turn mousse "cupcakes" over onto small plates; gently peel off papers. Spoon sauce around each mousse and a little on top. Set a few raisins on sauce.

Makes 9 servings

Triple-Chocolate Mousse Parfait

In this stunning new dessert, three chocolate mousses are layered, parfait-style, in stemmed glasses to show off the different hues of chocolate. The three delicious mousses of white chocolate, milk chocolate and dark chocolate are made from a single basic mixture.

Photo opposite.

2-1/4 cups whipping cream

6 large egg yolks

1 tablespoon sugar

4 oz. fine-quality white chocolate, chopped

6 tablespoons unsalted butter, cut in tablespoon-size pieces, room temperature

4 oz. fine-quality milk chocolate, chopped

4 oz. fine-quality bittersweet chocolate, chopped

White Quick Chocolate Curls, page 172, White Chocolate Leaves, page 177, or candied violets, if desired (for garnish)

Refrigerate 1-3/4 cups cream. Whisk egg yolks with sugar and 1/2 cup cream in a medium-size metal bowl. Set bowl in a pan of nearly simmering water. Heat, whisking constantly, until mixture reaches 160F (70C) on an instant-read or candy thermometer, about 4 minutes. Remove from heat and immediately whip with electric mixer until cool.

Melt white chocolate in a medium bowl over nearly simmering water. Stir until smooth. Remove from water. Add 3 tablespoons butter and stir to blend. Add 1/3 cup plus 1 tablespoon yolk mixture and stir until blended.

Melt milk chocolate. Remove from water. Add 2 tablespoons butter and stir to blend. Add 1/3 cup plus 1 tablespoon yolk mixture and stir until blended.

Melt bittersweet chocolate. Remove from water and add remaining butter and half of remaining yolk mixture. Stir quickly until blended. Stir in remaining yolk mixture.

In a large chilled bowl, whip chilled cream until stiff. Fold 1-1/3 cups cream into white chocolate mixture. Divide white chocolate mousse among 6 wine glasses or other 1-cup glasses, using about 1/3 cup mousse for each. Refrigerate about 15 minutes or freeze 10 minutes or until top is partially set.

Fold 1-1/3 cups whipped cream into milk chocolate mixture. Gently spoon milk chocolate mousse over white mousse in glasses in an even layer. Refrigerate 15 minutes or freeze 10 minutes.

Fold remaining whipped cream into bittersweet chocolate mixture. Gently spoon dark chocolate mousse into the glasses. Refrigerate about 2 hours or until set. Cover with plastic wrap when set. *Dessert can be kept 2 days in refrigerator.* Garnish with white chocolate curls or leaves or candied violets, or any combination, if using.

Makes 6 servings

Triple-Chocolate Mousse Parfait, above; White Chocolate Mousse with Strawberry Sauce, page 80; Molded Chocolate Mousse, page 83.

Chocolate-Apricot Terrine

A terrine is a loaf-shaped dish and the food served in it. This chocolate terrine is composed of a very rich, creamy mousse-like mixture. Like the classic Sachertorte, this dessert combines chocolate and apricots, but here the apricot flavor comes from dried apricots and apricot brandy and is more pronounced.

Photo on pages vi-vii.

1/3 cup dried apricots, very finely chopped with a knife (about 1-1/2 oz.)

5 tablespoons apricot-flavored brandy

4 oz. semisweet chocolate, chopped

4 egg yolks, room temperature

3/4 cup sugar

2 tablespoons water

3/4 cup (6 oz.) unsalted butter, slightly softened

3/4 cup unsweetened Dutch-process cocoa powder, sifted

1/2 pint whipping cream (1 cup), well-chilled

1 (3-oz.) pkg. ladyfingers (about 3 inches long) or about 6 oz. White Ladyfingers, page 137

About 9 dried apricot halves

Spirited Custard Sauce, page 169, flavored with apricot brandy

Put chopped dried apricots in a small jar. Pour 2 tablespoons brandy over apricots. Cover tightly; shake to mix. Cover and let stand 2 hours or up to overnight.

Oil an 8" x 4" loaf pan. Cut a 12" x 8" piece and an 18" x 12" piece of waxed paper. Fold 18-inch piece in 3 lengthwise; set lengthwise in loaf pan. Set second piece of waxed paper crosswise on top so pan is completely lined. Oil paper. Melt chocolate in a small bowl over nearly simmering water. Stir until smooth. Remove from water; let cool.

Whisk egg yolks with 1/4 cup sugar and 2 tablespoons water in a small metal bowl. Set in a pan of nearly simmering water. Heat, whisking, until mixture reaches 160F (70C) on an instant-read or candy thermometer, about 2 minutes. Remove from heat and immediately whip with electric mixer until cool.

Cream butter in a medium bowl until smooth. Beat in remaining 1/2 cup sugar. Beat in cocoa in 3 batches, followed by egg mixture. Beat in chocolate at low speed in 4 batches.

In a large chilled bowl, whip cream to soft peaks. Fold into chocolate mixture in 3 batches. Fold in chopped apricots with their brandy.

Set 4 packaged ladyfinger halves or homemade ladyfingers lengthwise in base of loaf pan, 1 at each corner. Arrange enough apricot halves, rounded-side down, on remaining area of base of pan to make 1 layer. Brush ladyfingers with apricot brandy. Pour 2 cups chocolate mixture into lined pan; spread smooth. Top with 1 layer of ladyfinger halves or whole homemade ladyfingers placed lengthwise, trimming them to fit if necessary. Brush with brandy. Pour in remaining chocolate mixture. Top with another layer of ladyfinger halves, spongy-side up, or whole homemade ladyfingers, placed lengthwise. Brush with remaining brandy. Cover and refrigerate overnight. *Terrine can be kept 1 week in refrigerator.*

To serve, unmold terrine onto a platter. Gently peel off paper. Serve in slices and spoon Spirited Custard Sauce around each slice.

Makes 8 servings

Variation

Omit apricots and their soaking brandy. Arrange a complete layer of ladyfingers on base of pan.

Cold Chocolate-Raspberry Soufflé

Chocolate and raspberries are a favorite American combination. In this cold soufflé, the vivid pink of the fresh-raspberry-mousse layers provides an exciting color and flavor contrast to the ribbon of dark chocolate mousse in the center. To show off the beauty of the colors to their greatest advantage, assemble and present this dessert in a glass soufflé dish and include all three layers in each portion when serving.

Photo on page iii.

Raspberry Mousse:

3 cups fresh or frozen unsweetened raspberries (about 12 oz.), thawed if frozen

1 (1/4-oz.) envelope unflavored gelatin (scant 1 tablespoon)

1/2 cup water

2/3 cup sugar

1/2 pint whipping cream (1 cup), well-chilled

Chocolate Mousse:

1-1/4 teaspoons unflavored gelatin

6 tablespoons water

7 oz. semisweet chocolate, chopped

5 tablespoons unsalted butter, cut in pieces

4 large egg yolks

2 tablespoons sugar

2 tablespoons plus 2 teaspoons clear raspberry brandy, if desired

1/2 pint whipping cream (1 cup), well-chilled

Garnish:

1/3 cup whipping cream, well-chilled

6 to 8 raspberries

1 heart-shaped, fluted or round Chocolate Cutout, page 175, about 1-1/2 to 2 inches across *or* a little grated chocolate

Raspberry Mousse: Puree raspberries in a food processor or blender until very smooth. Strain puree into a large bowl, pressing on pulp in strainer. Use a rubber spatula to scrape mixture from underside of strainer.

Sprinkle gelatin over 1/4 cup water in a small cup. In a small saucepan thoroughly mix sugar and remaining 1/4 cup water. Stir over low heat until sugar dissolves completely. Increase heat to medium and bring to a boil. Simmer 30 seconds without stirring. Remove from heat; immediately whisk in softened gelatin. Cool 3 minutes, stirring often. Gradually whisk mixture into raspberry puree.

Stirring very often, refrigerate mixture about 30 minutes, or set bowl of mixture in a larger bowl of iced water about 15 minutes, or until mixture is cold and thickened to the consistency of unbeaten egg whites but is not set.

In a large chilled bowl, whip cream until nearly stiff. Gently fold into berry mixture. Pour 2 cups mousse into a 1-quart soufflé dish. Cover and freeze 30 minutes. Keep remaining mousse at room temperature.

Chocolate Mousse: Sprinkle gelatin over 2 tablespoons water in a small cup. Melt chocolate with butter in a medium bowl in a shallow pan of nearly simmering water. Stir until smooth. Remove from water. Set cup of gelatin in pan of simmering water. Melt gelatin, stirring often, about 3 minutes. Stir into chocolate mixture.

Whisk yolks with sugar and 4 tablespoons water in a small metal bowl. Set bowl in pan of nearly simmering water. Heat, whisking constantly, until mixture reaches 160F (70C) on an instant-read or candy thermometer, about 1 minute. Immediately remove from water and whisk 2 minutes to cool. Gently stir into chocolate mixture. Stir in brandy.

In a large chilled bowl, whip cream until just stiff. Fold about 1/4 of cream into chocolate mixture. Spoon mixture over remaining cream; fold gently until blended.

Cut a 25-inch-long sheet of waxed paper; fold in half lengthwise. Wrap paper around soufflé dish containing raspberry mousse so it extends about 3 inches above rim to make a collar. Fasten tightly with tape. Pour Chocolate Mousse into soufflé dish; gently spread smooth. Freeze 10 minutes. Gently pour remaining Raspberry Mousse over Chocolate Mousse. Refrigerate 6 hours or until completely set. *Dessert can be kept, covered, 3 days in refrigerator.*

Garnish: In a small chilled bowl, whip cream until very stiff. To serve, carefully peel off paper collar. Using a pastry bag and large star tip, pipe rosettes of whipped cream at top edge of dessert. Top rosettes with raspberries. Set Chocolate Cutout in center or sprinkle with grated chocolate.

Makes 8 to 10 servings

Chocolate-Rum Bavarian Cream

In this incredibly creamy chocolate dessert, a favorite in my chocolate-dessert classes, rum or Grand Marnier provides a lively foil to the dessert's richness.

Bavarian Cream:

4 oz. semisweet chocolate, chopped

1 (1/4-oz.) envelope unflavored gelatin (scant 1 tablespoon)

1/4 cup water

1 cup milk

4 large egg yolks

6 tablespoons sugar

1/4 cup golden rum

1-1/4 cups whipping cream, well-chilled

Garnish:

1/2 cup whipping cream, well-chilled

1 teaspoon sugar

8 chocolate coffee beans or a little grated semisweet chocolate

Bavarian Cream: Melt chocolate in a medium bowl over nearly simmering water. Sprinkle gelatin over 1/4 cup water in a small cup.

Bring milk to a boil in a small heavy saucepan. Whisk egg yolks in a large bowl. Add sugar; whisk until smooth. Gradually whisk in hot milk. Return mixture to saucepan. Cook over medium-low heat, stirring and scraping bottom of pan constantly with a wooden spoon, until mixture reaches 165F to 170F (75C) on an instant-read or candy thermometer, about 5 minutes. To check without thermometer, see page 169. Remove from heat and immediately add softened gelatin; whisk until it completely dissolves. Pour into a large bowl; stir about 30 seconds to cool.

Remove chocolate from pan of water. Stir until smooth. Using a whisk, stir custard mixture, about 1/2 cup at a time, into chocolate. Return mixture to large bowl. Cool to room temperature, stirring occasionally. Gradually stir in rum. Lightly oil a 5-cup ring mold.

Refrigerate mixture about 20 minutes, or set bowl in a larger bowl of iced water and leave 10 minutes, stirring very often, or until mixture is cold and beginning to thicken but is not set. In a large chilled bowl, whip cream until nearly stiff. Fold into chocolate mixture, blending thoroughly.

Pour mixture into oiled mold; smooth top. Refrigerate at least 3 hours or until set. *Dessert can be kept, covered, 2 days in refrigerator; rum flavor weakens after 1 day.*

Garnish: Unmold dessert, see below. Refrigerate until ready to serve. In a chilled medium bowl whip cream with sugar until very stiff. Using a pastry bag and medium star tip, pipe rosettes of whipped cream at base of dessert. Garnish rosettes with chocolate coffee beans or with a sprinkling of grated chocolate.

Makes 8 servings

Variation

Chocolate-Grand Marnier Bavarian Cream: Follow recipe above, using 5 oz. fine-quality bittersweet chocolate, 1 (1/4-oz.) envelope plus 3/4 teaspoon unflavored gelatin, 5 tablespoons water, 1-1/4 cups milk, 5 large egg yolks, 7 tablespoons sugar, 5 tablespoons Grand Marnier and 1-1/2 cups whipping cream. Spoon mixture into a lightly oiled 7- or 8-cup mold. Makes 10 servings.

Tip

To unmold Bavarian cream: Run a thin-bladed flexible knife around edge of dessert, including inner edge if using a ring mold, gently pushing mixture slightly from edge of mold to let in air. Dip mold, nearly to depth of contents, in warm, not hot, water about 10 seconds. Dry base of mold. Set a platter on top of mold. Holding firmly together, quickly flip so dessert is right-side up. Shake mold gently downward; dessert should slip from mold onto platter. If dessert remains in mold, repeat dipping procedure. Carefully remove mold by lifting it straight upward.

White Chocolate Bavarian Squares

This dessert is inspired by a favorite restaurant dessert that my husband and I first enjoyed in Israel 15 years ago. The Israeli dessert is a vanilla Bavarian cream accompanied by dark chocolate sauce and sprinkled with chopped nuts. It is served right from the dish instead of being unmolded. This version is exceptionally creamy and delicately flavored with white chocolate, complemented by a sauce spiked with crème de cacao and by the crunch of pecans.

1-1/4 cups whipping cream

3 oz. fine-quality white chocolate, very finely chopped

1 (1/4-oz.) envelope unflavored gelatin (scant 1 tablespoon)

1/4 cup water

1 cup milk

4 large egg yolks

6 tablespoons sugar

1/4 cup white crème de cacao

Spirited Cold Chocolate Sauce, page 165

1/3 cup pecans, chopped

Refrigerate 1 cup cream. Put white chocolate in a medium bowl. Bring remaining 1/4 cup cream to a full boil in a small heavy saucepan. Pour over chocolate all at once. Stir with a whisk until mixture is smooth.

Sprinkle gelatin over 1/4 cup water in a small cup. Bring milk to a boil in a small heavy saucepan. Whisk egg yolks in a large bowl. Add sugar; whisk until blended. Gradually whisk in hot milk. Return mixture to saucepan. Cook over medium-low heat, stirring mixture and scraping bottom of pan constantly with a wooden spoon, until mixture thickens slightly and reaches 165F to 170F (75C) on an instant-read or candy thermometer, about 5 minutes. To check without thermometer, see page 169. Remove from heat and immediately add softened gelatin; whisk until it completely dissolves. Pour custard into a large bowl; stir about 30 seconds to cool. Cool 10 minutes.

Using a whisk, gradually stir custard mixture into chocolate mixture. Return mixture to large bowl; cool to room temperature, stirring occasionally. Gradually stir in creme de cacao.

Refrigerate mixture about 20 minutes, or set bowl in a larger bowl of iced water and leave 10 minutes, stirring very often, or until mixture is cold and beginning to thicken but is not set. Meanwhile, lightly oil an 8-inch-square baking dish or serving dish.

In a large chilled bowl, whip remaining 1 cup cream until nearly stiff. Gently fold into chocolate mixture. Pour into prepared dish; smooth top. Cover and refrigerate at least 3 hours or until set. *Dessert can be kept 2 days in refrigerator; liqueur flavor weakens after 1 day.*

Cut dessert in about 2-1/2-inch squares. Use a broad spatula to transfer to plates. Spoon chocolate sauce over each serving and sprinkle with pecans.

Makes about 8 servings

Truffled Bavarian Cream

Each of these individual Bavarian creams hides a soft chocolate truffle in its center. The vanilla molds dotted with chocolate resemble Italian Chocolate Chip Ice Cream, page 99, in appearance. They can be served surrounded by Raspberry Sauce, page 102, for a beautiful color contrast.

Soft Truffles:

1-1/2 oz. fine-quality semisweet chocolate, finely chopped

2 tablespoons whipping cream

1 tablespoon unsalted butter

Chocolate-Flecked Bavarian Cream:

1-1/2 cups milk

1 vanilla bean, split lengthwise

1 (1/4-oz.) envelope plus 1 teaspoon unflavored gelatin (scant 4 teaspoons)

1/4 cup water

5 large egg yolks

6 tablespoons sugar

1/2 pint whipping cream (1 cup), well-chilled

2 oz. semisweet chocolate, grated, chilled

Truffles: Melt chocolate with cream and butter in a small bowl over nearly simmering water. Whisk until smooth. Remove from pan of water; let cool. Cover and refrigerate at least 1 hour. Using 2 teaspoons, shape into 6 mounds on a plate, using 1 rounded teaspoon for each truffle. Freeze 10 minutes. Roll between palms to smooth. Freeze again 10 minutes. Refrigerate until ready to use.

Bavarian Cream: Bring milk and vanilla bean to a boil in a heavy medium saucepan. Remove from heat. Cover and let stand 15 minutes. Remove vanilla bean.

Sprinkle gelatin over water in a small cup. Reheat milk mixture to a boil. Whisk egg yolks in a large bowl. Add sugar; whisk until blended. Gradually whisk in hot milk. Return mixture to saucepan. Cook over medium-low heat, stirring mixture and scraping bottom of pan constantly with a wooden spoon, until mixture thickens slightly and reaches 165F to 170F (75C) on an instant-read or candy thermometer, about 5 minutes. To check without thermometer, see page 169. Remove from heat and immediately add softened gelatin; whisk until it completely dissolves. Pour custard into a large bowl; stir about 30 seconds to cool.

Cool to room temperature, stirring occasionally. Line bases of 6 (2/3-cup) ramekins with a round of waxed paper; lightly oil paper and sides of ramekins. Refrigerate custard about 20 minutes, or set bowl in a larger bowl of iced water for 10 minutes, stirring very often, or until mixture is cold and beginning to thicken but is not set.

Whip cream in a large chilled bowl until nearly stiff. Gently fold cream into custard, followed by grated chocolate. Spoon a scant 1/4 cup custard into each ramekin. Freeze ramekins 15 minutes. Keep remaining custard at room temperature.

Set a truffle in each ramekin. Spoon remaining custard on top. Tap firmly on work surface to distribute custard. Refrigerate at least 3 hours or until completely set. *Dessert can be kept, covered, 2 days in refrigerator.* Unmold desserts, page 88. Refrigerate until ready to serve.

Makes 6 servings

Variation

Chocolate-Flecked Bavarian Cream: Omit truffles. Spoon custard mixture into a lightly oiled 5-cup mold. Refrigerate at least 4 hours or until set. Unmold and serve with Raspberry Sauce, page 102.

Brown-Bottom Charlotte

The brown bottom of this rich charlotte is chocolate whipped cream.
It is topped by a layer of Bourbon Bavarian cream. The bourbon provides a zesty punch
on the first day and becomes delicate on the second day.

---

5 oz. packaged ladyfingers
  (3 inches long) or about 9 oz.
  White Ladyfingers, page 137

2 tablespoons bourbon whiskey

1 tablespoon water

Chocolate Cream Filling, page 164

Bourbon Bavarian Cream:

3/4 cup milk

1 vanilla bean

2 teaspoons unflavored gelatin

3 tablespoons water

3 large egg yolks

1/4 cup sugar

1 tablespoon plus 1 teaspoon
  bourbon whiskey

3/4 cup whipping cream,
  well-chilled

Quick Chocolate Curls, page 172, or
  grated chocolate, if desired
  (for garnish)

Lightly oil side of an 8-inch springform pan. If using packaged ladyfingers, which are usually split in half horizontally, stand ladyfinger halves up in a single row against side of pan, with spongy sides facing inward, forming a tight ring. If ladyfingers are joined in a row, there is no need to separate them. If using home-made ladyfingers, follow directions given in the tip following that recipe.

Arrange more ladyfingers in a layer on base of pan. Cut more ladyfingers so they fit as tightly as possible on base and fill any holes. Mix bourbon with water in a small dish. Brush ladyfingers in pan with bourbon mixture. Spoon choco-late filling into ladyfinger-lined pan. Smooth top. Refrigerate 1 hour.

Bavarian Cream: Bring milk and vanilla bean to a boil in a small heavy saucepan. Remove from heat. Cover and let stand 15 minutes. Sprinkle gelatin over water in a small cup. Reheat milk mixture to a boil. Remove vanilla bean.

Whisk yolks in a small bowl. Add sugar; whisk until blended. Gradually whisk in hot milk. Return mixture to saucepan. Cook over medium-low heat, stirring mixture and scraping bottom of pan constantly with a wooden spoon, until mixture reaches 160F to 165F (70C to 75C) on an instant-read or candy ther-mometer, about 5 minutes. To check without thermometer, see page 169. Remove from heat and immediately add softened gelatin; whisk until it com-pletely dissolves. Pour custard into a large bowl; stir about 30 seconds to cool.

Cool to room temperature, stirring occasionally. Slowly stir in bourbon. Refrigerate mixture about 15 minutes, or set bowl in a larger bowl of iced water and leave about 7 minutes, stirring very often, or until mixture is cold and beginning to thicken but is not set.

Whip cream in a small chilled bowl until nearly stiff. Fold into cold bourbon mixture. Carefully pour into charlotte mold. Refrigerate about 4 hours or until filling sets. *Dessert can be kept, covered, 3 days in refrigerator; bourbon flavor weak-ens after 1 day.*

To unmold dessert, release spring and remove side of pan. Garnish top with chocolate curls or grated chocolate, allowing white filling to show through.

Makes 6 servings

Chocolate Charlotte with Raspberries

Whole fresh raspberries accent the chocolate filling of this light-textured, easy-to-make charlotte that would be proudly served in the best of restaurants. Serve each slice surrounded by a ribbon of ruby-red Raspberry Sauce, page 102.

Photo opposite.

---

11 oz. semisweet chocolate, chopped

1 (1/4-oz.) envelope plus 1-1/4 teaspoons unflavored gelatin (4 teaspoons)

1/3 cup water

2 cups milk

6 large egg yolks

1/2 cup sugar

1 (3-oz.) pkg. ladyfingers (about 3 inches long) or about 6 oz. White Ladyfingers, page 137

1-1/2 cups whipping cream, well-chilled

2-2/3 cups fresh raspberries (about 11 oz.)

1/2 cup whipping cream, well-chilled, if desired (for garnish)

Melt chocolate in a large bowl over nearly simmering water. Stir until smooth. Remove from water. Sprinkle gelatin over 1/3 cup water in a small cup.

Bring milk to a boil in a heavy medium saucepan. Whisk yolks in a large heat-proof bowl. Add sugar; whisk until blended. Gradually whisk in hot milk. Return mixture to saucepan. Cook over medium-low heat, stirring mixture and scraping bottom of pan constantly with a wooden spoon, until mixture reaches 160F (70C) on an instant-read or candy thermometer, about 7 minutes. To check without thermometer, see page 169. Remove from heat and immediately add softened gelatin; whisk until it completely dissolves. Pour custard into a large bowl; stir about 30 seconds to cool. Whisk custard mixture, about 1 cup at a time, into chocolate. Cool to room temperature, stirring occasionally.

Lightly oil a 9-inch springform pan. If using packaged ladyfingers, which are usually split in half horizontally, stand ladyfinger halves up in a single row against side of oiled pan, with spongy sides facing inward, forming a tight ring. If ladyfingers are joined in a row, there is no need to separate them. If using homemade ladyfingers, follow directions in the tip accompanying that recipe.

Refrigerate chocolate mixture about 30 minutes, or set bowl of mixture in a larger bowl of iced water for about 15 minutes, stirring often, or until mixture is cold and beginning to thicken but is not set. In a large chilled bowl, whip 1-1/2 cups cream until nearly stiff. Fold into cold chocolate mixture.

Carefully pour 4 cups chocolate mixture into ladyfinger-lined pan. Freeze 10 minutes. Arrange 1-1/3 cups raspberries in 1 layer on chocolate. Carefully pour remaining chocolate mixture over them. Gently spread smooth. Refrigerate 10 minutes. Top with another layer of 1-1/3 cups raspberries. Refrigerate charlotte 3 hours or until filling sets. *Dessert can be kept, covered, 2 days in refrigerator.*

To unmold, carefully run a thin-bladed knife around charlotte; release spring and remove side of pan. Return dessert to refrigerator. In a chilled medium bowl, whip cream until very stiff. Using a pastry bag and medium star tip, pipe rosettes of whipped cream near bottom edge of dessert. Serve cold.

Makes 8 to 10 servings

Chocolate-Cognac Marquise

Like a charlotte, a marquise has a ladyfinger frame, but a marquise almost always has
a very rich chocolate filling and is usually loaf shaped.
This one is served with cognac custard sauce.

1 lb. semisweet chocolate, chopped

1 (3-oz.) pkg. ladyfingers
(3 inches long) or about 6 oz.
White Ladyfingers, page 137

1 cup (8 oz.) unsalted butter,
slightly softened

4 large egg yolks

3 tablespoons sugar

5 tablespoons water

2 tablespoons cognac

Spirited Custard Sauce, page 169,
flavored with cognac

Melt chocolate in a large bowl over nearly simmering water. Stir until smooth. Remove from water; let cool.

If using packaged ladyfingers, which are usually split in half horizontally, set ladyfinger halves crosswise in a single row on the base of an 8" x 4" loaf pan, with their spongy side facing up. If ladyfingers are joined in a row, there is no need to separate them. Stand more ladyfinger halves up against long sides of pan, with spongy sides facing inward, fitting them tightly. Stand more ladyfinger halves up against short sides of pan to complete case. Ladyfingers should be close together so pan is tightly lined. If using homemade ladyfingers, line pan as above, using whole ladyfingers and trimming them as necessary to fit tightly.

Cream butter in a large bowl until very smooth. Beat in chocolate in 4 batches until smooth.

Whisk egg yolks with sugar and 3 tablespoons water in a small metal bowl until blended. Set in a pan of nearly simmering water. Heat, whisking, until mixture reaches 160F (70C) on an instant-read or candy thermometer, about 2 minutes. Remove from water and immediately whisk about 2 minutes to cool. Beat into chocolate mixture in 2 batches.

Mix 2 tablespoons cognac and remaining 2 tablespoons water in a small bowl. Brush ladyfinger case lightly but evenly with cognac mixture. Pour chocolate mixture into lined pan without moving ladyfingers. Smooth top of mixture with a rubber spatula. Using a sharp knife, cut off ladyfinger ends above level of chocolate mixture; set on top of mixture near edges of pan. Add more ladyfinger pieces, if necessary, to make an even layer. Press gently so top is even. Refrigerate at least 2 hours or until set. *Dessert can be kept, covered, 3 days in refrigerator.*

Remove marquise from refrigerator about 30 minutes before serving. Run a thin-bladed knife around dessert; turn out onto a platter. Cut off short ends. Cut marquise in thin slices with a sharp knife. To serve, spoon a little sauce around each slice on plate. Serve remaining sauce separately.

Makes 10 to 12 servings

Royal Chocolate Charlotte

In this spectacular dessert fit for a royal feast, a classic-style frame of spiral-shaped slices
of raspberry jellyroll surrounds a chocolate Bavarian cream.
Serve this regal treat for extra-special occasions.

**Orange Sponge Cake, page 24, made
without orange zest**

3/4 cup raspberry preserves

Chocolate Bavarian Cream:

**6-1/2 oz. fine-quality bittersweet
chocolate, chopped**

1 cup milk

1 vanilla bean, split lengthwise

**1 (1/4-oz.) envelope unflavored
gelatin (scant 1 tablespoon)**

1/4 cup water

4 large egg yolks

5 tablespoons sugar

**1-1/2 cups whipping cream,
well-chilled**

Apricot Glaze:

1/2 cup apricot preserves

2 tablespoons water

Bake cake. Cool to room temperature. Spread raspberry preserves on cake. Beginning with a long side, roll up cake carefully but tightly; if it is not rolled tightly enough, slices will have holes. Wrap and refrigerate 30 minutes. *Cake can be kept 1 day in refrigerator.*

Using a serrated knife, cut cake in 3/8-inch slices. Oil base of a 9-inch spring-form pan. Line base with waxed paper; oil paper and sides of pan. Arrange cake slices in pan, 1 slice standing against side and 1 slice next to it on base to support it. When there are enough slices on base to prevent those on side from falling, begin gently pushing slices on base into place, side by side, and complete the layer. Squeeze slices at side and on base tightly into place so there are no holes. Patch any holes with small pieces of cake.

Bavarian Cream: Melt chocolate in a medium bowl over nearly simmering water. Stir until smooth. Remove from water. Bring milk and vanilla bean to a boil in a heavy medium saucepan. Remove from heat. Cover and let stand 15 minutes. In a small cup sprinkle gelatin over 1/4 cup water.

Reheat milk mixture to a boil. Remove vanilla bean. Whisk yolks in a large bowl. Add sugar; whisk until blended. Gradually whisk in hot milk. Return mixture to saucepan. Cook over medium-low heat, stirring mixture and scraping bottom of pan constantly with a wooden spoon, until mixture reaches 165F to 170F (75C) on an instant-read or candy thermometer, about 5 minutes. To check without thermometer, see page 169. Remove from heat and immediately add softened gelatin; whisk until it completely dissolves. Pour custard into a large bowl; stir about 30 seconds to cool. Cool 5 minutes.

Using a whisk, stir custard, 3/4 cup at a time, into melted chocolate. Pour into a large bowl; cool to room temperature, stirring occasionally.

Refrigerate mixture about 20 minutes, or set bowl of mixture in a larger bowl of iced water and leave about 10 minutes, stirring very often, or until mixture is cold and beginning to thicken but is not set. In a large chilled bowl, whip cream until nearly stiff. Fold into chocolate mixture. Pour into cake-lined bowl; smooth top. Refrigerate 10 minutes. Gently set remaining cake slices on top to make 1 layer. Cover and refrigerate at least 5 hours or until set. *Dessert can be kept, covered, 3 days in refrigerator.*

To unmold, turn dessert over onto serving platter. Gently release spring and remove side of springform. Remove base. Peel off paper.

Glaze: Combine preserves and water in a small saucepan. Heat over low heat until hot but not boiling. Strain into a small bowl, pressing on apricot pieces. Using a pastry brush, dab glaze on cake. *Glazed dessert can be kept, covered with a cake cover or overturned bowl, 1 day in refrigerator.* Serve cold.

Chocolate Chestnut Log

This favorite French family dessert is easy to prepare yet rich and sophisticated in taste. Canned or bottled chestnuts can be purchased at specialty food stores and in some supermarkets.

8 oz. semisweet chocolate, chopped

3-1/3 cups canned unsweetened whole chestnuts (1 lb.), drained well

2/3 cup milk, room temperature

1/2 cup (4 oz.) unsalted butter

1/2 cup plus 3 tablespoons powdered sugar, sifted

2 tablespoons rum

About 2 teaspoons unsweetened Dutch-process cocoa powder

Quick Chocolate Curls, page 172

About 1/2 teaspoon powdered sugar (for garnish)

1/2 pint whipping cream (1 cup), well-chilled (for accompaniment)

Melt chocolate in a medium bowl over nearly simmering water. Stir until smooth. Remove from water; let cool. Puree chestnuts with milk in a food processor until smooth.

Cream butter in a large bowl. Add powdered sugar and beat until smooth and fluffy. Stir in chestnut mixture and rum. Gradually stir in chocolate. Transfer to a bowl, cover and refrigerate 45 minutes. Spoon mixture onto a large piece of foil of about 20" x 12". Roll to a log, about 2-1/2 inches in diameter. Close ends of foil so log is wrapped. Refrigerate 8 hours or until firm. *Dessert can be kept 2 days in refrigerator.*

Remove foil from log, set log on a platter and press, if necessary, to give it a neater round shape. Put waxed paper on platter around log. Sift cocoa evenly over log. Make lines lengthwise on log with a fork to resemble bark. Top with chocolate curls. Sift powdered sugar over chocolate curls. Remove waxed paper from platter.

In a large chilled bowl, whip cream to soft peaks. Serve log in 1/2-inch-thick slices. Serve whipped cream separately.

Makes 8 servings

Cool, refreshing chocolate ice creams and frozen desserts are naturally the stars among summer sweet treats. Many are impressive yet easy to prepare, and most do not require baking and involve little or no last-minute work.

Chocolate Ice Creams

It is hard to imagine anything more delicious than homemade chocolate ice cream that has just been churned. Whether it is made the European way from custard mixtures, as in French-Italian Chocolate Ice Cream, or from easy blends of chocolate and cream, as in Chocolate-Mint Ice Cream or American Chocolate Ice Cream, its taste and smoothness are unparalleled.

Although ice cream keeps for several weeks in the freezer, when it is fresh it has the most wonderful soft creamy texture. If, however, your schedule does not allow you to churn the ice cream immediately before serving or you prefer a firmer texture, the ice cream can be left in the freezer for two to four hours and will still be at its best.

Frozen Chocolate Desserts

This group of desserts includes some of the most elegant of sweet finales. Smooth and frosty, they can be made in a multitude of shapes, colors and tastes.

Because these desserts are made from mixtures that are richer than ice cream, there is no need to stir them during the freezing process. They therefore do not require an ice cream machine to give them a velvety texture and prevent the formation of ice crystals. Instead, their smoothness is achieved by the addition of whipped cream, egg yolks, Italian meringue, butter or some combination of these elements.

Chocolate parfaits are made of a custard enriched with whipped cream; it is the chocolate that ensures that the parfait freezes to a silky texture. Frozen chocolate mousses, used in both Chocolate-Blackberry Loaf and Chocolate Mousse Ring with Fresh Berries, are prepared by a procedure similar to that for classic chocolate mousse but include a generous proportion of whipped cream for lightness. Iced soufflés consist of a special mousse-type mixture formed to resemble a hot soufflé. Bombes are traditionally rounded in shape, and are composed of an outer layer of ice cream and a creamy filling of a contrasting color and flavor. Chocolate can appear either in the ice cream, as in Chocolate-Strawberry Bombe, or in the filling, as in Rum-Raisin Chocolate Bombe.

Chocolate Ice Cream Cakes

A stroll from one pastry shop to the next in the cities of France and Italy will reveal that these favorite American treats are popular in southern Europe too, although they look much different.

In many ice cream cakes, the rich filling is balanced by layers of a light sponge cake. Another possibility is crisp meringues, which are traditionally paired with ice cream in Europe. Instead of cake, a quicker base can be made as in Brownie Ice Cream Cake, where fudge brownies are split and alternated with coffee and vanilla ice creams.

Ice cream cakes can be absolutely spectacular. One of the most dazzling cakes of France and Austria, both celebrated for their fabulous entremets, is the vacherin. This sensational castle of light meringues contains a rich filling. Contemporary versions are usually filled with ice cream. French pâtisseries often have ice cream- and sorbet-filled vacherins ready in their freezers, a useful tip for the home cook as well.

Ice cream cakes afford a wonderful opportunity for creativity. They can be shaped in different types of molds, cake pans or even mixing bowls. If, for example, you substitute coffee ice cream for vanilla in Chocolate-Pecan Sundae Pie and decorate the top with chocolate coffee beans, you'll have a delectable mocha sundae pie. Try rum-raisin ice cream instead of vanilla in Brownie Ice Cream Cake. The list could go on and on. Choose the flavor combinations you like best and be sure to have them on hand to make tasty substitutions. Your fabulous ice cream cakes will turn any get-together, from an elegant dinner to a casual meeting with friends, into a celebration.

French-Italian Chocolate Ice Cream

The French learned to make ice cream from the Italians but claim to be the first to have made chocolate ice cream! The finest Italian and French ice creams are made from the same mixture, a rich custard called *crème anglaise* or *English cream*. This luscious ice cream is extra-creamy, silky smooth and very chocolaty.

1-1/2 cups milk

1-1/2 cups whipping cream

9 large egg yolks

1 cup sugar

7 oz. fine-quality bittersweet chocolate, chopped

Bring milk and cream to a boil in a heavy medium saucepan. Whisk egg yolks in a large heatproof bowl. Add sugar; whisk until blended. Gradually whisk in hot milk mixture. Return mixture to saucepan. Cook over medium-low heat, stirring and scraping bottom of pan constantly with a wooden spoon, until mixture reaches 165F to 170F (75C) on an instant-read or candy thermometer, about 7 minutes. To check without thermometer, see page 169. Immediately pour into a bowl; stir about 30 seconds to cool. Cool 10 minutes.

Melt chocolate in a medium bowl over nearly simmering water. Stir until smooth. Remove from water; let cool. Whisk custard into chocolate, about 1/2 cup at a time, whisking until blended after each addition. Cool completely, stirring occasionally. Pour chocolate custard into an ice cream machine. Churn-freeze ice cream in machine until set. Serve soft ice cream immediately. Or, remove dasher and replace lid. Cover lid with foil. Place ice cream in freezer 2 to 4 hours or until firm. *To store ice cream up to 1 month, transfer to a chilled bowl; cover tightly. Place in freezer.* Serve ice cream slightly softened.

Makes about 1 quart

American Chocolate Ice Cream

When it first comes out of the machine, this delicious ice cream has a texture similar to that of custard-based ice cream. When stored, though, it freezes harder and colder. It is the easiest type of ice cream to prepare.

1-1/2 pints whipping cream (3 cups)

1 cup milk

3/4 cup sugar

1 vanilla bean, split lengthwise

10 oz. fine-quality bittersweet chocolate, chopped

Combine cream, milk and sugar in a heavy medium saucepan; stir to blend. Add vanilla bean. Cook over low heat, stirring, until sugar dissolves. Increase heat to medium-high. Bring to a simmer. Remove from heat. Cover and let stand 30 minutes. Remove vanilla bean. Melt chocolate in medium bowl over nearly simmering water. Stir until smooth. Remove from water; let cool. Whisk cool cream mixture into chocolate, about 1 cup at a time. Cool completely. Pour mixture into an ice cream machine. Churn-freeze ice cream in machine until set. Serve soft ice cream immediately. Or, remove dasher and replace lid. Cover lid with foil. Place ice cream in freezer 2 to 4 hours or until firm. *To store ice cream up to 1 month, transfer to a chilled bowl; cover tightly. Place in freezer.* Serve ice cream slightly softened.

Makes about 5 cups

Italian Chocolate Chip Ice Cream

A favorite *gelato* throughout Italy, where it is known as *stracciatella,*
this light vanilla ice cream is accented by tiny bits of chocolate
that easily melt in your mouth.

1 cup milk

1 pint whipping cream (2 cups)

1 vanilla bean, split lengthwise

6 large egg yolks

1/2 cup sugar

4 oz. fine-quality semisweet
    chocolate, coarsely grated

Combine milk, 1 cup cream and vanilla bean in a heavy medium saucepan. Bring to a boil. Remove from heat. Cover and let stand 20 minutes. Remove vanilla bean. Bring milk mixture to a boil. Whisk yolks in a large bowl. Add sugar; whisk until blended. Gradually whisk in hot milk. Return mixture to saucepan. Cook over medium-low heat, stirring mixture and scraping bottom of pan constantly with a wooden spoon, until mixture thickens slightly and reaches 165F to 170F (75C) on an instant-read or candy thermometer, about 7 minutes. Immediately pour into a bowl; stir about 30 seconds to cool. Cool completely, stirring occasionally. Stir in remaining cream. Pour mixture into an ice cream machine. Churn-freeze ice cream in machine until nearly set. Add grated chocolate; stir gently. Continue churning until ice cream is firm. Serve soft ice cream immediately. Or, remove dasher and replace lid. Cover lid with foil. Place ice cream in freezer 2 to 4 hours or until firm. *To store ice cream up to 1 month, transfer to a chilled bowl; cover tightly. Place in freezer.* Serve ice cream slightly softened.

Makes about 3-1/2 cups

Chocolate-Mint Ice Cream

Fresh mint is the secret to this light, easy-to-prepare ice cream. The mint leaves steep in the milk,
which absorbs their flavor, and then are strained out. This refreshing ice cream is irresistible!
Serve it garnished with fresh mint leaves or, for a novel touch,
with Half-Dipped Chocolate Mint Leaves, page 177.

1 medium bunch fresh mint
    (about 3-1/2 oz.)

1-1/2 cups milk

2-1/2 cups whipping cream

3/4 cup sugar

7 oz. semisweet chocolate, chopped

Remove mint leaves from stems; you will have about 2-1/2 cups leaves. Coarsely chop leaves. Bring 1 cup milk and 1 cup cream to boil in a heavy medium saucepan. Add mint. Remove from heat; stir. Cover and let stand 1 hour. Add sugar; stir over low heat until completely dissolved. Strain milk into a medium bowl, pressing on mint in strainer. Cool to room temperature. Melt chocolate in a medium bowl over nearly simmering water. Stir until smooth. Remove from water; let cool. Whisk cool milk mixture, about 1/2 cup at a time, into chocolate. Whisk in remaining 1/2 cup milk and 1-1/2 cups cream. Pour mixture into ice-cream machine. Churn-freeze ice cream in machine until set. Serve soft ice cream immediately. Or, remove dasher and replace lid. Cover lid with foil. Place ice cream in freezer 2 to 4 hours or until firm. *To store ice cream up to 1 month, transfer to a chilled bowl; cover tightly. Place in freezer.* Serve ice cream slightly softened.

Makes about 1 quart

Cappuccino-Chocolate Ice Cream

Like some versions of the famous drink, this ice cream combines a favorite flavor trio:
chocolate, coffee and cinnamon. Coffee and cinnamon are introduced by infusing
coffee beans and cinnamon sticks in the milk.
This keeps the tastes delicate and the ice cream satiny.

**1 cup coffee beans, preferably
Mocha Java (about 3 oz.)**

**About 2-3/4 cups plus 2 tablespoons
milk**

2 (3-inch) cinnamon sticks

6 large egg yolks

3/4 cup sugar

5 oz. semisweet chocolate, chopped

**1/2 pint whipping cream (1 cup),
well-chilled**

Place coffee beans in a bag; coarsely crush with a rolling pin. Heat 2-1/2 cups milk with coffee beans and cinnamon sticks in a heavy medium saucepan until bubbles form around edge of pan. Cover and let stand 30 minutes. Set aside cinnamon sticks. Strain milk through a double layer of cheesecloth. Squeeze hard. Measure strained milk; add enough milk to obtain 2 cups.

Bring flavored milk to a boil in a heavy medium saucepan. Whisk yolks in a large bowl. Add sugar; whisk until blended. Gradually whisk in hot milk. Return mixture to saucepan. Cook over medium-low heat, stirring and scraping bottom of pan constantly with a wooden spoon, until mixture thickens slightly and reaches 165F to 170F (75C) on an instant-read or candy thermometer, about 7 minutes. To check without thermometer, see page 169. Immediately pour into a bowl; stir about 30 seconds. Cool 10 minutes.

Melt chocolate in a medium bowl over nearly simmering water. Stir until smooth. Remove from water; let cool. Stir custard mixture, about 1/2 cup at a time, into chocolate. If mixture is not smooth, strain into a bowl. Return cinnamon sticks to mixture. Cool completely, stirring occasionally. Remove cinnamon sticks. Stir in cream.

Pour custard into ice cream machine. Churn-freeze ice cream in machine until set. Serve soft ice cream immediately. Or, remove dasher and replace lid. Cover lid with foil. Place ice cream in freezer 2 to 4 hours or until firm. *To store ice cream up to 1 month, transfer to a chilled bowl; cover tightly. Place in freezer.* Serve ice cream slightly softened.

Makes about 3-1/2 cups

Caramel-Chocolate Swirl Ice Cream

Creamy caramel flavors both the ice cream and the chocolate fudge sauce that is rippled through it. The caramel makes the ice cream stay soft-textured even when frozen.

2-1/2 cups whipping cream

1 cup water

2-1/4 cups sugar

1 cup milk

6 large egg yolks

3 oz. semisweet chocolate, chopped

Heat 1-1/2 cups cream in a medium saucepan until bubbles form around edge of pan. Remove from heat. Transfer to a 2-cup measure.

Combine water and 2 cups sugar in a heavy large saucepan that does not have a black interior. Heat mixture over low heat until sugar dissolves, gently stirring occasionally. Boil over high heat, without stirring, but occasionally brushing down any sugar crystals from side of pan with a brush dipped in water, until mixture begins to brown. Reduce heat to medium-low. Cook, swirling pan gently, until mixture is a rich brown and a trace of smoke begins to rise from pan. Do not let caramel get too dark or it will be bitter; if too light, it will be too sweet. Immediately remove from heat.

Standing at a distance, pour in hot cream, about 2 tablespoons at a time, without stirring; caramel will bubble furiously. When caramel stops bubbling, return mixture to low heat. Heat, stirring, 1 minute or until blended. Cool to lukewarm. Set aside 3/4 cup caramel for making fudge sauce.

Stir milk and 1/2 cup cream into remaining caramel. Bring to a simmer, whisking. Whisk yolks in a large bowl. Add remaining 1/4 cup sugar; whisk until blended. Gradually whisk in hot caramel mixture. Return mixture to saucepan. Cook over medium-low heat, stirring mixture and scraping bottom of pan constantly with a wooden spoon, until mixture reaches 165F to 170F (75C) on an instant-read or candy thermometer, about 7 minutes. To check without thermometer, see page 169. Immediately pour into a bowl; stir about 30 seconds. Cool to room temperature, stirring occasionally. Stir in remaining 1/2 cup cream. Chill a medium bowl or container in freezer.

Reheat reserved caramel mixture in a bowl above hot water until it is just warm and fluid. Melt chocolate in a medium bowl over nearly simmering water. Stir until smooth. Stir chocolate into caramel. Cool to room temperature.

Pour custard mixture into ice cream machine. Churn-freeze ice cream in machine until set. Spoon about 1/3 of ice cream into chilled bowl or container. Quickly spoon 1/3 of chocolate sauce over it in a layer. Repeat with remaining ice cream and sauce, adding each in 2 batches. Stir once to swirl; cover. Freeze ice cream at least 3 hours before serving. *Ice cream can be kept in tightly covered container 1 month in freezer.*

Makes about 1 quart

Chocolate-Raspberry Coupe

This *coupe,* or French sundae, dresses up chocolate and vanilla ice creams with raspberries and raspberry sauce. For an extra-special treat, spike the sauce with aromatic, clear raspberry brandy.

Raspberry Sauce:

3 cups fresh raspberries or 1 (12-oz.) package frozen, thawed

About 1/2 powdered sugar, sifted

3/4 pint French-Italian Chocolate Ice Cream, page 98, or other chocolate ice cream (1-1/2 cups)

3/4 pint vanilla ice cream (1-1/2 cups)

1 cup fresh raspberries (for garnish)

Sauce: Process raspberries and 1/2 cup powdered sugar in a food processor or blender until very smooth. Strain puree into a bowl, pressing on pulp in strainer. Use a rubber spatula to scrape mixture from underside of strainer. Taste sauce and whisk in more powdered sugar, if needed. Whisk sauce thoroughly so sugar is completely blended in. Cover and refrigerate 30 minutes. *Sauce can be kept, covered, 2 days in refrigerator.* Stir sauce before serving.

To serve, scoop chocolate and vanilla ice creams into 6 dessert dishes; pour sauce around ice cream. Garnish with raspberries. Serve immediately.

Makes 6 servings

Sabra Sundae

I was introduced to Sabra, the chocolate-orange liqueur, when I lived in Israel and was glad to find it available when I returned to the United States. For this sundae, the hot Chocolate-Sabra Sauce is poured over vanilla ice cream, which is garnished with fresh orange segments.

2 oranges, sectioned

6 tablespoons Sabra liqueur

4 oz. semisweet chocolate, chopped

1/3 cup whipping cream

1 pint vanilla ice cream

Combine oranges and 2 tablespoons liqueur in a bowl; toss lightly. Cover and refrigerate 10 to 30 minutes.

Sauce: Melt chocolate in cream in a medium bowl over nearly simmering water. Remove from pan of water; stir until sauce is smooth. *Sauce can be kept, covered, 1 week in refrigerator.* Reheat sauce over a pan of hot water before serving; stir in remaining liqueur.

To serve, scoop ice cream into 4 dessert dishes; arrange orange sections around it. Pour warm sauce over ice cream. Serve immediately.

Makes 4 servings

Meringata

This is an elegant sundae that my husband and I enjoyed at a cafe on the Italian Riviera
during our first trip to Italy. It combines the crunchiness of small star-shaped meringues,
the smoothness of ice cream and the lightness of whipped cream.
The whole glorious creation is topped off with a rich, dark, shiny, coffee-flavored chocolate sauce.

Meringue Kisses:

2 large egg whites

1/4 teaspoon cream of tartar

1/2 cup sugar

Coffee-Chocolate Sauce:

1/3 cup boiling water

1-1/2 teaspoons instant coffee
granules

1 tablespoon unsalted butter

4 oz. bittersweet chocolate, chopped

1-1/2 pints vanilla or
coffee ice cream

Whipped Cream, page 2

Meringue Kisses: Position rack in center of oven and preheat to 200F (95C). Lightly butter corners of 1 large baking sheet; line with foil or parchment paper. Butter and lightly flour foil or paper. Have ready a rubber spatula for folding and a pastry bag fitted with a medium star tip that has large points. Using a paper clip, close end of bag just above tip, so mixture will not run out while bag is being filled.

In a small dry bowl, whip egg whites with cream of tartar at medium speed until stiff. At high speed, gradually beat in sugar and whip until whites are shiny. Immediately spoon meringue into pastry bag. Remove paper clip. Pipe meringue in small kisses with points, about 3/4 inch in diameter and 1 inch high, spacing them about 1 inch apart.

Bake meringues about 1-1/2 hours or until firm and dry. To test, remove a meringue. Cool 2 minutes, then break meringue apart; it should be dry and crumbly and not sticky. Using a large metal spatula, immediately remove meringues from pan; cool on a rack. *Meringues can be kept in airtight containers at room temperature 1 week in dry weather. If they become sticky, they can be recrisped in a 200F (95C) oven about 20 minutes.*

Coffee-Chocolate Sauce: Pour boiling water over coffee; cool to room temperature. Combine coffee, butter and chocolate in a medium bowl over hot water. Leave until melted. Remove from water; stir until smooth. Cool to room temperature.

In each of 6 dessert dishes put 4 meringues, top with a scoop of ice cream and add 2 spoonfuls Whipped Cream on the sides. Spoon sauce over, allowing ice cream and whipped cream to show partially. Top with a few meringues on sides. Dip peak of 6 meringues in sauce and set 1 on top of each dessert. Serve any remaining sauce and Whipped Cream separately.

Makes 6 servings; about 60 meringues

Rum-Raisin-Chocolate Bombe

For this hemispherical dessert, a bowl is lined with ice cream and filled with
a special chocolate bombe mousse.
Vanilla, chocolate chip or coffee ice cream can be substituted for the rum-raisin.

**1-1/4 pints rum-raisin ice cream
(2-1/2 cups)**

Chocolate Bombe Mousse:

1/2 cup sugar

1/3 cup water

4 large egg yolks

4 oz. semisweet chocolate, chopped

**1/2 pint whipping cream (1 cup),
well-chilled**

**1/2 recipe Chocolate Chantilly
Cream, page 164, if desired**

Set freezer at coldest setting. Chill a 1-1/2-quart bowl in freezer 30 minutes. Slightly soften ice cream in refrigerator until spreadable. Quickly spread ice cream in an even layer on base and side of chilled bowl, using the back of a spoon and dipping spoon occasionally in lukewarm water. Cover and return to freezer.

Mousse: Heat sugar and water in a small saucepan over low heat, stirring, until sugar dissolves. Bring to a boil; remove from heat.

With a hand electric mixer or whisk, beat yolks in a large bowl. Gradually pour hot sugar mixture over yolks, beating constantly. Set bowl of yolk mixture in a pan of hot water over low heat. Beat at low speed about 5 minutes or until mixture increases in volume and lightens in color. Remove from heat. Beat at high speed until mixture is completely cool.

Melt chocolate in a small bowl over nearly simmering water. Stir until smooth. Remove from water; let cool. Check ice cream; if it slipped down from side of bowl, push it back up so it reaches rim of bowl. Return to freezer.

Stir about 1/2 cup yolk mixture into chocolate until smooth. Fold mixture into remaining yolk mixture. In a large chilled bowl, whip cream until nearly stiff. Fold into chocolate mixture in 2 batches. Pour into ice cream-lined bowl. Cover and freeze at least 6 hours. *Bombe can be kept, covered, 2 weeks.*

Unmold bombe; see below. Smooth top if necessary with a wet metal spatula. Immediately return bombe to freezer. Freeze at least 10 minutes or until ready to serve. Using a pastry bag and medium star tip, pipe a ruffle of Chocolate Chantilly Cream at base of dessert. Serve bombe by cutting in thin wedges.

Makes 8 to 10 servings

Tip

To unmold frozen desserts—mousses, bombes and parfaits: Run a metal spatula or thin-bladed knife around dessert's edge. If dessert is in a ring mold, run knife around center of ring also. Dip mold in room-temperature water to come halfway up its side about 5 seconds. Dry base of mold. Set a platter, or a plate, on top of mold. Holding firmly together, quickly flip so dessert is right-side up. Shake bowl gently downward; dessert should slip onto platter. If dessert remains in bowl, put a hot damp towel on top of bowl for a few seconds and tap mold with platter on a folded towel set on work surface until dessert comes out. Carefully lift up mold.

Frozen Chocolate Soufflé with Candied Ginger

Crystallized ginger adds zest and sweetness to this intensely chocolaty dessert.
The soufflé gains extra smoothness from shiny Italian meringue,
made of egg whites whipped with syrup.

Frozen Chocolate Soufflé:

4 large eggs, separated

1 cup sugar

6 oz. bittersweet chocolate, chopped

2 oz. unsweetened chocolate, chopped

1/2 cup plus 2 tablespoons water

1-1/2 cups whipping cream, well-chilled

1/2 cup finely chopped crystallized ginger (about 2-1/2 oz.)

Garnish:

1/2 cup whipping cream, well-chilled

2 tablespoons tiny squares of crystallized ginger

Chocolate Scrolls, page 176, if desired

Frozen Chocolate Soufflé: Cut a 25-inch-long sheet of waxed paper; fold in half. Wrap paper around a 1-quart soufflé dish so it extends about 3 inches above rim to make a collar. Fasten tightly with tape.

Whisk egg yolks with 1/4 cup sugar and 2 tablespoons water in a small metal bowl. Set bowl in a pan of nearly simmering water. Heat, whisking constantly, until mixture reaches 160F (70C) on an instant-read or candy thermometer. Remove from heat and immediately whip with electric mixer until cool. Transfer to a large bowl.

Melt chocolates in a medium bowl over nearly simmering water. Stir until smooth. Remove from water; let cool. Meanwhile, put egg whites in a large bowl.

Combine 1/2 cup water and remaining 3/4 cup sugar in a small heavy saucepan. Cook over low heat, gently stirring often, until sugar dissolves. Bring to a boil over medium-high heat. Boil, without stirring, 3 minutes. Meanwhile, whip egg whites until stiff but not dry. Continue boiling syrup until a candy thermometer registers 238F (115C) (soft-ball stage), about 3 minutes. See page 169 for soft-ball test. Immediately remove from heat.

Gradually beat hot syrup into center of whites, with mixer at high speed. Beat until cool and shiny. Fold 1/4 of meringue into yolk mixture. Return mixture to remaining meringue; fold until blended. Gently fold in chocolate in 3 batches.

In a large chilled bowl, whip cream to soft peaks. Fold into chocolate mixture in 3 batches. Fold in ginger. Pour into prepared mold. Freeze about 5 hours or until firm. Cover when firm. *Soufflé can be kept, covered, 1 month in freezer.*

Garnish: A short time before serving, carefully peel off and discard paper collar. Return dessert to freezer. In a small chilled bowl, whip 1/2 cup cream until very stiff. Using a pastry bag and medium star tip, pipe cream in a ruffle or rosettes near edge of soufflé. Top cream with crystallized ginger. Garnish dessert with Chocolate Scrolls, if using.

Makes 10 to 12 servings

Frozen Chocolate Mousse Ring with Fresh Berries

A medley of blueberries, blackberries and strawberries is encircled by a kirsch-scented chocolate mousse to make a colorful, quick and easy summer dessert.

Photo opposite.

Chocolate Mousse:

8 oz. fine-quality bittersweet chocolate, chopped

4 large egg yolks

5 tablespoons sugar

2 tablespoons water

2 tablespoons kirsch

1-2/3 cups whipping cream, well-chilled

Berries & Cream:

1/2 pint whipping cream (1 cup), well-chilled

2 tablespoons sugar

1/2 cup blackberries

1/2 cup blueberries

1 cup small strawberries, quartered lengthwise

Mousse: Lightly oil a 5-cup ring mold. Melt chocolate in a medium bowl over nearly simmering water. Stir until smooth. Remove from water.

Whisk yolks with 4 tablespoons sugar and water in a small metal bowl. Set bowl in a pan of nearly simmering water. Heat, whisking constantly, until mixture reaches 160F (70C) on an instant-read or candy thermometer. Remove from heat and immediately whip with electric mixer until cool. Add to chocolate all at once; stir until smooth. Add kirsch.

In a large chilled bowl, whip cream with remaining 1 tablespoon sugar until nearly stiff. Fold into chocolate mixture. Pour mousse into oiled mold. Smooth top. Cover and freeze at least 6 hours or until set. *Mousse can be kept, covered, 2 weeks in freezer.*

Unmold mousse, page 104. Smooth top of mousse with a metal spatula. Return to freezer 5 minutes or until ready to serve.

Berries & Cream: In a large chilled bowl, whip cream with sugar until very stiff. Set aside several of each type of berry for garnish. Gently mix together remaining berries. Spoon fruit mixture into center of chocolate ring. Using a pastry bag with a medium star tip, pipe whipped cream in a ruffle around outer base of dessert. Garnish ruffle with reserved berries. Serve any remaining cream separately.

Makes 8 servings

Chocolate-Strawberry Bombe

A shell of chocolate ice cream encases a surprise of refreshing, pink strawberry mousse.
Chocolate-dipped strawberries add a festive finishing touch.

Photo on page iii.

---

2 pints fine-quality chocolate ice
   cream

Strawberry-Bombe Mousse:

3 cups strawberries (about 12 oz.)

3 large egg whites

1 cup sugar

1/2 cup water

3/4 cup whipping cream, well-
   chilled

Garnish:

2/3 cup whipping cream,
   well chilled, if desired

10 Chocolate-Dipped Strawberries,
   page 150, if desired

Set freezer at coldest setting. Chill a 2-1/2-quart bowl in freezer 30 minutes. Slightly soften ice cream in refrigerator until spreadable. Quickly spread ice cream in an even layer on base and up side of chilled bowl, using the back of a spoon and dipping spoon occasionally in lukewarm water. Cover and return to freezer.

Mousse: Process strawberries in a food processor or blender until very smooth. There will be about 1-1/3 cups puree. Set aside 1/2 cup puree.

Bring remaining puree to a boil in a heavy small saucepan. Simmer over medium heat, stirring often, about 6 minutes or until reduced to 1/3 cup. Transfer to a bowl; cool completely. Put egg whites in a large dry bowl.

Cook sugar and water in a heavy small saucepan over low heat, gently stirring often, until sugar dissolves. Bring to a boil over medium-high heat. Boil, without stirring, 3 minutes. Meanwhile, whip egg whites until stiff but not dry. Continue boiling syrup until a candy thermometer registers 238F (115C) (soft-ball stage), about 3 minutes. See page 161 for soft-ball test. Gradually beat hot syrup into center of whites with mixer at high speed. Beat until meringue is cool and shiny.

Check ice cream; if it slipped down from side of bowl, push it back up so it reaches rim of bowl. Return to freezer.

Stir reserved fresh and reduced strawberry purees into meringue. In a chilled bowl, whip 3/4 cup cream to soft peaks. Fold into strawberry mixture. Pour into ice cream-lined bowl. Cover and freeze at least 6 hours. *Bombe can be kept, covered, 2 weeks in freezer.*

Garnish: Unmold bombe, page 104. Smooth top with a wet metal spatula. Immediately return bombe to freezer. Freeze at least 10 minutes or until ready to serve. In a chilled bowl, whip 2/3 cup cream, if using, until very stiff. Using a pastry bag with a large star tip, pipe a ruffle of whipped cream around base of bombe. Serve bombe in thin wedges, with strawberries, if using.

Makes 10 servings

Individual Chocolate Parfaits with Caramel-Fudge Sauce

These are parfaits in the French style, meaning creamy molded desserts. Dark caramel gives the rich shiny sauce an intriguing, not overly sweet flavor.

---

6 oz. semisweet chocolate, chopped

4 large egg yolks

2/3 cup sugar

1/2 cup milk

1/2 pint whipping cream (1 cup), well-chilled

Hot Caramel-Fudge Sauce, page 166

Melt chocolate in a medium bowl over nearly simmering water. Stir until smooth. Remove from water.

Whisk yolks lightly in a medium bowl. Add sugar; whisk until blended. Bring milk to a boil in a small, heavy saucepan. Gradually whisk hot milk into yolk mixture. Return mixture to saucepan. Cook over very low heat, stirring mixture and scraping bottom of pan constantly with a wooden spoon, about 4 minutes or until it is thick enough to coat a spoon and reaches 160F (70C). To check without a thermometer, see page 169. Do not overcook custard or it will curdle. Immediately pour into a bowl; stir about 30 seconds to cool. Cool 5 minutes, stirring occasionally. Whisk custard, about 2/3 cup at a time, into melted chocolate until smooth. Cool to room temperature, stirring occasionally. Lightly oil 6 (2/3-cup) ramekins.

In a large chilled bowl, whip cream until stiff. Fold into chocolate mixture in 3 batches. Ladle mixture into ramekins, filling them nearly to top. Cover and freeze about 6 hours or until firm. *Parfaits can be kept, covered, 2 weeks.*

Unmold parfaits, page 104. Smooth top with a spatula, if necessary. Return to freezer for at least 5 minutes. About 10 minutes before serving, transfer parfaits to refrigerator.

Reheat sauce in a medium bowl above nearly simmering water until it is just warm and fluid. If it is too thick, stir in 1 tablespoon lukewarm water. Keep sauce warm above water. To serve, spoon 2 or 3 tablespoons sauce around base of each parfait and a little sauce on top.

Makes 6 servings

Chocolate-Blackberry Loaf

This dessert is a frozen chocolate-blackberry mousse molded in a loaf pan.
For a beautiful reddish-chocolate hue, choose blackberries that have a touch of red or
substitute olallieberries. The loaf makes an especially festive dessert when the slices are served with
two sauces of contrasting colors—blackberry sauce and crème de cacao sauce—or
serve it with a double quantity of either sauce.

Chocolate-Blackberry Mousse:

3 cups fresh or frozen unsweetened blackberries (about 12 oz.), thawed if frozen

12 oz. fine-quality semisweet chocolate, chopped

3 large egg yolks

7 tablespoons sugar

2 tablespoons water

1-1/3 cups whipping cream, well-chilled

Blackberry Sauce, page 168

Crème de Cacao Sauce, page 170

Mousse: Lightly oil an 8" x 4" loaf pan. Process blackberries in a food processor or blender until smooth. Push puree through a strainer, pressing on pulp. Use a rubber spatula to scrape mixture from underside of strainer.

Melt chocolate in a medium bowl over hot water. Stir until smooth. Remove from water; let cool. Add blackberry puree; whisk until blended.

Whisk egg yolks with 4 tablespoons sugar and 2 tablespoons water in a small metal bowl until blended. Set bowl in a pan of nearly simmering water. Heat, whisking constantly, until mixture reaches 160F (70C) on an instant-read or candy thermometer. Remove egg mixture from water and immediately whisk 2 minutes to cool. Stir into chocolate mixture.

In a large chilled bowl, whip cream and remaining 3 tablespoons sugar until nearly stiff. Fold into chocolate mixture. Spoon into oiled loaf pan. Cover and freeze overnight. *Mousse can be kept, covered, 2 weeks in freezer.*

To serve: Unmold mousse, page 104. Return to freezer until ready to serve. Cut loaf into about 5/8-inch-thick slices. Set slices on rimmed dessert plates. Spoon 2 tablespoons Blackberry Sauce on 1 side of each plate. Tilt plate so sauce runs around dessert to cover half of plate; spoon 2 tablespoons Crème de Cacao Sauce over other half of plate so it barely meets Blackberry Sauce. Do not move plate much after adding second sauce because it is thinner than Blackberry Sauce and could run into it. Serve any remaining sauce separately.

Makes 10 servings

Chocolate Baked Alaska

The pleasing contrast of warm meringue and cold ice cream inspired several desserts with names of snowy countries. Ours is called *Baked Alaska*, the French often call theirs *Norwegian Omelet*, and there is an Austrian version called *Icelandic Omelet*.
Here a cake is layered with two ice creams and kept in the freezer so there is little last-minute work. The meringue is spread on the dessert and baked just before serving.

Light Cocoa Cake:

1/4 cup plus 2 tablespoons all-purpose flour

3 tablespoons unsweetened cocoa powder

1/4 teaspoon baking powder

4 large egg yolks

1/2 cup plus 1 tablespoon sugar

3 large egg whites

1/4 teaspoon cream of tartar

2 tablespoons unsalted butter, melted and cooled

Filling:

1 pint vanilla ice cream

3 tablespoons hazelnut, praline or coffee liqueur

1 pint chocolate ice cream

Meringue Topping:

4 large egg whites

1 cup sugar

Cake: Position rack in center of oven and preheat to 350F (175C). Lightly butter a 9" x 5" loaf pan. Line base of pan with parchment paper or foil. Butter paper or foil and flour lined pan. Sift flour, cocoa and baking powder into a small bowl.

Beat egg yolks lightly in a large bowl. Add 7 tablespoons sugar and beat at high speed about 5 minutes or until mixture is pale and very thick.

In a large dry bowl, whip egg whites with cream of tartar to soft peaks. Beat in remaining 2 tablespoons sugar. Whip at high speed until whites are stiff and shiny but not dry.

Sprinkle about 1/2 of cocoa mixture over yolk mixture; fold gently until nearly incorporated. Gently fold in 1/2 of whites, then remaining cocoa mixture, then remaining whites. When batter is nearly blended, gradually pour in cool melted butter while folding. Fold lightly but quickly, just until blended.

Transfer batter to prepared pan. Bake about 30 minutes or until top springs back when pressed lightly and a cake tester inserted into center of cake comes out clean. Unmold onto a rack. Carefully remove paper; cool. *Cake can be kept, covered, 1 day at room temperature.*

Filling: Soften vanilla ice cream in refrigerator until spreadable. Cut cake in 2 layers with a serrated knife. Put 1 cake layer on a platter. Brush with 1-1/2 tablespoons liqueur. Spoon vanilla ice cream onto cake. Spread quickly to cover layer evenly. Freeze about 30 minutes or until firm. Cover and set second cake layer aside.

Soften chocolate ice cream in refrigerator until spreadable. Spread it over layer of vanilla ice cream. Freeze 1 hour or until nearly firm. Sprinkle soft side of second cake layer with remaining liqueur. Set layer, crust-side up, on ice cream; press to adhere. If necessary, smooth ice cream to a neat layer. Freeze until firm. Wrap and freeze at least 8 hours. *Dessert can be kept 2 weeks in freezer.*

Topping: Have ready a pastry bag and medium star tip. Preheat oven to 500F (260C). In a large dry bowl, whip egg whites until stiff. At high speed, beat in sugar, about 2 tablespoons at a time. Whip until whites are shiny.

Transfer ice cream cake to a large, heavy, shallow baking dish, such as an oven-proof platter or oval gratin dish. With a large metal spatula, spread meringue to cover ice cream and cake completely. Use pastry bag to pipe meringue in a few rosettes on top. If more meringue remains, pipe a few rosettes around base.

Bake 4 minutes or until meringue is lightly browned. Do not let rosettes burn. Serve immediately. Cut with a heavy knife. Any leftovers can be quickly returned to freezer and served frozen.

Makes 8 servings

Chocolate-Pecan Sundae Pie

This is a very easy-to-make sundae of vanilla ice cream and thick chocolate sauce in a crunchy nutty crust. The sauce sets upon contact with the ice cream. If you like, substitute chocolate chip, chocolate, coffee or rum-raisin ice cream for the vanilla.

Cocoa-Pecan Crust:

1-1/4 cups pecan halves (about 4 oz.)

2 tablespoons powdered sugar

1 tablespoon unsweetened cocoa powder

2 tablespoons unsalted butter, very soft

7 to 9 pecan halves (for garnish)

1-1/2 pints vanilla ice cream (for filling)

Chocolate Sauce:

3 oz. semisweet chocolate, finely chopped

1/4 cup plus 2 tablespoons whipping cream

Crust: Preheat oven to 400F (205C). Lightly butter an 8-inch pie pan. In a food processor, chop pecans, sugar and cocoa using quick on/off pulses until nuts are finely chopped but small pieces remain; do not grind to a powder. Transfer to a bowl. Add butter; crumble mixture with your fingers until well blended. Press mixture in a thin even layer on base and side of buttered pan, using the back of a spoon. Bake about 6 minutes or until light brown. Cool completely. Freeze 10 minutes.

Reduce oven temperature to 350F (175C). Toast pecan halves for garnish in a small shallow baking pan in oven 7 minutes. Remove and cool. Slightly soften ice cream in refrigerator until spreadable. Spoon into crust in pie pan, mounding ice cream slightly towards center and quickly spreading it smooth. Freeze about 2 hours or until firm. Cover if not serving immediately.

Sauce: Melt chocolate in cream in a small heatproof bowl over nearly simmering water. Remove from water; stir until smooth. Cool sauce to room temperature or until thick enough to pipe. Using a pastry bag and small star tip, pipe a little sauce in center of pie, then in lines radiating outward like spokes of a wheel. Pipe a ribbon of sauce about 1/2 inch from edge. If any sauce remains, pipe a dot of sauce between each "spoke."

Set toasted pecans on pie at equal intervals near edge and 1 in center; press so they adhere. Serve immediately; to serve later, freeze about 15 minutes or until sauce is very firm, then cover. *Pie can be frozen up to 1 month.*

Makes 6 to 8 servings

Shown on next page is Two-Toned Vacherin, pages 114-115.

Two-Toned Vacherin

A vacherin is a spectacular meringue case with a mysterious origin—the French attribute
its creation to the Swiss, while the Austrians give credit to the Spanish. It can be filled with ice cream,
whipped cream or mousse. This one is made using a method of putting together meringue fingers
that I learned from Albert Jorant, the great pastry chef of La Varenne Cooking School in Paris.
Fill it with one or several of your favorite ice creams in layers.

Photo on page 113.

Baked White & Cocoa Meringues:

2 tablespoons unsweetened
  cocoa powder

2 tablespoons powdered sugar

9 large egg whites

1/2 teaspoon cream of tartar

2-1/4 cups granulated sugar

Cooked Meringue:

4 large egg whites

1-1/4 cups granulated sugar

Ice Cream Filling:

5 pints chocolate ice cream
  (10 cups)

2-1/2 pints vanilla ice cream
  (5 cups)

Garnish:

1/2 cup whipping cream, if desired,
  well-chilled

Candied violets, if desired

Baked Meringues: Preheat oven to 180F (80C). Lightly butter corners of 3 baking sheets; line with foil. Butter and lightly flour foil. Using a 9-inch cake pan or lid as a guide, mark a circle in flour on 1 baking sheet. On 2 baking sheets, mark crosswise lines, 4 inches apart, as a guide for lengths of meringue fingers. Have ready a rubber spatula for folding and a pastry bag with a 1/2-inch plain tip. Using a paper clip, close end of bag just above tip so mixture will not run out while you fill bag. Sift cocoa and powdered sugar into a medium bowl.

In a large bowl, beat egg whites with cream of tartar at medium speed until stiff. At high speed, beat in 1-1/4 cups granulated sugar, pouring it into whites in a fine stream. Beat 30 seconds longer until meringue is very shiny. Sprinkle about 1/4 of remaining granulated sugar over whites; fold in as lightly and quickly as possible. Fold in remaining granulated sugar in 3 batches, folding lightly but thoroughly. Transfer 2 cups meringue to bowl of cocoa mixture; fold gently until blended.

Immediately spoon white meringue into pastry bag. Push it down towards tip so there are no air bubbles. Remove paper clip. Beginning in center of marked circle on baking sheet, pipe meringue in a tight spiral until marked circle is completely covered.

Pipe remaining meringue into "fingers," 4 inches long and about 1-1/4 inches wide, on remaining baking sheets. To end each finger, stop pressing and turn tip sharply upward. Do not worry about "tails" at end of fingers; they will be cut off later.

Squeeze out remaining meringue from pastry bag. Spoon cocoa meringue into bag and squeeze out a few tablespoons so any white meringue remaining in bag will come out with it. Pipe cocoa mixture in fingers as above.

Place meringue base and full sheet of meringue fingers in center of oven, if possible; put remaining baking sheet on rack underneath. Bake until firm and dry, about 2-1/2 hours for fingers and about 3 hours for base. Do not open oven for first 2 hours. To test meringue fingers, remove one and cool 3 minutes, then break it apart; it should be dry and crumbly and not sticky.

Carefully remove meringue fingers from foil. Release base from foil with a large metal spatula. Gently peel off any foil. If meringue base is still sticky on bottom, bake 30 minutes longer. Cool meringues on a rack. Put in airtight containers as soon as they are cool. *Baked meringue fingers and base can be stored 1 week in an airtight container in dry weather. If they become sticky from humidity, they can be baked in a 200F (95C) oven about 30 minutes to recrisp.* Rinse and dry pastry bag.

Cooked Meringue: Combine egg whites and sugar in a large heatproof bowl. Set bowl in a pan of hot water over low heat. Beat with a hand mixer at low speed 5 minutes, then at medium speed about 3 minutes or until mixture is warm to touch. Beat at high speed about 2 minutes or until very thick. Remove mixture from water. Beat at high speed until completely cooled. Meringue will be very shiny and sticky. *Cooked meringue can be kept, tightly covered, 1 day in refrigerator.*

Assembly: With sawing motion of a small sharp knife, cut small piece from "tail" end of each meringue finger so finger is 3-1/2 inches long and end is straight. If edge of meringue base is not of an even height, trim it carefully with sawing motion of knife. Line a baking sheet with foil or parchment paper. Set meringue base on lined baking sheet.

Using a pastry bag and small star tip, pipe a border of Cooked Meringue on meringue base as close to edge as possible. Stand 2 meringue fingers, 1 white and 1 cocoa, upright at edge of base, touching each other; press flat end of meringue fingers into Cooked Meringue. Rounded sides of fingers should face outward. Stand meringue fingers upright, alternating white and cocoa fingers. After every group of 4 fingers, pipe a line of Cooked Meringue going upwards between each pair of fingers, on both their outer and inner edges, pressing hard to fill in cracks between fingers. Trim last meringue finger lengthwise, if necessary, to make it fit. Pipe a border of Cooked Meringue at inner bases of fingers, on inside of case, pressing hard; border will help support fingers.

Pipe a decorative line of Cooked Meringue to cover line attaching each pair of fingers, piping upward from base. Pipe a continuous decorative line of meringue along bases of fingers, all around bottom edge of case. Pipe a decorative line or continuous row of points of Cooked Meringue across top edges of fingers. If desired, crown top with additional meringue rosettes above divisions between fingers. Return to 180F (80C) oven. Bake 1-1/2 hours to dry Cooked Meringue. Cool case completely before filling. *Baked unfilled case can be kept, uncovered, in a dry place 2 days.*

Filling: Slightly soften chocolate and vanilla ice creams in refrigerator. Spoon about 2-1/2 pints chocolate ice cream into case. Press ice cream with your fingers up to edges of case so filling is compact; press gently to avoid cracking case. Spread with the back of a ladle to a smooth layer. Fill with vanilla ice cream in the same way. Freeze dessert 10 minutes. Spread remaining chocolate ice cream in case; smooth top. Freeze about 1 hour or until firm. *Vacherin can be kept, covered, 2 weeks in freezer. Let soften slightly in refrigerator before serving.*

Garnish: Just before serving, whip cream in a chilled medium bowl to stiff peaks. Set vacherin on platter. Using a pastry bag and medium star tip, pipe rosettes of cream in a circle on top of filling. Top rosettes with candied violets.

Makes about 15 servings

Brownie Ice Cream Cake

Ice cream sandwiched between fudgy brownies is a delightful dessert.
Very thin brownies are used, so the ice cream cake can be cut easily.
For a more intense chocolate experience, substitute chocolate ice cream
for the vanilla or coffee ice creams.

Thin Fudge Brownies:

2 oz. semisweet chocolate, chopped

3 tablespoons unsalted butter

1/4 cup plus 2 teaspoons all-purpose flour

1/4 teaspoon baking powder

Pinch of salt

1 large egg

1/2 cup sugar

1/2 teaspoon pure vanilla extract

1/3 cup walnuts, chopped

Ice Cream Filling:

1 pint coffee ice cream (2 cups)

1-1/4 pints vanilla ice cream (2-1/2 cups)

Garnish:

1/2 pint whipping cream (1 cup), well-chilled

2 teaspoons sugar

1 teaspoon pure vanilla extract

9 chocolate coffee beans

Thin Brownies: Position rack in center of oven and preheat to 350F (175C). Line base and sides of a 7-1/2- to 8-inch-square baking pan with a single piece of waxed paper or foil; butter paper or foil. Melt chocolate and butter in a medium bowl over nearly simmering water. Stir until smooth. Remove from pan of water; cool slightly. Sift flour, baking powder and salt into a small bowl.

Beat egg lightly. Add sugar; beat just until blended. Beat in vanilla. Add chocolate mixture in 3 batches, beating until blended after each addition. Stir in flour mixture, then walnuts.

Transfer batter to prepared pan; spread carefully to corners of pan in an even layer. Bake about 19 minutes or until a cake tester inserted in center of mixture comes out dry. Cool in pan on a rack to room temperature. Turn out onto a board; remove paper or foil. Cut carefully in 16 squares, using a sharp knife.

Ice Cream Filling: Clean square pan; line its base with waxed paper. Chill pan about 15 minutes in freezer. Slightly soften coffee ice cream in refrigerator until spreadable. Spoon ice cream into pan; spread smooth. Freeze 15 minutes or until firm. Slightly soften 1 cup vanilla ice cream in refrigerator until spreadable. Add to pan in spoonfuls; carefully spread until smooth. Freeze 15 minutes or until firm.

Use a sharp thin-bladed knife to split brownies carefully in 2 layers; press on bottom layer, so smoother top comes out in 1 piece. Do not worry if some of brownies crumble. Keep more attractive brownie halves separate. Arrange a layer of less attractive brownie halves on ice cream in pan, first placing brownies next to sides of pan, then filling in center. Press brownies into ice cream. Freeze 15 minutes or until firm.

Slightly soften remaining 1-1/2 cups ice cream in refrigerator until spreadable. Add to pan; carefully spread until smooth. Freeze 15 minutes. Set attractive brownie halves on top, smooth-side up, first arranging them against edge of pan, then in center. Press into ice cream so top surface is as even as possible. Cover and freeze about 8 hours or overnight. *Cake can be kept 1 week in freezer.*

Garnish: Just before serving, whip cream with sugar and vanilla in a large chilled bowl until stiff. Run a thin-bladed knife around edge of cake; turn out onto a platter. Carefully peel off paper. Using a pastry bag and medium star tip, pipe ruffles of whipped cream to cover sides of cake. Pipe 9 rosettes on top of cake, spacing them equally. Top each rosette with a chocolate coffee bean. To serve, cut in squares with a heavy knife.

Makes 9 servings

In the realm of baked small-size sweets, those flavored with chocolate are undoubtedly the best-loved. Chocolate cookies and brownies are the supreme snack when accompanied by a glass of milk or a cup of coffee or tea. Chocolate macaroons and other elegant chocolate cookies suit a variety of occasions and are good partners for fresh or poached fruit and creamy desserts.

Crisp cookies make delightful presents. Favorites are chocolate chip cookies, airy nut meringues, or the moist coconut peaks that decorate the windows of fine pâtisseries. An assortment of a few types of cookies, arranged attractively in a box or basket, is always welcome.

Chocolate Cookies

So many popular cookies contain chocolate in some form. First and foremost are the chocolate chip cookies. Traditionally made with walnuts, now they are prepared in an impressive array of flavors, including macadamia nuts and chunks of white chocolate.

Instead of appearing as chips or chunks, chocolate can flavor the cookie dough throughout. Cookies can be crunchy and nutty or soft and cake-like. Melted chocolate makes a delightful frosting for cookies as well, as in the Chocolate-Coated Coconut Kisses.

Careful baking is the crucial step in the preparation of chocolate chip cookies, macaroons and any cookies that should be slightly soft to ensure that the cookies are moist and slightly chewy inside but not too sticky. They should brown only lightly and should be just firm enough to be removed from the baking sheet but still soft in the center. When hot, they might appear too soft, but it is amazing how much they harden as they cool. If the texture of a cookie seems just right when it is hot, it will be too hard, dry and brittle when cool.

Cookies, Brownies & Petit Fours

Brownies & Other Chocolate Bar Cookies

Whenever I want to show off an American sweet to friends from other lands, I make brownies. It is hard to imagine that something that involves so little work could taste so good. Because they are baked for a relatively short time, they remain very moist inside.

Today's brownies are intensely chocolaty rather than being overly sweet. They are delicious plain, especially when flavored with exotic ingredients such as Brazil nuts, but are even more festive when frosted, as in Brandied Brownies topped with brandy-flavored butter frosting, or Bittersweet Brownies topped with French ganache.

Chocolate makes a wonderful contribution to other bar cookies as well. It can be chopped and sprinkled over a crisp cookie dough base, as in Chocolate-Walnut Bars, or it can be a center for Chocolate-Cinnamon Squares, where the chocolate is sandwiched between a delicate almond cake base and a light meringue topping.

Chocolate Petits Fours, Macaroons & Meringues

Although for some people petits fours are limited to very sweet frosted squares of sheet cakes, here the term is used in a broader sense. We have included elegant small cakes, such as Almond Truffle Petits Fours, and also cookies, like Chocolate Macaroons, which are served at the finest of restaurants with the coffee after dessert.

Chocolate-flavored meringues have a special crunchy texture that makes them a good accompaniment for ice cream and other smooth creamy desserts. Both macaroons and meringues are quite sweet and this explains their small size, because one or two bites is the perfect portion.

Triple Chocolate Chip Cookies

Full of morsels of white, milk and dark chocolate, these nutty cookies sweetened with brown sugar are crisp on their edges and moist inside.

---

1 cup all-purpose flour

1/2 teaspoon baking soda

1/4 teaspoon salt

1/2 cup (4 oz.) unsalted butter, slightly softened

1/2 cup firmly packed dark-brown sugar

1/4 cup granulated sugar

1 large egg

1 teaspoon pure vanilla extract

1/2 cup pecans, coarsely chopped

3/4 cup semisweet real chocolate pieces

3/4 cup milk chocolate pieces

3/4 cup white chocolate pieces

Position rack in center of oven and preheat to 350F (175C). Lightly butter 2 baking sheets. Sift flour, baking soda and salt into a medium bowl.

Cream butter in a medium bowl. Add sugars; beat until smooth and fluffy. Add egg; beat until smooth. Add vanilla; beat until blended. Stir in flour mixture until blended. Stir in nuts and all chocolate pieces.

Push batter from a teaspoon with a second teaspoon onto buttered baking sheets, using about 1 tablespoon batter for each cookie and spacing them about 2 inches apart. Bake about 10 minutes or until browned around edges and nearly set but still soft to touch in center. Using a metal spatula, carefully transfer cookies to racks; cool completely. Cool baking sheets; clean off any crumbs and butter sheets again. Bake remaining cookies. *Cookies can be kept 1 week in an airtight container at room temperature.*

Makes about 48 cookies

Variation

Chocolate-Chunk Cookies: Chop 4-1/2 ounces semisweet chocolate and 4-1/2 ounces milk chocolate in chunks and substitute for chocolate pieces; or use packaged chocolate chunks.

From upper right: Ganache-Frosted Bittersweet Brownies, page 122; Triple Chocolate Chip Cookies, above; Golden Pine Nut-Chocolate Chip Bars, page 125.

Chocolate-Almond Sandwiches

White chocolate ganache is the filling of these thin, extra-crisp, cocoa-almond cookies.
The cookies are easy to shape—the dough is simply formed into cylinders and sliced.

Cocoa-Almond Cookies:

3/4 cup whole blanched almonds
(about 4 oz.)

3/4 cup sugar

1-3/4 cups all-purpose flour

3 tablespoons unsweetened
Dutch-process cocoa powder

1 teaspoon baking powder

1 cup (8 oz.) unsalted butter,
slightly softened

White Chocolate Ganache:

6 oz. fine-quality white chocolate,
very finely chopped

1/2 cup whipping cream

Cookies: Grind almonds with sugar in a food processor to a fine powder. Sift flour, cocoa and baking powder into a medium bowl.

Cream butter in a large bowl. Add almond mixture; beat until smooth and fluffy. Using a wooden spoon, stir in cocoa mixture. Dough will seem dry at first, but stir until it comes together. Divide dough in half. Spoon each half onto a sheet of waxed paper. Roll in a log, about 1-1/2 inches in diameter. Wrap in waxed paper. Refrigerate 2 hours. Roll each log again to an even round shape. Refrigerate 4 hours or until firm.

Position rack in center of oven and preheat to 375F (190C). Cut each log in about 1/4-inch-thick slices with a thin sharp knife. Put slices on ungreased baking sheets, about 1-1/2 inches apart. Bake 10 to 11 minutes or until cookies are just set; they burn easily on the bottom. Carefully transfer to racks with a metal spatula; cool completely.

Ganache: Put white chocolate in a small bowl. Bring cream to a full boil in a small heavy saucepan. Pour over chocolate all at once. Stir with a whisk until mixture is smooth. Cool to room temperature. Refrigerate 30 minutes, stirring occasionally with whisk, until cold and thick but not set. Whip mixture at high speed 3 minutes or until lighter in color and thickened.

Spread about 2 teaspoons ganache on flat sides of half the cookies. Sandwich each with flat side of a second cookie, choosing cookies of same size to pair together. Refrigerate 15 minutes to set before serving. *Cookies can be kept, covered, 1 week in refrigerator.* Serve at room temperature.

Makes 28 cookie sandwiches

Crisp Chocolate Chip-Macadamia Nut Cookies

Unlike many chocolate chip cookies, these are not chewy but are crisp and delicate. They are a perfect accompaniment for ice cream, a cup of coffee or a glass of milk.

1 cup all-purpose flour

1/2 teaspoon salt

1/2 teaspoon baking soda

1/2 cup (4 oz.) unsalted butter, slightly softened

1/2 cup firmly packed brown sugar

1/4 cup granulated sugar

1 large egg

1/2 teaspoon pure vanilla extract

1 cup coarsely chopped unsalted macadamia nuts or desalted macadamia nuts, page 178 (about 5 oz.)

3/4 cup semisweet real chocolate pieces

Position rack in center of oven and preheat to 350F (175C). Lightly butter 2 baking sheets. Sift flour, salt and baking soda into a medium bowl.

Cream butter in a medium bowl. Add sugars; beat until smooth and fluffy. Add egg; beat until smooth. Add vanilla; beat until blended. Stir in flour mixture until blended. Stir in nuts and chocolate pieces.

Push batter from a teaspoon with a second teaspoon onto buttered baking sheets, using about 1-1/2 teaspoons batter for each cookie and spacing them about 2 inches apart. Flatten each cookie by pressing it firmly with the bottom of a fork dipped in water.

Bake about 8 minutes or until lightly browned. Using a metal spatula, carefully transfer cookies to racks; cool completely. Cool baking sheets; clean off any crumbs and butter sheets again. Bake remaining cookies. *Cookies can be kept 1 week in an airtight container at room temperature.*

Makes about 48 cookies

Variation

Crisp Chocolate Chip-Walnut Cookies: Substitute 1 cup walnut pieces for macadamia nuts.

Ganache-Frosted Bittersweet Brownies

The best of both worlds: American brownies with the finest French chocolate frosting—ganache.

Photo on page 119.

Bittersweet Brownies:

6 oz. bittersweet chocolate, chopped

1/2 cup plus 2 tablespoons (5 oz.) unsalted butter, cut in pieces

3/4 cup all-purpose flour

1/2 teaspoon baking powder

1/4 teaspoon salt

3 large eggs

1 cup sugar

2 teaspoons vanilla extract

3/4 cup coarsely chopped walnuts

Semisweet Ganache:

6-1/2 oz. semisweet chocolate, very finely chopped

1/2 cup whipping cream

Brownies: Position rack in center of oven and preheat to 350F (175C). Line base and sides of a 9- to 9-1/2-inch-square baking pan with a single piece of waxed paper or foil; butter paper or foil. Melt chocolate with butter in a medium bowl over nearly simmering water. Stir until smooth. Remove from water; cool 5 minutes. Sift flour, baking powder and salt into a small bowl.

Beat eggs lightly. Add sugar; whip at high speed about 5 minutes or until thick and light. Beat in vanilla. Add chocolate mixture in 3 batches, beating at low speed until blended after each addition. Stir in flour mixture, then walnuts.

Transfer batter to prepared pan; carefully spread to corners of pan in an even layer. Bake about 35 minutes or until a wooden pick inserted 1/2 inch from center of mixture comes out nearly clean. Cool in pan on a rack to room temperature. Turn out onto a tray; remove paper or foil. Turn back over onto another tray.

Ganache: Put chocolate in a small heatproof bowl. Bring cream to a full boil in a small heavy saucepan. Pour over chocolate all at once. Stir with a whisk until and mixture is smooth. Refrigerate about 20 minutes, stirring occasionally with whisk, until cold and thick enough to spread but not set. Spread ganache over top of brownies. Refrigerate 1 hour or until set. Carefully cut in 16 to 20 squares, using a sharp knife. *Brownies can be kept, covered, 3 days in refrigerator.*

Makes 16 to 20 brownies

Tip

For extra-shiny glaze, cool ganache at room temperature. Let glazed brownies set at cool room temperature about 2 hours.

Brandied Brownies

These "adult" brownies make delicious petits fours. They are dark and cakelike and are topped with white, brandy butter frosting and pecan halves.

Brandied Chocolate-Pecan Brownies:

5 oz. fine-quality semisweet chocolate, chopped

1/2 cup (4 oz.) unsalted butter, cut in 8 pieces, room temperature

3/4 cup plus 2 tablespoons all-purpose flour

1/2 teaspoon baking soda

1/4 teaspoon salt

3 large eggs

1/2 cup packed brown sugar

6 tablespoons granulated sugar

2 tablespoons brandy or Cognac

1-1/3 cups pecans, coarsely chopped (4 oz.)

Brandy Butter Frosting:

1/2 cup (4 oz.) unsalted butter, slightly softened

1-1/2 cups powdered sugar, sifted

2 tablespoons brandy or Cognac

20 pecan halves (for garnish)

Brownies: Position rack in center of oven and preheat to 350F (175C). Line base and sides of a 9- to 9-1/2-inch-square baking pan with a single piece of waxed paper or foil; butter paper or foil. Melt chocolate in a medium bowl over nearly simmering water. Stir until smooth. Add butter in 2 batches, stirring until blended after each addition. Remove from pan of water; let cool. Sift flour, baking soda and salt into a small bowl.

Beat eggs lightly. Add sugars; beat at low speed until blended. Whip mixture at high speed about 7 minutes or until thick and light. Gradually fold in chocolate mixture just until blended. Stir in brandy. Fold in flour mixture, then chopped pecans.

Pour batter into prepared pan. Bake about 30 minutes or until a wooden pick inserted into center of mixture comes out nearly clean. Cool in pan on a rack to room temperature. Turn out onto a tray; remove paper or foil.

Frosting: Cream butter in a large bowl. Add powdered sugar; beat at low speed until blended. Gradually beat in brandy. Spread frosting over top of brownies. Mark 2-inch squares with a knife.

Set a pecan half in center of each square. Refrigerate about 1 hour or until frosting sets. Follow marks to cut in 2-inch squares using sharp knife. *Brownies can be kept, covered, 3 days in refrigerator; brandy flavor gradually weakens.*

Makes 20 brownies

Hazelnut Fudge Brownies

A generous quantity of toasted hazelnuts add an interesting twist to these moist brownies.
Unsalted macadamia nuts, pecans or walnuts would be good alternatives.

---

1 cup hazelnuts (about 4-1/2 oz.)

4-1/2 oz. semisweet chocolate, chopped

6 tablespoons unsalted butter

1/2 cup plus 1 tablespoon all-purpose flour

Pinch of salt

2 large eggs

3/4 cup plus 2 tablespoons sugar

1 teaspoon pure vanilla extract

Position rack in center of oven and preheat to 350F (175C). Toast hazelnuts and remove skins, page 179; cool nuts completely. Chop nuts coarsely. Line base and sides of a 7-1/2- to 8-inch-square baking pan with a single piece of waxed paper or foil; butter paper or foil. Melt chocolate with butter in a medium bowl over nearly simmering water. Stir until smooth. Remove from water; cool 5 minutes. Sift flour and salt into a small bowl.

Beat eggs lightly in a medium bowl at medium speed. Add sugar; beat just until blended. Beat in vanilla. Add chocolate mixture in 3 batches, beating until blended after each addition. Stir in flour mixture, then nuts. Transfer batter to prepared pan; carefully spread to corners of pan in an even layer. Bake about 24 minutes or until a wooden pick inserted 1/2 inch from center of mixture comes out nearly clean. Cool in pan on a rack to room temperature. Turn out onto a board; remove paper or foil. Carefully cut in 16 squares, using the point of a sharp knife. Turn each brownie back over to serve. *Brownies can be kept 3 days in an airtight container at room temperature.*

Makes 16 brownies

Fudgy Brazil Nut Brownies

Brazil nuts and a hint of orange flavor these rich, super-chocolaty brownies.
For a special treat, serve these brownies with vanilla ice cream.

1/2 cup plus 2 tablespoons (5 oz.) unsalted butter, cut in pieces

3 oz. semisweet chocolate, chopped

3 oz. unsweetened chocolate, chopped

3/4 cup all-purpose flour

1/4 teaspoon salt

3 large eggs

1-1/4 cups sugar

1 tablespoon grated orange zest

3/4 cup Brazil nuts, chopped (4 oz.)

Position rack in center of oven and preheat to 350F (175C). Line base and sides of a 7-1/2- to 8-inch-square baking pan with a single piece of waxed paper or foil; butter paper or foil. Melt butter with chocolates in a medium bowl over nearly simmering water. Stir until smooth. Remove from pan of water; let cool. Sift flour and salt into a medium bowl.

Beat eggs lightly at medium speed. Add sugar; beat just until blended. Beat in orange zest. Add chocolate mixture in 3 batches, beating until blended after each addition. Stir in flour mixture, then chopped nuts.

Transfer batter to prepared pan; carefully spread to corners of pan in an even layer. Bake about 32 minutes or until a wooden pick inserted 1/2 inch from center of mixture comes out nearly clean. Cool in pan on a rack to room temperature. Turn out onto a board; remove paper or foil. Carefully cut in 16 squares, using point of sharp knife. *Brownies can be kept 3 days in an airtight container at room temperature.*

Makes 16 brownies

Golden Pine Nut-Chocolate Chip Bars

This type of bar cookie, often called a blond brownie or golden brownie, is light-textured but rich and buttery. These are sweetened with brown sugar and studded with chocolate chips and pine nuts.

Photo on page 119.

1 cup plus 2 tablespoons
   all-purpose flour

1 teaspoon baking powder

1/4 teaspoon salt

1/2 cup plus 2 tablespoons (5 oz.)
   unsalted butter, slightly softened

1/4 cup granulated sugar

3/4 cup packed light brown sugar

2 large eggs

1 teaspoon pure vanilla extract

2/3 cup pine nuts (about 3 oz.)

1 cup semisweet real chocolate
   pieces (6 oz.)

1/4 cup pine nuts, if desired
   (for sprinkling)

Position rack in center of oven and preheat to 350F (175C). Butter a 9- to 9-1/2-inch-square baking pan. Sift flour, baking powder and salt into a medium bowl.

Cream butter in a large bowl. Add sugars; beat until smooth and fluffy. Add eggs, 1 at a time, beating very thoroughly after each addition. Beat in 2 tablespoons flour mixture at low speed. Add vanilla; beat until blended. Using a wooden spoon, stir in remaining flour mixture. Stir in 2/3 cup pine nuts and chocolate pieces.

Transfer batter to prepared pan; spread evenly. Sprinkle evenly with 1/4 cup pine nuts, if using. Bake 30 to 35 minutes or until mixture is brown on top, pulls away slightly from sides of pan and a wooden pick inserted into center comes out nearly clean. Cool in pan on a rack. Cut into approximately 1-1/4" x 1-3/4" bars, using the point of a sharp knife. *Cookies can be kept 3 days in an airtight container at room temperature.*

Makes 16 to 20 bars

Chocolate-Walnut Bars

With an extra-buttery dough made in a food processor and patted out by hand in a baking pan, these are very quick and easy bar cookies. Part of the dough is turned into a crumbly topping that is sprinkled over the chocolate-raspberry filling.

Walnut Cookie Dough:

1 cup walnuts (about 3-3/4 oz.)

3 large egg yolks

1/2 cup sugar

1/4 teaspoon salt

2 teaspoons pure vanilla extract

2 teaspoons grated lemon zest

1 cup (8 oz.) unsalted butter,
   well-chilled, cut in 16 pieces

1-3/4 cups all-purpose flour, sifted

Chocolate-Raspberry Filling:

1/2 cup raspberry preserves

6 oz. semisweet chocolate,
   cut into very small chunks

Nutty Crumble Topping:

2 tablespoons sugar

1/4 cup all-purpose flour

1/4 cup walnuts, coarsely chopped

Dough: Chop nuts fairly fine in a food processor. Transfer to a bowl. Combine yolks, sugar, salt, vanilla, lemon zest and butter in food processor. Process using 10 quick on/off pulses, then process continuously 5 seconds until nearly blended. Add flour and walnuts; process 2 seconds. Scrape down and process about 3 seconds or until the dough begins to form sticky crumbs but does not come together in a ball. Put dough in a plastic bag or in plastic wrap. Press dough together; shape in a rectangle. Refrigerate 1 hour. Clean and dry food processor.

Position rack in center of oven and preheat to 350F (175C). Cut off 1/4 of dough; set aside in refrigerator. Pat out remaining dough in bottom of an unbuttered 13" x 9" baking pan.

Filling: Stir preserves. Using a rubber spatula, spread gently over dough, leaving a border of about 1/4 inch. Sprinkle chocolate evenly over preserves.

Topping: Cut reserved dough in 10 pieces. Return to food processor. Add sugar and flour; process using a few quick on/off pulses until sugar and flour are blended in but dough is still very crumbly. Crumble dough quickly between your fingers to separate any lumps. Sprinkle crumbs evenly over chocolate. Sprinkle with chopped walnuts.

Bake 30 to 35 minutes or until crumbs are firm and light brown. Cool in pan on a rack until lukewarm. Cut in 1-1/2" x 2" bars in pan, using sharp knife. *Cookies can be kept 3 days in an airtight container at cool room temperature.*

Makes about 24 bars

Variation

To make dough by hand: Follow variation at the end of Sweet Pie Pastry, page 59. For Topping, rub refrigerated dough pieces with sugar and flour between your fingers until dough becomes very crumbly.

Chocolate-Marzipan Rosettes

Made of homemade marzipan, these cookies have a nutty, fudgy interior and can be made in a variety of pretty shapes. Colorful and festive when decorated with a variety of candied fruit, they keep well and make lovely gifts for the holidays.

Photo on page 133.

Chocolate-Marzipan Cookies:

2 oz. semisweet chocolate, chopped

1 oz. unsweetened chocolate, chopped

1-1/2 cups whole blanched almonds (about 7-1/2 oz.)

3/4 cup sugar

3 large egg whites, beaten to mix

Garnish:

About 1/2 cup of any or all of the following: sliced almonds; green or red candied cherries, quartered; crystallized ginger, cut in small squares

Quick Glaze:

1 tablespoon powdered sugar

2 tablespoons milk or water

Cookies: Position rack in center of oven and preheat to 350F (175C). Line 2 baking sheets with parchment or waxed paper; lightly butter paper. Melt chocolates in a small bowl over nearly simmering water. Stir until smooth. Remove from pan of water; let cool.

Grind almonds with 1/4 cup sugar in a food processor to a fine powder. Add remaining 1/2 cup sugar; process until blended. Add egg whites; process until blended. Add chocolate; process again until blended.

Using a pastry bag and large star tip with points far apart, pipe mixture in rosettes or rings onto prepared baking sheet. Mixture is stiff so press firmly. For better control, hold pastry bag high so tip is not too close to baking sheet. If mixture does not detach easily from tip, cut it off with the point of a knife.

Garnish: Decorate cookies with sliced almonds, candied cherries or crystallized ginger. Bake 12 minutes or until firm on outside. Leave cookies on baking sheet.

Glaze: Mix powdered sugar with milk in a very small saucepan. Heat until sugar dissolves. Brush glaze lightly over hot cookies. Carefully remove cookies from baking sheet with a metal spatula or pancake turner; cool on a rack. *Cookies can be kept 1 week in an airtight container at room temperature.*

Makes 40 small cookies

Meringue Mushrooms

Serve these as a decorative addition to a platter of petits fours, as cookies or
in their traditional role as a garnish and accompaniment for Chocolate Yule Log, page 24.

Photo on pages vi-vii.

---

3 large egg whites

1/4 teaspoon cream of tartar

3/4 cup sugar

**1 to 2 tablespoons unsweetened
  cocoa powder, sifted**

Position rack in center of oven and preheat to 225F (105C). Lightly butter corners of a large baking sheet; line with foil or parchment paper. Butter and very lightly flour foil or paper. Have ready a spatula for folding and pastry bag fitted with plain 1/2-inch tip. Using a paper clip, close end of bag just above tip so mixture will not run out while you fill bag.

In a small bowl, beat egg whites and cream of tartar at medium speed until stiff. At high speed, add sugar 1 tablespoon at a time and beat until meringue is very stiff and shiny. Immediately spoon into pastry bag. Remove paper clip. To form mushroom caps, pipe about 1/2 of mixture onto prepared baking sheet in small mounds, about 3/4 inch in diameter, 1 inch high and about 1 inch apart; finish with a quick rounded motion so they will be smooth. Push down any points with your dampened finger.

Pipe remaining mixture in pointed bases, lifting pastry bag upward to form points about 1-1/2 inches high and of slightly smaller diameter than caps. You should have about as many pointed bases as mounds.

Sprinkle mounds, not points, very lightly with cocoa through a small strainer. Bake 35 to 40 minutes or until mounds can just be lifted from foil; if overbaked, they will not stick to bases. Insert the point of a thin sharp knife in flat side of a mound; turn knife point to make a hole. Stick mound on top of a pointed base, inserting point in hole. Press gently to be sure top, which should still be slightly sticky, adheres to base; otherwise tops will fall off. Repeat with remaining tops and bases. Return to oven.

Bake about 1-1/2 hours or until firm and dry. To check, remove a meringue. Cool 2 minutes and break apart; meringue should be dry and crumbly and not sticky. Using a large metal spatula, immediately remove meringues from foil or paper; cool on a rack. Put cookies in airtight containers as soon as they are cool. *Meringues can be kept in airtight containers at room temperature 2 weeks in dry weather. If they become sticky from humidity, recrisp in a 200F (95C) oven about 20 minutes.*

Makes 45 cookies

Variation

Bake mushroom caps and bases separately 2 hours and 10 minutes or until firm and dry; cool completely. Make holes with knife as in fourth paragraph. Spread a dab of melted chocolate on pointed end of each base and stick caps on top.

Chocolate Meringue Fingers

These light cookies are shaped like ladyfingers but their taste and texture are completely different. They are sweet, crunchy and chocolaty and delightful with vanilla ice cream.

Photo on page 133.

1/4 cup unsweetened Dutch-process cocoa powder

1/2 cup powdered sugar

3 large egg whites

1/4 teaspoon cream of tartar

1/4 cup plus 2 tablespoons granulated sugar

Position rack in center of oven and preheat to 225F (105C). Lightly butter corners of 2 baking sheets; line with foil. Butter and lightly flour foil. Have ready a rubber spatula for folding and a pastry bag fitted with a 1/2-inch plain or star tip. Using a paper clip, close end of bag just above tip so mixture will not run out while you fill bag. Sift cocoa and powdered sugar into a medium bowl.

In a medium dry bowl, beat egg whites with cream of tartar at medium speed until stiff. At high speed, gradually beat in granulated sugar and beat until whites are very shiny. Gently fold in cocoa mixture as quickly as possible.

Immediately spoon meringue into pastry bag. Remove paper clip. Pipe mixture in thin fingers 2-1/2 inches long, spacing them about 1 inch apart. To finish each finger, use a quick sharp upward movement of tip.

Bake about 1 hour and 10 minutes or until firm and dry. To check, remove a meringue. Cool 2 minutes and break apart; meringue should be dry and crumbly and not sticky. Using a large metal spatula, immediately transfer meringue fingers to a rack; cool completely. Put cookies in airtight containers as soon as they are cool. *Meringues can be kept in airtight containers at room temperature 2 weeks in dry weather. If they become sticky from humidity, they can be baked in a 200F (95C) oven for about 20 minutes to recrisp.*

Makes about 45 cookies

Chocolate-Cinnamon Squares

These triple-layer bar cookies are made in the Eastern European style: the base is
a delicate almond cake, the center is sprinkled with chocolate pieces and
the top is a cinnamon-flavored meringue. The result is a light, delicious cookie
that is perfect for teatime or as a petit four.

Almond-Cinnamon Dough with Chocolate Chips:

1 cup all-purpose flour

1/2 teaspoon baking powder

2 teaspoons ground cinnamon

1/2 cup whole blanched almonds (about 2-1/2 oz.)

1/2 cup sugar

1/2 cup (4 oz.) unsalted butter, slightly softened

1 large egg, beaten

1 large egg yolk

1 cup semisweet real chocolate pieces (6 oz.)

Light Chocolate-Cinnamon Topping:

3-1/2 oz. semisweet chocolate, coarsely chopped, chilled

1 large egg white

1/4 cup granulated sugar

1 teaspoon ground cinnamon

Powdered sugar (for sprinkling)

Dough: Position rack in center of oven and preheat to 350F (175C). Butter a 9- to 9-1/2-inch-square baking pan. Sift flour, baking powder and cinnamon into a medium bowl. Grind almonds with 2 tablespoons sugar in a food processor to a fine powder. Transfer to a medium bowl.

Cream butter in a medium bowl. Add remaining 6 tablespoons sugar; beat until smooth and fluffy. Add egg in 2 batches, beating thoroughly after each. Add yolk; beat until blended. Beat in almond mixture at low speed. Using a wooden spoon, stir in flour mixture. Spread evenly in cake pan. Sprinkle evenly with chocolate pieces. Refrigerate while preparing topping.

Topping: Chill a food processor and metal blade for chopping chocolate. Chop chocolate in food processor until as fine as possible.

In a small bowl, beat egg white to soft peaks. Gradually beat in granulated sugar; beat at high speed about 30 seconds or until mixture is very shiny. Beat in cinnamon. Fold in chopped chocolate. Gently spoon mixture over chocolate pieces; spread carefully and evenly over dough.

Bake about 25 minutes or until dough is firm and lightly browned at edges and topping is set. Cool in pan on a rack until lukewarm. Carefully cut in 2-inch squares or 2" x 1-1/4" bars, using a sharp knife. Sift powdered sugar over cookies just before serving. *Cookies can be kept 3 days in an airtight container at cool room temperature.*

Makes 20 to 24 cookies

Almond-Truffle Petits Fours

Unlike many traditional petits fours, these do not have a sweet fondant coating and are simple to prepare. They are made of light, tender, white almond cake and a rich chocolate-truffle mixture. The frosting and filling are made from the same mixture, but for the topping the mixture is whipped to give a lighter texture and color.

Photo on page 133.

Light Almond Cake:

1 cup whole blanched almonds (about 4-1/2 oz.)

3/4 cup plus 2 tablespoons sugar

6 tablespoons all-purpose flour

8 large egg whites

1/3 cup milk

Coffee-Flavored Ganache:

10 oz. semisweet chocolate, very finely chopped

2 teaspoons instant coffee granules

3/4 cup whipping cream

24 whole blanched almonds, if desired (for garnish)

Cake: Position rack in center of oven and preheat to 375F (190C). Line a 17" x 11" baking sheet with parchment paper or foil; butter paper or foil. Grind almonds with 1/2 cup plus 2 tablespoons sugar in a food processor to a fine powder. Transfer to a medium bowl. Sift flour over ground almonds; stir until blended.

In a large dry bowl, beat egg whites to soft peaks. Gradually beat in remaining 1/4 cup sugar; beat at high speed until whites are stiff and shiny but not dry.

Using a wooden spoon, stir milk into almond mixture. Stir in about 1/4 of whites. Gently fold remaining whites into almond mixture in 3 batches. Fold lightly but quickly, just until batter is blended. Spread batter evenly on prepared baking sheet. Bake 15 minutes or until cake is light brown on top and golden-brown at edges. Cool in pan on a rack.

Ganache: Combine chocolate and coffee in a heatproof medium bowl. Bring cream to a full boil in a small heavy saucepan. Pour over chocolate all at once. Stir with a whisk until mixture is smooth. Refrigerate about 20 minutes, stirring occasionally with whisk, until cold and thick but not set.

Cut cake in half crosswise with a sharp knife; each piece will be about 8 inches wide. Carefully remove 1 piece from paper. Set on a platter; cake will feel slightly sticky. Spread with about 1/3 cup ganache in a thin layer. Top with second piece of cake, positioning it so cut sides of cake are even with each other. Refrigerate 10 minutes.

Whip remaining ganache in a medium bowl at high speed about 5 minutes or until thickened and slightly lighter in color. Spread over top cake layer. Set almonds, if using, on top, about 1-1/2 inches apart. Refrigerate 1 hour or until frosting sets. Trim edges of cake. Cut in 1-1/2-inch squares, using the point of a sharp knife. *Petits fours can be kept, covered, 5 days in refrigerator.* Serve at room temperature.

Makes 24 petits fours

Chocolate-Coated Coconut Kisses

Macaroonlike, white coconut peaks are dipped in dark bittersweet chocolate,
which forms a topping of a contrasting color and a flavor that offsets the cookie's sweetness.

Photo opposite.

---

3 large egg whites

1/2 cup sugar

**1-3/4 cups flaked or grated coconut
(about 5-1/2 oz.)**

**4 oz. bittersweet chocolate, chopped
(for dipping)**

Position rack in center of oven and preheat to 300F (150C). Lightly butter corners of a large baking sheet; line with foil. Butter foil.

Combine egg whites and sugar in a medium bowl. Set bowl in a pan of hot water over low heat. Beat with a hand mixer at low speed 5 minutes, then at medium speed about 6 minutes or until mixture is warm to touch. Remove from pan of water. Beat at high speed until cool. Stir in coconut.

Using about 1 tablespoon batter for each cookie, push batter from a spoon with a second spoon onto prepared baking sheets, spacing about 1 inch apart. Shape each with your dampened fingers into a rounded peak. Bake about 25 minutes or until set and very light brown; cookies should feel soft inside. Transfer to a rack; cool completely.

Melt chocolate in a small deep bowl over nearly simmering water. Stir until smooth. Remove from water; cool to body temperature. Line a tray with foil or waxed paper.

Holding each cookie from its base, gently dip peak into chocolate so about 2/3 of cookie is coated. Hold briefly upside down so chocolate drips back into bowl. Set on a lined tray, peak-side up. If chocolate begins to thicken during dipping, set briefly above pan of hot water to soften. Refrigerate cookies 20 minutes or until chocolate sets. *Cookies can be kept in 1 layer in a shallow covered container 4 days in refrigerator.* Serve at room temperature.

Makes about 22 cookies

Clockwise from left: Row of Florentines alternately arranged with chocolate-frosted side up, page 136; ring-shaped almond-garnished Chocolate-Marzipan Rosettes, page 127; Almond Truffle Petits Fours, page 131; Chocolate-Coated Coconut Kisses, above; Chocolate Meringue Fingers, page 129; variation of Chocolate-Marzipan Rosettes topped with a cherry.

Devil's Food Cupcakes

Bake this batter either as tender cupcakes or as 8-inch cake layers.
Its rich frosting is simple to prepare and has a pure chocolate flavor,
quite different from the powdered-sugar icings often found on cupcakes.

Cocoa Cupcakes:

2 cups cake flour

2/3 cup unsweetened cocoa powder

1-1/4 teaspoons baking soda

1/4 teaspoon salt

1/2 cup buttermilk

1/3 cup water

3/4 cup (6 oz.) unsalted butter, slightly softened

1-3/4 cups sugar

2 large eggs

1-1/2 teaspoons pure vanilla extract

Rich Chocolate Frosting:

5 oz. semisweet chocolate, chopped

1/3 cup whipping cream

2 tablespoons unsalted butter, well-chilled, cut in 2 pieces

Cupcakes: Position rack in center of oven and preheat to 350F (175C). Line 24 muffin cups with paper baking cups. Sift flour, cocoa, baking soda and salt into a large bowl. Mix buttermilk and water in a medium bowl.

Cream butter in a large bowl. Add sugar; beat until smooth and fluffy. Add eggs, 1 at a time, beating thoroughly after each addition. Add vanilla; beat until blended. At lowest speed, blend in about 1/4 of cocoa mixture, then about 1/3 of buttermilk mixture. Alternately add remaining cocoa mixture in 3 batches and remaining buttermilk mixture in 2 batches. Mix just until batter is blended.

Fill paper baking cups 2/3 full, using about 1/4 cup batter for each. Bake about 20 minutes or until a cake tester inserted into center of a cupcake comes out clean. Cool in pan on a rack. Remove cupcakes with their paper baking cups.

Frosting: Melt chocolate in cream in a medium bowl over nearly simmering water. Remove from pan of water; stir until smooth. Add butter; stir until blended. Refrigerate 15 minutes. Beat at high speed 8 minutes or until frosting is thick enough to spread. Frost top of each cupcake. Refrigerate 1 hour or until frosting sets. *Cupcakes can be kept, covered, 4 days in refrigerator.* Serve at room temperature.

Makes 20 to 24 cupcakes

Variation

Devil's Food Cake: Butter 2 round 8-inch layer cake pans; line base of each pan with foil. Butter foil and sides of pans. Transfer batter to pans; spread smooth. Bake about 35 minutes or until a cake tester inserted into center of each cake comes out clean. Cool 5 minutes in pans. Carefully invert onto racks; cool. Frosting is enough to fill cake and cover top. To obtain enough frosting for side of cake as well, use the following amounts: 7-1/2 ounces semisweet chocolate, 1/2 cup whipping cream, 3 tablespoons butter.

Chocolate Macaroons

Dense chewy macaroons, made mainly of ground almonds, are among the first types of
cookie known in the history of food and remain one of the most popular sweets.
Bittersweet chocolate adds just the perfect touch for the traditionally sweet flavor of macaroons.

4-1/2 oz. bittersweet or semisweet chocolate, chopped

1-1/2 cups whole blanched almonds (about 6 oz.)

1 cup sugar

3 large egg whites

2 teaspoons grated orange zest, if desired

Position rack in center of oven and preheat to 325F (165C). Line 3 baking sheets with parchment paper or waxed paper; lightly butter paper. Melt chocolate in a medium bowl over nearly simmering water. Stir until smooth. Remove from water; let cool.

Grind almonds with 3 tablespoons sugar in a food processor to a fine powder. Add egg whites and remaining sugar alternately, each in 2 batches, processing about 10 seconds after each addition or until smooth. Add orange zest; process to blend. Transfer to a large bowl. Gradually add chocolate, stirring until mixture is smooth.

Using a pastry-bag fitted with a 1/2-inch plain tip, pipe mixture in mounds of about 1 inch diameter onto baking sheets, spacing them about 1 inch apart. Flatten any points with your lightly moistened finger. Bake 5 minutes. Wedge oven door slightly open with handle of a wooden spoon. Bake about 7 minutes longer or until just firm to touch; centers should still be soft. Remove from oven.

Lift 1 end of paper and pour about 2 tablespoons water under it onto baking sheet; water will sizzle on contact with hot baking sheet. Lift other end of paper and pour 2 tablespoons water under it. When water stops boiling, carefully remove macaroons from paper with a metal spatula. Cool on a rack.

Bake remaining macaroons. If necessary, bake on 2 racks. Halfway through baking time, switch positions of baking sheets from lower to upper racks so all macaroons bake evenly. *Macaroons can be kept 1 week in an airtight container at room temperature.*

Makes about 60 small cookies

Florentines

Named for Florence, where it probably originated, this crisp, chewy, candylike cookie is a favorite in Italy, France, Austria and Germany. It is a lacy holiday cookie, studded with colorful candied fruits and almonds, flavored with honey and glazed with chocolate.

Photo on page 133.

1/2 cup whipping cream

1/4 cup unsalted butter

1/2 cup sugar

2 tablespoons honey

1/3 cup diced candied orange peel, finely chopped

1/3 cup red candied cherries, rinsed in hot water, drained and chopped

1-2/3 cups sliced almonds (about 5 oz.)

6 tablespoons all-purpose flour

8 oz. bittersweet chocolate, chopped (for glaze)

Position rack in center of oven and preheat to 350F (175C). Butter and flour 2 baking sheets, preferably nonstick, tapping to remove excess flour.

In a heavy medium saucepan, mix cream with butter, sugar, honey, candied peel and cherries. Cook over low heat, stirring, until butter melts. Bring to a boil over medium-high heat, stirring. Remove from heat; stir in almonds and flour. Drop rounded teaspoons of mixture onto prepared baking sheets, spacing them 3 inches apart. Flatten each cookie until very thin by pressing it with the bottom of a fork dipped in water.

Bake 5 minutes. Remove from oven. Using a 3-inch cookie cutter, pull in any uneven edges of each cookie to give it an even round shape. Bake 4 minutes longer or until edges of cookies are golden brown. Watch carefully—they burn easily; but do not underbake or cookies quickly become sticky. Cool to lukewarm on baking sheet. Remove cookies to a rack with a metal pancake turner.

Melt chocolate in a medium bowl over nearly simmering water. Stir until smooth. Remove from water; cool, stirring often, about 5 minutes or until slightly thickened. Line a tray with foil or waxed paper. Spread chocolate on flat side of each cookie; set on tray.

Refrigerate cookies 5 minutes or until chocolate is thickened but not set. Using a cake-decorating comb or a fork, mark wavy lines on chocolate coating of each cookie. Refrigerate about 10 minutes or until set. *Cookies can be kept in an airtight container 1 week in refrigerator.* To serve, arrange cookies on a platter, alternating some with chocolate facing up, others with chocolate facing down.

Makes about 42 cookies

Chocolate Ladyfingers

Use these to make frames for charlottes or to accompany mousses or ice creams.

3 tablespoons plus 1 teaspoon unsweetened Dutch-process cocoa powder

1-1/2 teaspoons powdered sugar

3/4 cup all-purpose flour

4 large eggs, separated

2/3 cup granulated sugar

3/4 teaspoon pure vanilla extract

1/4 teaspoon cream of tartar

Position rack in center of oven and preheat to 350F (175C). Butter and lightly flour 2 nonstick baking sheets. Designate length of ladyfingers by marking crosswise lines 3-1/2 inches apart on baking sheets. Ladyfingers will be piped lengthwise between lines. Have ready a rubber spatula for folding and a pastry bag with a large plain tip of 5/8 inch diameter. Using a paper clip, close end of bag just above tip so mixture will not run out while you fill bag.

Mix 2-1/2 teaspoons cocoa with powdered sugar in a small bowl; set aside for sprinkling. Sift flour and remaining 2 tablespoons plus 1-1/2 teaspoons cocoa into a medium bowl.

Beat egg yolks lightly in a large bowl. Beat in 6 tablespoons granulated sugar; whip at high speed about 5 minutes or until mixture is pale and very thick. Beat in vanilla.

In a large dry bowl, beat egg whites with cream of tartar to soft peaks. Gradually beat in remaining 2-2/3 tablespoons granulated sugar; beat at high speed until whites are stiff and shiny but not dry.

Sift about 1/4 of flour mixture over yolk mixture; fold gently until nearly incorporated. Gently fold in about 1/4 of whites. Repeat with remaining flour mixture and whites, each in 3 batches, adding each batch when previous one is nearly blended in. Fold lightly but quickly, just until batter is blended.

Immediately spoon into prepared pastry bag. Remove paper clip. Pipe 3-1/2" x 1-1/4" ladyfingers onto prepared baking sheets between marked lines, spacing them about 1 inch apart. Sift cocoa-powdered sugar mixture lightly but evenly over ladyfingers.

Bake in center of oven about 12 minutes or until ladyfingers are just firm on outside and spring back when pressed very lightly but are slightly soft inside. Transfer to a rack; cool. *Ladyfingers can be kept 1 day in an airtight container in 1 layer; or they can be frozen in layers separated with waxed paper about 2 months.*

Makes about 30 ladyfingers; about 10 ounces

Variation

White Ladyfingers: Omit cocoa. Increase powdered sugar to 1 tablespoon plus 1 teaspoon; set aside for sprinkling on ladyfingers. When preparing baking sheets, mark crosswise lines 3 inches apart. Pipe 3-inch ladyfingers. Sift powdered sugar lightly but evenly over ladyfingers. Makes about 48 small ladyfingers; about 10 ounces.

Tip

To line a mold or pan with ladyfingers: Trim ladyfingers at their sides so they can fit tightly in mold. Trim them flat at 1 end to sit squarely on base of pan. Line side of mold with ladyfingers standing upright. If using chocolate ladyfingers, smooth bottom side should face outward; if using white ladyfingers, smooth side should face inward. Fit them in mold as tightly as possible.

Chocolate truffles and other homemade chocolate candies give the most intense chocolate experience and are among the most luxurious of food gifts.

Some people hesitate to make truffles and other chocolate candies because dipping them in chocolate appears complicated. But the truth is that making dipped truffles delicious is easy; only making them beautiful takes practice. Many quick-to-prepare truffles and chocolate candies do not even need to be dipped.

Truffles, chocolate candies and chocolate drinks are sweet snacks rather than desserts, although they can be served instead of dessert after a rich dinner. Truffles can be used to make desserts, such as Truffled Bavarian Cream, page 90.

Chocolate Truffles

Made primarily of pure chocolate and cream, Europe's most popular candies, truffles, are fast becoming favorites here too.

In France, classic truffles are round and have three parts: a filling of ganache, made of chocolate and cream; a coating of pure chocolate; and a second coating of cocoa.

Although the pure flavor of fine chocolate is the most important quality of a good truffle, other secondary flavors, such as coffee or ginger, can be added. In many parts of the country, truffles cannot be sold when flavored with liqueurs and therefore the liqueur flavor is often imitated with extract, which is no match for the real thing. At home, you can prepare some of the most delicious truffles, flavored with Grand Marnier, raspberry brandy or other spirits.

Some chocolatiers boast that their truffles are largest but I find that the small, European-style truffles give the most pleasure. The chocolate is so rich that one or two bites are usually enough and—you can always have a second or third truffle! However, this is a matter of taste and how large you want to make your truffles is up to you.

Many popular candies, from rich truffles to simple pieces of dried fruit, are superior when dipped in fine chocolate. A special type of chocolate called *couverture* is best-suited for this purpose (see also "What is Chocolate," pages viii-ix, and mail order information, page 179). This chocolate has a relatively high cocoa butter content and is more fluid than other types of chocolate when warm, which results in a thinner, more delicate coating. It is also easier to use because other chocolates become too thick when they reach the correct temperature for dipping, which must be relatively cool so the creamy center of the truffle does not melt.

Other Chocolate Candies

Of course, chocolate candies do not have to be round. With the aid of inexpensive plastic candy molds, an endless array of different shaped chocolate candies can be made with ease.

Colorful chocolate-dipped fruit is another popular candy that is simple to prepare and makes an amusing activity for all ages. Chocolate coatings can be striped or even marbled for a beautiful treat.

There are many delicious, easy-to-make chocolate candies that do not require dipping. Take the Quick Cognac Truffles, for example, in which the chocolaty center is simply rolled in chopped nuts; or Coconut-Coated Chocolate Balls where the outer coating is coconut. Grand Marnier Chocolate Cups are another example; after small paper candy cups are lined with chocolate and filled with a chocolate-Grand Marnier ganache, the paper cups are simply peeled away from the chocolate.

Chocolate Drinks

Easy-to-make chocolate drinks can be served as warm treats in winter or refreshing beverages in summer. Both cocoa and melted chocolate give rich-tasting results. These range from spiced Mexican Hot Cocoa flavored with cinnamon and cloves, to liqueur- or rum-spiked drinks, such as silky smooth Chocolate Egg Nog.

Truffles, Candies & Drinks

To Dip Truffles:

Melt chocolate in a medium bowl over hot water over low heat, stirring very often with a rubber spatula. Stir until smooth. Remove from pan of water. Either temper chocolate, page 174, for a professional finish; or cool melted chocolate, stirring often, until it reaches 88F (30C) or slightly cooler than body temperature, for dark chocolate, or 84F (29C) for white or milk chocolate.

Set container of chocolate in a bowl of warm water off heat, making sure it sits squarely in bowl and does not move around. Set 1 truffle center in melted chocolate. Turn over with 2 fingers or a dipping utensil until completely coated. Lift out and gently shake a few times so excess chocolate drips back into bowl. Gently wipe truffle against rim of bowl to remove excess chocolate.

Occasionally replace warm water in bowl to maintain temperature of chocolate. If chocolate gets thick, set bowl of chocolate over pan of hot water 2 or 3 minutes to soften.

For dipping, use one of the following three techniques:

- *Using your fingers:* This is messy but you do not need any special equipment. Hold the candy with your index finger and third finger while dipping.

- *Using a regular fork:* Bend the two middle tines of a fork upward so they are perpendicular to the others. Scoop up candy with lower tines and let it rest against those bent upward.

- *Using a professional dipping fork:* Use a straight three-tined fork for solid candies and a loop-ended utensil for truffles.

DIPPING TECHNIQUES & TIPS

- For best results work in a cool room.
- Keep all utensils for stirring and dipping and containers for melting chocolate completely dry. At all stages of dipping, be very careful not to splash any water into the chocolate; a drop of water could cause the chocolate to harden.
- Soft creamy mixtures, like ganache, should be cool or cold so they do not melt from the warmth of the chocolate coating. Other ingredients, such as nuts or candied fruit, should be at room temperature.
- Use a bowl or top of a double boiler that is relatively small so the chocolate is deep enough to cover the candies.
- Dipped candies should be set on a completely flat surface after dipping. The easiest to use is a foil-lined tray. The foil should fit very tightly and smoothly so the candies cannot roll.
- When setting the dipped candy on the tray, take care not to drip any coating on the tray; drips will form "feet." Large "feet" can be broken off when the candy is set.

Traditional Truffles

Classic French truffles are dipped in chocolate, then rolled in cocoa so they look earthy like real truffles. Their charm lies in the wonderful contrast between the creamy center, crisp chocolate shell, and bittersweet powdery cocoa. Tempering is less important than for some other truffles because the cocoa coating covers up any streaks or other imperfections in the chocolate shell. To make truffles the easiest way, omit the dipping; simply roll the truffle centers in cocoa.

Photo on page 144.

Ganache Centers:

9 oz. fine-quality semisweet chocolate, very finely chopped

2/3 cup whipping cream

Coating:

1 cup unsweetened Dutch-process cocoa powder

12 oz. fine-quality semisweet chocolate, preferably *couverture*, chopped

Ganache Centers: Put 9 ounces chocolate in a medium bowl. Bring cream to a full boil in a small heavy saucepan over medium-high heat. Pour cream over chocolate all at once. Stir with a whisk until mixture is smooth; cool to room temperature. Scrape down mixture with a rubber spatula. Cover with a paper towel and plastic wrap; refrigerate, occasionally stirring gently, about 1 hour or just until thick enough to pipe.

Line 2 trays with foil. Have ready a pastry bag with a large plain tip, about 5/8-inch in diameter. Using a paper clip, close end of bag just above tip so mixture will not run out. Fill bag. Remove paper clip. Pipe mixture in small mounds or "kisses," about 3/4 inch in diameter and 1 inch high, onto prepared trays, spacing mounds about 1 inch apart. Cover and refrigerate 30 to 45 minutes or until firm.

Carefully remove a mound from tray, keeping second tray in refrigerator. Press mound into a ball; return to tray. Repeat with remaining mounds. Quickly roll each ball between your palms until smooth. If truffles soften too much during rolling, refrigerate about 5 minutes and continue. Cover and refrigerate at least 3 hours or until very firm. *Truffle centers can be kept, covered, 3 days in refrigerator; or they can be frozen 2 months.*

Coating: Spread cocoa in a small tray or shallow bowl so it is about 1/2 inch deep. Line 2 trays with foil.

Melt 12 ounces chocolate and dip a truffle according to directions, page XXX. Set dipped truffle in tray of cocoa; spoon enough cocoa over truffle to cover it. Dip and coat 4 or 5 more centers. Gently shake tray of cocoa to be sure truffles are coated with cocoa. Very gently transfer truffles to foil-lined tray.

Continue with remaining truffles. Let truffles stand at room temperature to set. If coating does not set within 10 minutes, refrigerate truffles about 10 minutes or until set. Gently transfer truffles to a rack. Gently brush off excess cocoa with a pastry brush. Refrigerate truffles 1 hour. *Truffles can be kept in an airtight container 1 week in refrigerator; or they can be frozen 2 months.* Serve at room temperature in white or gold candy papers.

Makes about 48 small truffles

Bittersweet Belgian Truffles

When making truffles, it is particularly important to use top-quality chocolate; some of the finest chocolate available comes from Belgium. These truffles have an intense chocolate flavor with a hint of vanilla and rum. They are richer and denser than Traditional Truffles because of the addition of butter and the higher proportion of chocolate.

Photos on pages vi-vii and 144.

Bittersweet Ganache Centers:

1/2 cup whipping cream

1 vanilla bean, split lengthwise

10 oz. fine-quality bittersweet chocolate, chopped

2 tablespoons unsalted butter, room temperature, cut in 6 pieces

2 tablespoons rum

Coating:

12 oz. fine-quality bittersweet chocolate, preferably *couverture*, chopped

Ganache Centers: Bring cream and vanilla bean to a boil in a heavy medium saucepan. Remove from heat. Cover and let stand 15 minutes. Melt 10 ounces chocolate in a medium bowl over nearly simmering water. Stir until smooth. Remove from pan of water; cool slightly.

Remove vanilla bean from cream. Pour cream into a medium bowl. Gradually whisk chocolate into cream. Add butter; whisk until blended. Cool to room temperature. Stir in rum. Cover mixture with a paper towel and plastic wrap; refrigerate about 1 hour or until firm.

Line 2 trays with foil. Using 2 teaspoons, shape mixture in rough 3/4-inch mounds, using about 2 teaspoons of mixture for each and spacing about 1 inch apart on prepared trays for easy handling. Cover and refrigerate about 30 minutes or until firm.

Carefully remove a mound from tray, keeping second tray in refrigerator. Press mound into a ball; return to tray. Repeat with remaining mounds. Quickly roll each ball between your palms until smooth. If truffles soften too much during rolling, refrigerate about 5 minutes and continue. Cover and refrigerate at least 2 hours or until very firm. *Truffle centers can be kept, covered, 3 days in refrigerator; or they can be frozen 2 months.*

Coating: Line 2 trays with foil. Melt 12 ounces chocolate and dip a truffle according to directions, page 139. Gently set truffle on prepared tray. Swirl top for a decorative finish, if desired. Dip remaining truffles. Let coated truffles stand at room temperature until set. If coating does not set within 10 minutes, refrigerate truffles about 10 minutes or until set. Remove from foil. *Truffles can be kept in an airtight container 1 week in refrigerator; or they can be frozen 2 months.* Serve cool.

Makes about 38 truffles

Variation

For garnish: Melt 3 ounces white chocolate and cool. Use to drizzle a design on the truffles with a fork, or to pipe a design with a pastry bag and fine plain tip.

Extra-Creamy Truffles

A high proportion of cream makes the centers of these truffles so soft
they melt quickly in your mouth. Their velvety texture is a wonderful contrast for
the crisp dark chocolate coating and the crunch of toasted pecans.

Chocolate-Orange Centers:

2 large navel oranges

1/2 pint whipping cream (1 cup)

10 oz. fine-quality bittersweet
chocolate, very finely chopped

Coating:

2/3 cup pecans, if desired

1 lb. fine-quality bittersweet
chocolate, preferably *couverture*,
chopped

Chocolate-Orange Centers: Using a vegetable peeler, pare colored part of
orange peel in long strips, without including white pith. Heat cream with
orange strips in a heavy medium saucepan over medium heat until bubbles
form around edge of pan. Remove from heat. Cover and let stand 20 minutes.
Strain into a medium bowl.

Melt 10 ounces chocolate in a medium bowl over nearly simmering water. Stir
until smooth. Remove from water; cool 5 minutes. Add cream all at once; whisk
until blended. Cool to room temperature. Scrape down mixture with a rubber
spatula. Cover with a paper towel and plastic wrap and refrigerate, occasionally
stirring gently, about 1-1/2 hours or until just thick enough to pipe.

Line 2 trays with foil. Have ready a pastry bag with a large plain tip, about 5/8-
inch diameter. Using a paper clip, close end of bag just above tip so mixture will
not run out. Fill bag. Remove paper clip. Pipe mixture in small mounds or
"kisses," about 3/4 inch in diameter and 1 inch high, onto prepared trays, spacing mounds about 1 inch apart. Cover and refrigerate 3 hours or until firm.

Remove a mound from tray, keeping second tray in refrigerator. Press mound
into a ball; return to tray. Repeat with remaining mounds. Quickly roll each ball
between your palms until smooth. If truffles soften too much during rolling,
refrigerate about 5 minutes and continue. Cover and refrigerate at least 6 hours
or until very firm. *Truffle centers can be kept, covered, 3 days in refrigerator; or they
can be frozen 2 months.*

Coating: Preheat oven to 350F (175C). Lightly toast pecans in a shallow baking
pan in oven 4 minutes. Transfer to a plate; cool completely. Using a sharp knife,
chop pecans into tiny cubes.

Line 2 trays with foil. Melt 1 pound chocolate in a medium bowl over hot water
over low heat, stirring very often with a rubber spatula. Stir until smooth.
Remove from water. Either temper chocolate, page 174, for a professional finish; or cool melted chocolate, stirring often, until it reaches 88F (30C) or slightly cooler than body temperature. Stir pecans into chocolate. Dip truffles, page
139. Set on prepared trays. Let coated truffles stand at room temperature until
set. If coating does not set within 10 minutes, refrigerate truffles about 10 minutes or until set. Carefully remove from foil. *Truffles can be kept in an airtight container 1 week in refrigerator; or they can be frozen 2 months.* Serve cool.

Makes about 48 small truffles

Variations

Easy Chocolate Kisses: Instead of rolling truffle centers into balls, leave them
shaped as "kisses." Omit coating.

Easy Pecan-Coated Truffles: Roll truffles in balls, then in chopped pecans.
Omit melted chocolate coating.

Spirited White Chocolate Truffles

Fruit brandies contribute "spirit" to these sweet, white chocolate truffles. My favorites are raspberry brandy and pear brandy. Use any brandy you like, but the most assertive ones are best. Make these truffles small because of their concentrated flavor.

White Ganache Centers:

9 oz. fine-quality white chocolate, very finely chopped

6 tablespoons whipping cream

1 tablespoon unsalted butter, room temperature

2 tablespoons fine-quality fruit brandy, such as clear raspberry brandy, pear brandy, kirsch or calvados

White Chocolate Coating:

Small pieces of candied violets, if desired (for garnish)

1 lb. fine-quality white chocolate, preferably *couverture*, chopped

Ganache Centers: Put 9 ounces chocolate in a medium bowl. Bring cream to a full boil in a small heavy saucepan over medium-high heat. Pour cream over chocolate all at once. Stir with whisk until smooth. Add butter; whisk until blended. Gradually whisk in fruit brandy. Scrape down mixture with a rubber spatula. Cover with a paper towel and plastic wrap; refrigerate about 3 hours or until firm.

Line 2 trays with foil. Using 2 teaspoons, shape mixture in rough 3/4-inch mounds, using about 2 teaspoons of mixture for each mound and spacing about 1 inch apart on prepared trays. Cover with paper towels and plastic wrap; refrigerate about 1 hour or until firm.

Remove a mound, keeping second tray in refrigerator. Press mound into a ball; return to tray. Repeat with remaining mounds. Quickly roll each ball between your palms until smooth. If truffles soften too much during rolling, refrigerate a few minutes and continue. Cover and refrigerate at least 3 hours or until very firm. *Truffle centers can be kept, covered, 3 days in refrigerator; or they can be frozen 2 months.*

Coating: Line 2 trays with foil. Break candied violets, if using, into small pieces. Melt white chocolate and dip a truffle according to directions, page 139. Set on prepared tray. Swirl top of coating with your finger for a decorative finish, if desired. Immediately put a piece of candied violet on top.

Dip and garnish remaining truffles. Let coated truffles stand at room temperature until set. If coating does not set within 10 minutes, refrigerate truffles about 10 minutes or until set. Very carefully remove from foil so center does not stick. *Truffles can be kept in an airtight container 1 week in refrigerator; or they can be frozen 2 months.* Serve cool in brown candy papers.

Makes about 22 truffles

Variation

Almond-Coated White Chocolate Truffles: Omit candied violets. Toast 1 cup slivered almonds, page 179, and cool. Chop almonds into tiny cubes. Transfer to a tray. After dipping each truffle, set on tray of chopped almonds. Spoon more chopped almonds from tray over truffle so nuts stick to top.

Café au Lait Truffles

In these milk-chocolate and coffee truffles, a richly flavored coffee center is offset by a sweet milk-chocolate coating. The truffles are decorated with small coffee bean candies but can instead be drizzled with dark chocolate using the same technique as in the variation after Bittersweet Belgian Truffles, page 141.

Photo opposite.

Chocolate-Coffee Centers:

6 oz. fine-quality milk chocolate, very finely chopped

4 oz. fine-quality bittersweet chocolate, very finely chopped

1 tablespoon instant coffee granules

1/2 cup whipping cream

Coating:

12 oz. fine-quality milk chocolate, preferably *couverture*, chopped

About 32 small chocolate coffee beans (about 5/8 inch long) or coffee-flavored candy drops, if desired (for garnish)

Chocolate-Coffee Centers: Combine 6 ounces milk chocolate, 4 ounces bittersweet chocolate and coffee in a heatproof medium bowl. Bring cream to a full boil in a small heavy saucepan over medium-high heat. Pour cream over chocolate mixture all at once. Stir with a whisk until mixture is smooth; cool to room temperature. Scrape down mixture with a rubber spatula. Cover with a paper towel and plastic wrap; refrigerate, occasionally stirring gently, about 1 hour or until firm.

Line 2 trays with foil. Using 2 teaspoons, shape mixture into rough 3/4-inch mounds, using about 2 teaspoons of mixture for each and spacing about 1 inch apart on prepared trays for easy handling. Cover and refrigerate 30 to 45 minutes or until firm.

Remove a mound from tray, keeping second tray in refrigerator. Press mound into a ball; return to tray. Repeat with remaining mounds on tray. Roll each ball between your palms until smooth. If truffles soften too much during rolling, refrigerate about 5 minutes and continue. Cover and refrigerate at least 3 hours or until very firm. *Truffle centers can be kept, covered, 3 days in refrigerator; or they can be frozen 2 months.*

Coating: Line 2 trays with foil. Melt milk chocolate and dip a truffle according to directions, page 139. Set truffle on prepared tray. If desired, garnish with a chocolate coffee bean or candy drop.

Dip and garnish remaining truffles. Let coated truffles stand at room temperature until set. If coating does not set within 10 minutes, refrigerate truffles about 10 minutes or until set. Carefully remove from foil. *Truffles can be kept in an airtight container 1 week in refrigerator; or they can be frozen 2 months.* Serve cool.

Makes about 32 truffles

Upper dish: Double-Dipped Strawberries, page 150. Middle dish: assorted truffles—Traditional, page 140; Spirited White Chocolate, page 143; Café au Lait, above; Bittersweet Belgian, page 141; Quick Cognac, page 146. In lower tray: Grand Marnier Chocolate Cups, page 148.

Quick Cognac Truffles

A walnut coating provides a complementary taste and crunchy texture for the intense cognac-chocolate flavor of the interior of these truffles. No dipping is required, making these rich, creamy truffles easy to prepare. The truffle mixture is chilled several times because the cognac makes it soft.

Photo on page 144.

---

8 oz. fine-quality semisweet chocolate, chopped

6 tablespoons unsalted butter, slightly softened

1/3 cup whipping cream

1/4 cup cognac

About 3 tablespoons unsweetened Dutch-process cocoa powder

3/4 cup finely chopped walnuts

Melt chocolate in a medium bowl over nearly simmering water. Stir until smooth. Remove from water; cool slightly. In a small bowl, cream butter until smooth.

Heat cream in a very small heavy saucepan over medium-high heat until bubbles form around edge of pan; cool 3 minutes. Pour cream over chocolate all at once. Whisk until blended. Whisk in butter; cool mixture to room temperature. Gradually stir in cognac. Cover with a paper towel and plastic wrap; refrigerate about 5 hours or until firm.

Line 2 trays with foil. Using 2 teaspoons, shape mixture in rough 3/4-inch mounds, using about 2 teaspoons of mixture for each and spacing about 1 inch apart on prepared trays. Cover and refrigerate about 3 hours or until firm.

Remove a mound, keeping second tray in refrigerator. Press mound into a ball; return to tray. Repeat with remaining mounds. Quickly roll each ball between your palms until smooth, occasionally dipping your palms in cocoa to prevent sticking. If truffles begin to soften too much, refrigerate about 5 minutes and continue. Cover and refrigerate at least 2 hours or until firm.

Line 2 trays with foil. Put walnuts in a shallow bowl or tray. Roll truffles in walnuts, 1 at a time, pressing so walnuts adhere. Transfer to trays; refrigerate 1 hour or until firm. *Truffles can be kept in an airtight container 1 week in refrigerator; or they can be frozen 2 months.* Serve cold in candy papers.

Makes about 25 truffles

Molded Gianduja-Filled Chocolates

Beautiful, professional-looking molded chocolates can be made in an endless variety of shapes. These treats have a chocolate coating that is brushed on candy molds and a creamy filling made of *gianduja*, a mixture of toasted nuts and chocolate used in Italy and France. Plastic candy molds can be purchased at candy-supply stores or by mail order. Small ones are best because these candies are very rich.

Hazelnut-Gianduja Filling:

3/4 cup hazelnuts (about 3 oz.)

3/4 cup powdered sugar

3 oz. semisweet chocolate, chopped

1/2 cup whipping cream

1 tablespoon unsalted butter, room temperature

Coating:

12 oz. fine-quality semisweet or bittersweet chocolate, preferably *couverture*, chopped

Filling: Preheat oven to 350F (175C). Toast hazelnuts and remove skins, page 179; cool nuts completely. Grind nuts with powdered sugar in a food processor to a fine powder. Transfer to a medium bowl.

Melt 3 ounces chocolate in a small bowl over nearly simmering water. Stir until smooth. Remove from water; cool 5 minutes. Add to hazelnut mixture; stir until blended. Grind chocolate mixture in food processor until it begins to stick together; leave in food processor. Bring cream to a simmer in a small saucepan. Pour over chocolate mixture in processor. Add butter; process until blended. Transfer to a bowl; cool to room temperature.

Coating: Melt 12 ounces chocolate in a medium bowl over hot, not simmering, water over low heat, stirring very often with a rubber spatula. Stir until smooth. Remove from water. Either temper chocolate, page 174, for a professional finish; or cool melted chocolate, stirring often, until it reaches 88F (30C) or slightly cooler than body temperature.

Choose small, plastic candy molds, each holding up to 1 tablespoon. Using a small brush about 3/4 inch long and 1/4 inch in diameter, brush a thin even layer of chocolate in each mold. Wipe off any drips. Refrigerate about 5 minutes or until slightly firm. Repeat brushing, making a second layer. Hold mold up to the light to check that there are no holes. Wipe off any drips. Refrigerate 5 minutes.

Using a pastry bag and medium plain tip or a spoon, add enough filling to each mold to come to within about 1/4 inch of top. Refrigerate 5 minutes to set filling. Spoon more chocolate on top. Use brush to spread chocolate gently just to edges and to enclose filling. Wipe off any drips. Refrigerate molds about 30 minutes or until set.

To unmold candies, invert mold onto waxed paper. Press each mold gently; if candy does not come out refrigerate a few minutes longer and try again. *Candies can be kept in an airtight container 1 week in refrigerator.*

Makes 20 to 60 candies, depending on size of molds

Tip

To care for the candy molds, wash them with lukewarm water without soap, then dry with paper towel.

Grand Marnier Chocolate Cups

It is hard to believe that such elegant candies as these could be so simple to prepare.
The chocolate cups are made by painting chocolate into little candy papers using a small brush
bought from an art supply store. The cups are filled with a creamy
Grand Marnier chocolate ganache, then the papers are simply peeled off.
Photo on page 144.

Chocolate Cups:

4 oz. fine-quality bittersweet
chocolate, chopped

Grand Marnier-Chocolate Filling:

8 oz. semisweet chocolate,
very finely chopped

2/3 cup whipping cream

3 tablespoons plus 1 teaspoon
Grand Marnier

Tiny squares or triangles of
candied orange peel, if desired
(for garnish)

Chocolate Cups: Line 2 trays with foil. Melt 2 ounces bittersweet chocolate in a very small heatproof bowl over hot water over low heat, stirring very often with a rubber spatula. Stir until smooth. Remove from water; cool to slightly less than body temperature.

Using a very small brush, about 3/4 inch long and 1/4 inch in diameter, brush a thin layer of melted chocolate into 1-inch or 1-1/2-inch sturdy paper or foil candy cups. Coat each cup without leaving any holes and without dripping chocolate onto outside of cup. Set cups on prepared trays; refrigerate 12 minutes or freeze 7 minutes or until set.

Melt remaining 2 ounces bittersweet chocolate and cool as above. Repeat coating on chilled cups, handling them as little as possible. Refrigerate about 15 minutes or until set.

Filling: Put semisweet chocolate in a medium bowl. Bring cream to a full boil in a small heavy saucepan over medium-high heat. Pour cream over chocolate all at once. Stir with a whisk until smooth; cool to room temperature. Gradually whisk in Grand Marnier. Cover with a paper towel and plastic wrap; refrigerate about 30 minutes or until cold but not set. Whip mixture at high speed, scraping down occasionally, about 3 minutes or until lightened in color.

Using a pastry bag and medium star tip, fill each chocolate cup with a large rosette of filling. If desired, set a piece of candied orange peel on center of rosette. Refrigerate about 1 hour or until set. *Candies can be kept in an airtight container 1 week in refrigerator.* Serve in foil candy cups or gently peel off paper.

Makes 16 to 24 small candies, depending on size of cups

Dried Fruit Chocolate Medallions

Dried fruit is easy to dip because you can hold onto half the fruit and dip the other half.
These are good as candy and the smaller pieces make pretty garnishes for cakes and other desserts.
For a special effect, try two-tone and marble-dipped fruit as in the variations below.

1 lb. mixed dried or candied fruit, such as: dried apricots; dried pears; dried peaches; small, dark, dried figs (Mission figs); dried dates; pitted prunes; candied-ginger pieces; candied-pineapple wedges; thin strips of candied orange peel, about 1/4 inch wide

6 oz. fine-quality bittersweet or semisweet chocolate, preferably *couverture*, chopped

6 oz. fine-quality milk chocolate, preferably *couverture*, chopped

6 oz. fine-quality white chocolate, preferably *couverture*, chopped

Select attractive pieces of fruit and set aside. Line 3 or 4 trays with foil.

Melt bittersweet chocolate in a medium bowl over hot water over low heat, stirring very often with a rubber spatula. Stir until smooth. Remove from water. Either temper chocolate, page 174, for a professional finish; or cool melted chocolate, stirring often, until it reaches 88F (30C) or slightly cooler than body temperature. Set container of chocolate in a bowl of warm water off heat, making sure it sits squarely in bowl and does not move around.

Holding a piece of fruit at 1 end, dip half of fruit in chocolate. Gently shake fruit and let excess chocolate drip into bowl. Gently wipe fruit against rim of bowl to remove excess chocolate. Set fruit on prepared tray. Dip more fruit. If chocolate thickens, set it briefly over hot water so it becomes fluid.

Melt milk chocolate above hot water. Stir until smooth. Remove from water. Either temper milk chocolate; or cool it, stirring often, until it reaches 84F (29C) or cooler than body temperature. Dip fruit in milk chocolate. Melt and cool white chocolate in same way, and dip fruit in it.

Let dipped fruit stand at room temperature until set. If coating does not set within 10 minutes, refrigerate fruit about 10 minutes or until set. Carefully remove from foil. *Dipped fruit can be kept in an airtight container 1 week in refrigerator.*

Makes 1 pound dipped fruit

Variations

Marble-Dipped Dried Fruit: Melt equal amounts of white chocolate and either dark chocolate or milk chocolate. Cool dark chocolate, stirring often, until it reaches 88F (30C). Cool white or milk chocolate until it reaches 84F (29C). Spoon cooled white and dark chocolates into the same bowl next to each other. Run a knife through chocolates to marble them slightly. Dip fruit into marbled chocolate, dipping it straight down and lifting it straight up so pattern in chocolate is reproduced on fruit.

Two-Tone Dipped Dried Fruits:

Dip peaches, pears or apricots by 1/3 in melted bittersweet or milk chocolate; let set. Using tongs to hold fruit in center, dip opposite end of fruit in white chocolate by 1/3, leaving center 1/3 of fruit showing. Or dip by 2/3 in melted bittersweet or milk chocolate; let set. Dip coated side of fruit in white chocolate by 1/3.

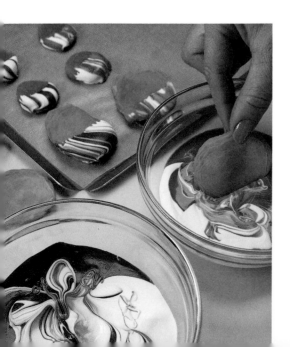

Double-Dipped Strawberries

I always assumed that strawberries dipped in chocolate, which are so popular here,
were an American creation but recently I discovered this sweet treat in Vienna, where the locals claimed
it was a Viennese specialty. This version makes a delightful three-tone confection to serve as dessert after a
rich meal, to accompany ice cream or to add freshness and color to a tray of petits fours or chocolates.
Photo on cover and page 144.

---

10 large strawberries, preferably with stems and leaves

5 oz. fine-quality white chocolate, chopped

2 oz. fine-quality bittersweet or semisweet chocolate, chopped

Rinse strawberries, leaving stems on. Pat completely dry with paper towels. Let dry on paper towels on a rack 30 minutes. Line a tray with foil or waxed paper.

Melt white chocolate in a small deep bowl over hot, not simmering, water over low heat, stirring very often with a rubber spatula. Stir until smooth. Remove from pan of water. Cool chocolate, stirring very often, until it reaches 84F (29C) on an instant-read thermometer, or cooler than body temperature.

Pat a strawberry dry again with paper towels. Holding it by its stem end, dip pointed 2/3 of berry in chocolate. Gently shake berry and let excess chocolate drip back into bowl. Set berry on prepared tray. Continue dipping remaining berries. If chocolate thickens, set it briefly over hot water again so it becomes fluid. Refrigerate berries about 30 minutes or until chocolate sets. Carefully lift strawberries from foil to unstick and replace on tray.

Melt dark chocolate as above; cool until 88F (30C) or slightly cooler than body temperature. Dip bottom 1/3 of each berry in chocolate. Set berries on tray. Refrigerate about 15 minutes to set. *Dipped strawberries can be kept, uncovered, 2 hours in refrigerator.* Remove from refrigerator about 10 minutes before serving.

Makes 10 dipped berries

Variation

Chocolate-Dipped Strawberries: Use 3 ounces of only 1 type of chocolate: bittersweet, semisweet or white. Melt and cool dark chocolate to 88F (30C) or white chocolate to 84F (29C). Dip 1/2 of each berry in chocolate.

Chocolate-Dipped Orange Sections

These make a delicious and beautiful garnish for Chocolate Cake à l'Orientale, page 2,
or for vanilla or chocolate ice cream.

Photo on pages vi-vii.

---

1 small orange, sectioned

**2 oz. fine-quality bittersweet or
semisweet chocolate, chopped**

Line rack with paper towels. Put orange sections on lined rack. Let dry 1 hour, patting often with paper towels, turning fruit over occasionally and changing towels as needed. A small amount of moisture can make chocolate solidify suddenly.

Line a tray or plate with waxed paper. Melt chocolate in a small deep heatproof bowl set over nearly simmering water over low heat. Stir until smooth. Remove from heat; cool to slightly less than body temperature.

Dip 1/2 of one orange section in chocolate. Let excess chocolate drip into bowl. Transfer orange section to waxed paper. Dip remaining sections, setting on waxed paper with chocolate half of all oranges pointing in same direction. Let stand at cool room temperature or refrigerate 30 minutes until chocolate sets. *Orange sections can be kept, uncovered, 4 hours in refrigerator.* Remove from refrigerator about 10 minutes before serving.

Makes 6 to 8 dipped sections

Chocolate-Dipped Almonds

A lovely decoration for chocolate-almond cakes with creamy frostings, such as Chef Chambrette's Chocolate Macaroon Cake, page 17. You can make chocolate-dipped pecans the same way.

**1 oz. fine-quality bittersweet
chocolate, chopped**

8 whole blanched almonds

Melt chocolate in a very small heatproof bowl over hot water over low heat. Stir until smooth. Remove from pan of water; cool to body temperature. Line a plate with waxed paper. Dip pointed end of each almond in chocolate; let excess drip into bowl. Gently set on paper-lined plate. Refrigerate to set chocolate.

Makes 8 dipped almonds

Chocolate-Macadamia Triangles

These are toasted, caramelized, macadamia nuts stuck together in triangles and dipped in chocolate. The recipe was inspired by a fabulous hazelnut confection I enjoyed in fine chocolate shops in Switzerland, France and Italy. For the prettiest candies, choose as many whole nuts as possible because the form of the nuts shows through the chocolate coating.

2/3 cup macadamia nuts, unsalted or desalted, page 178

1/3 cup sugar

3 tablespoons water

1 teaspoon unsalted butter

9 oz. fine-quality bittersweet chocolate, preferably *couverture*, chopped

Preheat oven to 350F (175C). Toast nuts in a shallow baking pan in oven 3 minutes. Remove from oven; leave in pan to keep warm. Lightly oil a baking sheet.

Combine sugar and water in a heavy, very small saucepan that does not have a black interior. Heat over low heat until sugar dissolves, gently stirring occasionally. Boil over high heat without stirring, but occasionally brushing down any sugar crystals from side of pan with a brush dipped in water, until mixture reaches soft-ball stage, page 161.

With pan off heat, stir nuts into syrup, being careful not to splash, until they are well-coated. Stir until syrup crystallizes. Cook over medium-high heat, stirring frequently and scraping sugar down from sides, until syrup becomes golden-brown. Do not let mixture get too dark or it will burn and candies will be bitter.

Remove from heat. Add butter; stir until blended. Transfer immediately to oiled baking sheet. Using 2 forks, separate nuts into groups of 3; press together to form triangles. Do not touch them with your fingers. Cool nuts completely. Break off any extra bits of caramel so shape of each triangle is neat. Gently remove from baking sheet; put on a plate.

Line 2 trays with foil. Melt chocolate and dip candies, page 139. Gently set on prepared trays. Let candies stand at room temperature until coating sets. If coating does not set within 10 minutes, refrigerate candies about 10 minutes or until set. Carefully remove from foil. *Candies can be kept in an airtight container 1 week in refrigerator.*

Makes about 15 candies

Chocolate-Walnut Bourbon Balls

With a burst of bourbon in every bite, balanced by the richness of chocolate and of nuts,
this candy has another advantage—it is quick and simple to make.

7 oz. semisweet chocolate, chopped

1/4 cup unsalted butter

2 cups walnut pieces (about 7 oz.)

1/2 cup plus 2 tablespoons
powdered sugar, sifted

6 tablespoons bourbon whiskey

1/4 cup unsweetened Dutch-process
cocoa powder

2/3 cup walnut halves

Melt chocolate with butter in a medium bowl over nearly simmering water. Stir until smooth. Remove from water; cool 5 minutes, stirring occasionally.

Finely chop walnuts with powdered sugar in a food processor, leaving some small walnut pieces. Add nut mixture to chocolate; mix well. Stir in bourbon. Transfer to a bowl. Cover and refrigerate 1-1/2 hours or until firm.

Line 2 trays with foil. Using 2 teaspoons, shape mixture in rough 3/4-inch mounds, using about 2 teaspoons of mixture for each. Set on prepared trays. Roll mounds to smooth balls. Return to prepared trays; refrigerate 20 minutes. Roll each ball lightly in cocoa. Decorate each top with a walnut half; press firmly so it adheres. Refrigerate until ready to serve. *Candies can be kept in an airtight container 1 week in refrigerator.* Serve in candy papers.

Makes 36 candies

Coconut-Coated Chocolate Balls

I learned to make these candies from my mother.
They are quick and easy to prepare and are still a favorite of mine.
Rolling them in coconut gives them a lacy coating.

4 oz. bittersweet chocolate, chopped

1/4 cup unsalted butter, slightly
softened

1/2 cup powdered sugar

1 cup pecans, finely ground (about
3-1/2 oz.)

1 cup plus 2 tablespoons flaked
coconut

1 teaspoon pure vanilla extract

Melt chocolate in a medium bowl over nearly simmering water. Stir until smooth. Remove from water; let cool.

Cream butter in a medium bowl. Add powdered sugar; beat until smooth and fluffy. Stir in melted chocolate. Add nuts, 2 tablespoons coconut and vanilla; mix thoroughly. Refrigerate 1 hour or until firm.

Shape mixture in small balls, using about 2 teaspoons mixture for each. Put remaining flaked coconut in a shallow bowl or tray; roll balls in coconut. Set candies on plates or trays. Refrigerate 1 hour before serving. *Candies can be kept in an airtight container 1 week in refrigerator.*

Makes about 20 candies

Angelina's Hot Chocolate

A favorite late-morning treat when we lived in Paris was going to a cafe or tearoom for hot chocolate.
A great place to have the drink was the chic tearoom *Angelina,* off Place de la Concorde.
This version can be brought to the table in two elegant pitchers. Each person combines the milk and
chocolate to his own taste in a mug and tops it with a spoonful of whipped cream.
Photo opposite.

---

6 oz. fine-quality semisweet or bittersweet chocolate, chopped

1/4 cup water, room temperature

3 tablespoons hot water

3 cups hot milk

Sugar to taste

Whipped cream

Melt chocolate in 1/4 cup water in a medium bowl over nearly simmering water. Stir until smooth. Remove from pan of water. Whisk in 3 tablespoons hot water. Pour into a pitcher or 4 mugs.

Stir 3/4 cup hot milk into each mug; or serve milk in a separate pitcher. Pass sugar to taste and whipped cream.

Makes 4 servings

Spiced Mexican Hot Cocoa

Chocolate originated in Mexico and was first used in drinks. In this version of hot chocolate, a touch of
cloves is added to the traditional Mexican combination of cocoa and cinnamon.
The spices are delicate and the drink remains smooth because their flavors infuse into it.

1/3 cup unsweetened cocoa powder

1/2 cup sugar

1/4 cup water

8 whole cloves

4 (3-inch) cinnamon sticks

1 qt. milk

1/2 pint whipping cream (1 cup)

Mix cocoa, sugar, water, cloves and cinnamon sticks in a medium saucepan. Bring to a simmer, stirring constantly. Cook over low heat 3 minutes.

Heat milk in a large saucepan over medium-high heat until bubbles form around edge of pan. Gradually whisk milk and 1/2 cup cream into cocoa mixture. Cook until hot; do not boil. Strain mixture into a bowl, reserving cinnamon sticks. Rinse cinnamon sticks and pat dry.

In a small chilled bowl, whip remaining cream to soft peaks.

Whisk hot cocoa until frothy. Pour into 4 mugs. Gently spoon whipped cream on top of each serving and set a cinnamon stick in center.

Makes 4 servings

Chocolate-Cinnamon-Raisin Rolls, page 55; Angelina's Hot Chocolate, above.

Chocolate Egg Nog

Known as *bavaroise* in France, this smooth drink is rich in chocolate.
Made from a light custard with a punch of rum, it is good hot or cold.

---

9 oz. fine-quality semisweet chocolate, chopped

1 qt. milk

6 egg yolks

2/3 cup sugar

6 tablespoons rum

Combine chocolate with 2/3 cup milk in a large bowl over nearly simmering water. Leave until nearly melted. Remove from water. Stir until smooth.

Heat remaining 3-1/3 cups milk in a large saucepan over medium-high heat until bubbles form around edge of pan.

Whisk egg yolks in a large bowl. Add sugar; whisk about 3 minutes or until well-blended and slightly thickened. Gradually whisk in hot milk. Return mixture to saucepan. Cook over medium-low heat, stirring and scraping bottom of pan constantly with a wooden spoon, until mixture reaches 160F (70C) on an instant-read or candy thermometer, about 7 minutes. Pour into a bowl and stir 1 minute to cool. Gradually whisk yolk mixture into chocolate mixture. Whisk in rum.

If serving hot, pour into mugs and serve immediately. If serving cold, refrigerate 2 hours or until cold and serve. *Drink can be kept, covered, 1 day in refrigerator if it will be served cold.*

Makes 6 servings

The information and recipes in this chapter are referred to throughout the book, as they are helpful in preparing all sorts of chocolate desserts. Here you will find instructions for making chocolate decorations to use as beautiful garnishes; recipes for basic frostings, fillings and sauces; and tips on beating egg whites, using nuts, and recommended equipment.

Chocolate Decorations

Simply decorated desserts are often the most elegant. Many of the desserts in this book are garnished with whipped cream and, in the case of cakes, with their frosting. Still there are special occasions when we want something extra.

A quick but effective garnish is nuts, berries or slices of fruit of the type that was used to make the dessert, so that they act not only as a decoration but also give a hint of the flavors to expect. Nuts and some fruit for garnish can be half-dipped in chocolate. Chocolate coffee beans provide an easy and attractive finishing touch for desserts. Grated chocolate also makes a very simple, fast and lovely decoration.

Following are a variety of chocolate garnishes that will give a special touch to almost any chocolate dessert. They add not only beauty, but a delicious flavor, because chocolate tastes wonderful when it is thin and crisp, as it is when made into Chocolate Leaves or Chocolate Cutouts.

Making chocolate garnishes takes some time and often is not practical on the day you prepare an elaborate dessert, but you can make them ahead and have them on hand. They can be kept in the freezer and used when needed.

A convenient time to make special chocolate garnishes is when you have already melted or tempered a generous quantity of chocolate for dipping truffles, candies or fruit. When you have finished dipping, the chocolate is cool and perfect for making garnishes.

The chocolate you choose affects the tone of the decorations. Some chocolates have a reddish tinge, while others are very dark, almost black. For an interesting contrast, you can also make decorations with white chocolate. For ease of preparation, it is best to use "couverture" because it is fluid and tends to break less.

Chocolate Techniques

For preparing even the most exquisite, sophisticated looking chocolate desserts in this book, the culinary techniques to master are minimal. They include properly beating egg whites, folding ingredients and cooking custard sauce.

In this reference section are some useful dessert-making techniques and procedures for handling chocolate. The recipes in the book are clear in themselves but here are several techniques explained in greater detail. Tempering chocolate, a technique limited to several candy recipes, might interest advanced cooks.

Frostings, Sauces & Basics

Chocolate Truffle Frosting

Delicious with Queen of Sheba Cake, page 11, or Hazelnut Truffle Cake, page 26.

1/3 cup whipping cream

4 oz. semisweet chocolate, very finely chopped

1/4 cup unsalted butter, slightly softened but still cool

Bring cream to a full boil in a small heavy saucepan. Remove from heat; immediately add chopped chocolate. Using a small whisk, stir quickly until chocolate is completely melted and mixture is smooth. Transfer to a bowl. Cool to room temperature. Whip mixture at high speed about 3 minutes or until it thickens and becomes paler.

Cream butter in a medium or large bowl until very soft and smooth. Add chocolate mixture in 3 batches, beating constantly until mixture is smooth.

Makes about 1 cup

Chocolate-Honey Frosting

This easy-to-prepare frosting makes a luscious topping for
Chocolate-Brazil Nut Cake, page 9, or for other nut cakes or chocolate cakes.
The raspberry variation is the frosting and filling for Checkerboard Cake, page 21.

1/2 cup whipping cream

6 oz. semisweet chocolate, very finely chopped

6 tablespoons (3 oz.) unsalted butter, slightly softened but still cool

3 tablespoons plus 1 teaspoon honey

Bring cream to a full boil in a small heavy saucepan. Remove from heat; immediately add chopped chocolate. Using a small whisk, stir quickly until chocolate is completely melted and mixture is smooth. Transfer to a bowl. Cool to room temperature.

Cream butter in a medium bowl until very soft and smooth. Add chocolate mixture in 3 batches, beating constantly until mixture is smooth. Gradually beat in honey.

Makes about 1-1/2 cups

Variation

Raspberry Chocolate Frosting:

Prepare as above, using only 1/3 cup whipping cream. Omit honey. Strain 1/2 cup red raspberry preserves and gradually beat into finished frosting.

Fudge Frosting

Delicious on Chocolate-Hazelnut Cake, page 14.

1/2 cup whipping cream

1/4 cup sugar

2 oz. semisweet chocolate, very finely chopped

1 oz. unsweetened chocolate, very finely chopped

1/2 cup (4 oz.) unsalted butter, slightly softened but still cool

1/2 teaspoon pure vanilla extract

Combine cream and sugar in a heavy medium saucepan. Cook over low heat, stirring constantly, until sugar dissolves. Bring to a boil over medium-high heat, stirring constantly. Reduce heat and simmer 1 minute.

Remove from heat; cool 2 minutes. Immediately add semisweet chocolate. Stir quickly with a whisk until chocolate is completely melted and mixture is smooth. Add unsweetened chocolate; whisk until smooth. Refrigerate mixture, stirring often, until cool but not set.

Cream butter in a medium bowl until soft and smooth. Add chocolate mixture in 3 batches, beating constantly at low speed until mixture is smooth. Beat in vanilla.

Makes about 1-1/2 cups

Chocolate Velvet Frosting

This rich, creamy frosting is perfect with light-textured cakes like
Chocolate-Coconut Chiffon Cake, page 6.

---

6 oz. semisweet chocolate, chopped

2 large egg yolks

2 tablespoons sugar

3 tablespoons water

1-1/4 cups whipping cream, well-chilled

Melt chocolate in a medium bowl over nearly simmering water. Stir until smooth. Remove from water.

Whisk yolks with sugar and water in a small metal bowl. Set bowl in a pan of nearly simmering water. Heat, whisking, until mixture reaches 160F (70C) on an instant-read or candy thermometer, about 1 minute. Immediately remove from water and whisk until cool. Add to chocolate mixture and stir until blended. Let stand 15 minutes or until cool but not set; mixture will be very thick.

In a large chilled bowl, whip cream until stiff. Stir about 1/2 cup whipped cream into chocolate mixture. Return mixture to bowl of cream; fold gently until blended. If frosting is too soft, refrigerate a few minutes until it is easy to spread.

Makes about 3-1/3 cups

Classic Buttercream

Use for Chocolate Yule Log, page 24, and other traditional cakes.
Remember that this frosting is rich, and is best when spread in a thin layer.

4 large egg yolks

1/2 cup sugar

1/3 cup water

1 cup (8 oz.) unsalted butter,
    slightly softened but still cool

Beat egg yolks in bowl of mixer until blended. In a small heavy saucepan combine sugar and water. Cook over low heat, stirring gently, until sugar dissolves. Increase heat to medium-high and bring to a boil. Boil without stirring until a candy thermometer registers 238F (115C) or soft-ball stage, about 4 minutes. To test without a thermometer, see page 169. Immediately remove from heat.

Using a whisk, gradually beat hot syrup in a very thin stream into egg yolks. Immediately beat at high speed of mixer until completely cool and thick.

Cream butter in a large bowl until smooth and fluffy. Add yolk mixture in 4 batches, beating thoroughly after each addition.

Makes about 2 cups

Variations

To make 3 cups buttercream: Use 6 egg yolks, 3/4 cup sugar, 1/2 cup water and 1-1/2 cups (12 oz.) butter.

Classic Chocolate Buttercream: Melt 8 oz. fine-quality bittersweet or semisweet chocolate and let cool. Whisk into buttercream.

Chocolate Glaze

An easy way to dress up cakes like Marbled Chocolate Coffeecake, page 7, or
to spoon over Chocolate-Mint Cream Puffs, page 49.

4 oz. semisweet chocolate, chopped

2 tablespoons water

2 tablespoons unsalted butter

Melt chocolate with butter and water in a medium bowl over nearly simmering water. Stir until smooth. Remove from pan of water; cool until thickened.

Makes about 2/3 cup

Chocolate Meringue Buttercream

This luscious frosting is ideal with light-textured cakes, like the chocolate-nut sponge cake in Chocolate-Pecan Gâteau, page 4. The white chocolate variation is perfect with Chocolate Angel Layer Cake, page 25

---

7 oz. fine-quality bittersweet or extra-bittersweet chocolate, chopped

2/3 cup sugar

1/3 cup water

2 egg whites, room temperature

3/4 cup (6 oz.) unsalted butter, cut in pieces, slightly softened but still cool

2 tablespoons rum

Melt chocolate in a medium bowl over nearly simmering water. Stir until smooth. Remove from pan of water; let cool.

Combine sugar and water in a small heavy saucepan. Cook over low heat, stirring gently, until sugar dissolves. Increase heat to medium-high and bring to a boil. Boil, without stirring, 3 minutes. Meanwhile, beat egg whites in a large bowl until stiff but not dry. Continue boiling syrup until a candy thermometer registers 238F (115C) (soft-ball stage), about 4 minutes. To test without thermometer see below. Immediately remove from heat.

Using mixer at high speed, gradually pour hot syrup into center of whites; continue beating until meringue is cool and shiny.

Cream butter in a large bowl until soft and smooth. Beat in chocolate in 3 batches. Beat in meringue in 3 batches. Gradually beat in rum, 1 teaspoon at a time.

Variation

White Chocolate Meringue Buttercream: Substitute 3 oz. fine-quality white chocolate for the bittersweet chocolate. Omit rum.

Tip

To test syrup for soft ball stage without a thermometer: Remove pan from heat. Take a little hot syrup on a teaspoon and dip spoon into a cup of iced water, keeping spoon level. With your fingers in water, remove syrup from spoon. CAUTION: Do not touch syrup unless your fingers are in iced water. If syrup is ready, it will form a soft ball. If syrup dissolves into water, continue cooking and test again; if syrup was overcooked and forms firm ball, you can still use it. If syrup goes far beyond desired degree, quickly add 1/4 cup water and stir gently to combine it with syrup; temperature will decrease. Return to a boil and cook to correct temperature. Do not attempt to save syrup if it has begun to brown.

Maple Frosting

A traditional American flavor is used in a new way in this rich and easy frosting,
perfect for chocolate-nut cakes like Chocolate-Cashew-Maple Cake, page 28.

1/2 cup pure maple syrup

3 egg yolks, room temperature

**3/4 cup (6 oz.) unsalted butter,
slightly softened but still cool**

Bring maple syrup to a boil in a small saucepan. Using a hand whisk or hand mixer, beat egg yolks in a large bowl until blended. Gradually pour syrup onto yolks, whisking constantly. Whip at high speed of mixer until completely cool and very thick.

Cream butter in a large bowl until smooth and fluffy. Beat in maple mixture in 5 batches, beating thoroughly after each addition.

Makes about 1-1/2 cups

Chantilly Cream

The classic French whipped cream—serve it with any rich or light chocolate cake, or
pipe it in the center of a glazed Chocolate Crown, page 5.

**1/2 pint whipping cream (1 cup),
well-chilled**

1 tablespoon sugar

1 teaspoon pure vanilla extract

Prepare cream up to 30 minutes before using. In a large chilled bowl, whip cream with sugar and vanilla until stiff. Refrigerate until ready to use.

Makes about 2 cups

Kirsch Whipped Cream

Kirsch, the clear European cherry brandy, flavors this traditional frosting and filling for Black Forest Cherry Torte, which marries cherries and chocolate. The variation, used for Black Forest Trifle, includes a higher proportion of Kirsch, because trifle is traditionally a spirited dessert.

---

1 pint whipping cream (2 cups), well-chilled

2 tablespoons plus 1 teaspoon sugar

4-1/2 teaspoons kirsch

Prepare cream a short time before using. In a large chilled bowl whip cream with sugar until stiff. Add kirsch; beat at low speed until just blended. Refrigerate until ready to use.

Makes about 4 cups

Variation

Kirsch Whipped Cream for Trifle: Use 1 cup whipping cream, 1 tablespoon sugar and 2 tablespoons kirsch. Makes about 2 cups.

Amaretto Whipped Cream: Use 3/4 cup whipping cream, 1 teaspoon sugar and 2 tablespoons amaretto liqueur. Makes about 1-1/2 cups

Chocolate & Macadamia Liqueur Whipped Cream

Use to frost Hawaiian Chocolate-Flecked Nut Cake, page 1, or serve with nut cakes, vanilla sponge cakes or dark chocolate cakes.

1-1/4 oz. semisweet chocolate, chopped

3/4 cup whipping cream, well-chilled

2-1/4 teaspoons sugar

4-1/2 teaspoons macadamia nut or hazelnut liqueur

Prepare cream a short time before using. Melt chocolate in a small bowl over nearly simmering water. Stir until smooth. Remove from heat but leave bowl of chocolate over hot water.

In a large chilled bowl, whip cream with sugar until stiff. Add liqueur; beat just until blended.

Remove chocolate from pan of water; cool 30 seconds. Quickly stir about 1/3 cup whipped cream into chocolate. Quickly fold mixture into remaining cream until smooth. Work quickly so chocolate does not harden upon contact with the cold whipped cream. Use as soon as possible; cream stiffens when refrigerated.

Makes about 1-1/2 cups

Chocolate Whipped Cream

Light but flavorful, this cream is used to make Chocolate Dream, page 20, and is also wonderful with chocolate or vanilla sponge cakes. The first variation, Chocolate Cream Filling, is richer in chocolate and makes the chocolate layer of Brown-Bottom Charlotte, page 91.

---

3 oz. semisweet chocolate, chopped

1-1/4 cups whipping cream, well-chilled

Prepare cream a short time before using. Melt chocolate in a small bowl over nearly simmering water. Stir until smooth. Remove from heat but leave bowl of chocolate over hot water.

In a large chilled bowl, whip cream until stiff. Remove chocolate from pan of water; cool 30 seconds. Quickly stir about 1/2 cup whipped cream into chocolate. Quickly fold mixture into remaining cream until smooth. Work quickly so chocolate does not harden upon contact with the cold whipped cream. Use as soon as possible as filling or frosting; cream stiffens when refrigerated.

Variations

Chocolate Cream Filling: Use 4 oz. chocolate and 1 cup cream.

Chocolate Chantilly Cream: Prepare as Chocolate Whipped Cream, using 1-1/2 cups cream and beating it with 2 tablespoons sugar and 1 teaspoon pure vanilla.

Bourbon Sauce

A perfect partner for Dark Chocolate Bourbon Soufflé, page 62.

---

1 cup milk

3 large egg yolks

3 tablespoons sugar

1 tablespoon bourbon whiskey

Bring milk to a boil in a small heavy saucepan. Whisk egg yolks lightly in a medium bowl. Add sugar; whisk until well-blended. Gradually whisk in hot milk. Return mixture to saucepan, whisking constantly. Cook over medium-low heat, stirring mixture and scraping bottom of pan constantly with a wooden spoon, until mixture thickens slightly and reaches 170F to 175F (75C to 80C) on an instant-read or candy thermometer, about 5 minutes. To check without a thermometer, see page 169. Do not overcook sauce or it will curdle. Pour immediately into a bowl. Stir about 30 seconds to cool; let cool completely. Stir in bourbon. *Sauce can be kept, covered, 2 days in refrigerator.* Serve cold or cool.

Makes about 4 servings (about 1 cup)

Dark Chocolate Sauce

Serve hot with vanilla, coffee or rum-raisin ice cream or use for Crêpes Belle Hélène, page 76.

---

3 oz. semisweet chocolate, chopped

1 oz. unsweetened chocolate, chopped

1/3 cup water

3 tablespoons sugar

3 tablespoons unsalted butter, cut in pieces

Combine chocolates and water in small saucepan set over hot, not simmering, water over low heat. Leave until melted, stirring occasionally.

Stir in sugar. Place over direct heat. Cook over low heat 2 minutes, stirring constantly, until sugar dissolves and mixture thickens slightly. Remove from heat. Add butter; stir until blended. Serve immediately or refrigerate. *Sauce can be kept, covered, up to 1 week in refrigerator.*

Reheat refrigerated sauce in a double boiler or a bowl set in a pan of hot water over low heat.

Makes about 3/4 cup sauce

Spirited Cold Chocolate Sauce

The flavor of the liqueur seems strong when this sauce is tasted plain but it beautifully complements White Chocolate Bavarian Squares, page 89, and other creamy desserts.
It is also good spooned over ice cream or pieces of plain cake.

---

8 oz. bittersweet chocolate, chopped

1/4 cup unsalted butter, cut in 8 pieces

1/4 cup water

1/2 cup creme de cacao

Melt chocolate with butter and water in a medium bowl over nearly simmering water. Stir until smooth. Remove from pan of water; cool 10 minutes. Gradually stir in liqueur. Serve immediately or refrigerate. *Sauce can be kept, covered, up to 1 week in refrigerator.*

Reheat refrigerated sauce in a double boiler or a bowl set in a pan of hot water over low heat. Cool sauce to room temperature. If sauce is removed from refrigerator and brought to room temperature without reheating, it will be too thick.

Makes 1-1/3 cups

Hot Caramel Fudge Sauce

This dark, shiny and very rich sauce is perfect with vanilla or coffee ice cream.
Photo opposite.

3/4 cup whipping cream

1 cup sugar

1/2 cup cool water

3 oz. semisweet chocolate, chopped

3 tablespoons lukewarm water

Scald cream in a medium saucepan over medium-high heat by heating until bubbles form around edge of pan. Remove from heat. Transfer to a 2-cup measure. Cover to keep warm.

Combine sugar and cool water in a heavy medium saucepan that does not have a black interior. Heat mixture over low heat until sugar dissolves, gently stirring occasionally. Increase heat to high and boil, without stirring, but occasionally brushing down any sugar crystals from side of pan with a brush dipped in water, until mixture begins to brown. Reduce heat to medium-low. Continue cooking, swirling pan gently, until mixture is a rich brown color and a trace of smoke begins to rise from pan. Do not let caramel get too dark or it will be bitter; if caramel is too light it will be too sweet. Immediately remove from heat.

Standing at a distance, pour in hot cream, about 2 tablespoons at a time, without stirring; caramel will bubble furiously. When caramel stops bubbling, return mixture to low heat and heat, stirring, 1 minute or until it is well-blended. Increase heat if mixture does not appear to be blending. Cool to room temperature or refrigerate. *Sauce can be kept, covered, up to 2 weeks in refrigerator.*

Melt chocolate in a small bowl over nearly simmering water. Stir until smooth. Remove from pan of water. Stir chocolate, then lukewarm water, into caramel sauce. Keep sauce warm above hot water until ready to serve.

Makes about 1-1/4 cups

Blackberry Sauce

A bright, fruity sauce to serve with Chocolate-Blackberry Loaf, page 110,
or with chocolate, berry or vanilla ice cream.

---

1 qt. fresh or frozen unsweetened
　　blackberries (about 1 lb.),
　　thawed if frozen

3/4 to 1 cup powdered sugar, sifted

3 to 4 tablespoons blackberry-
　　flavored brandy or kirsch

Process blackberries and 3/4 cup powdered sugar in a food processor or blender until very smooth. Push puree through a strainer into a bowl, pressing on pulp. Use a rubber spatula to scrape mixture from underside of strainer. Taste sauce and whisk in more powdered sugar, if needed. Stir in 3 tablespoons brandy or kirsch. Taste and add remaining 1 tablespoon brandy or kirsch if desired. Cover and refrigerate at least 1 hour. *Sauce can be kept, covered, 2 days in refrigerator.* Stir before serving.

Makes about 1-1/4 cups

Raspberry-Brandy Sauce

A lovely complement to Flourless Fudge Cake, page 12.

---

2 cups milk

7 large egg yolks

1/3 cup sugar

3 tablespoons clear raspberry
　　brandy

Bring milk to boil in a heavy medium saucepan. Remove from heat. Whisk egg yolks lightly in a large bowl. Add sugar; whisk until thick and smooth. Gradually whisk in hot milk. Return mixture to pan, whisking constantly. Cook over medium-low heat, stirring mixture and scraping bottom of pan constantly with a wooden spoon, until mixture thickens slightly and reaches 170F to 175F (75C to 80C) on an instant-read or candy thermometer, about 5 minutes. To check without a thermometer, see page 169. Do not overcook sauce or it will curdle.

Pour immediately into a bowl. Stir about 30 seconds to cool; let cool completely. Cover and refrigerate. *Sauce can be kept, covered, 2 days in refrigerator.* Stir in brandy a short time before serving.

Makes about 12 servings (about 2-1/3 cups)

Vanilla Bean Custard Sauce

Known also as *crème anglaise,* custard sauce is one of the most popular sauces for accompanying very rich chocolate desserts and unfrosted chocolate cakes of all types. Making it is one of the most important dessert techniques to master because the sauce is also the base for the finest ice creams and Bavarian creams.

1-1/2 cups milk

1 vanilla bean, split lengthwise

5 or 6 large egg yolks

1/4 cup sugar

Bring milk and vanilla bean to a boil in a heavy medium saucepan. Remove from heat. Cover and let stand 15 minutes. Reheat to a boil.

Whisk egg yolks lightly in a large bowl. Add sugar; whisk until smooth. Gradually whisk in hot milk. Return mixture to saucepan, whisking. Cook over medium-low heat, stirring mixture and scraping bottom of pan constantly with a wooden spoon, until mixture thickens slightly and reaches 170F to 175F (75C to 80C) on an instant-read or candy thermometer, about 5 minutes. Do not overcook sauce or it will curdle.

Immediately strain sauce into a bowl. Stir about 30 seconds to cool; cool completely. Refrigerate at least 30 minutes before serving. *Sauce can be kept, covered, up to 2 days in refrigerator.*

Makes 6 to 8 servings (about 1-3/4 cups)

Variations

Spirited Custard Sauce: Omit vanilla bean, if desired. In Step 1, bring milk to a boil and proceed to next step. Just before serving, stir in 2 tablespoons liqueur or liquor of choice, such as brandy, Cognac, apricot-flavored brandy, Grand Marnier or hazelnut liqueur.

Coffee Custard Sauce: Omit vanilla bean. Bring milk to a boil. Remove from heat. Whisk in 4 teaspoons instant coffee granules.

Crème de Cacao Sauce: Substitute 1-1/3 cups whipping cream for the milk. Omit vanilla bean. Increase sugar to 1/3 cup. Just before serving, stir in 1/4 cup white crème de cacao liqueur.

Tip

To check whether custard sauce is thick enough without a thermometer: Remove pan from heat. Dip a metal spoon in sauce and draw your finger across back of spoon. Your finger should leave a clear path in mixture that clings to spoon. If it does not, continue cooking another 30 seconds and check again.

Rum Syrup

A favorite in Europe for moistening light cakes, such as sponge cakes and genoise, before they are frosted.
The Cointreau variation is ideal with orange-flavored cakes,
and the raspberry brandy version complements a raspberry-garnished cake.

1/4 cup sugar

1/4 cup water

2 tablespoons rum

Heat sugar and water in a small heavy saucepan over low heat, stirring, until sugar dissolves. Increase heat to medium-high and, without stirring, bring to a boil. Pour into a bowl; cool completely. Stir in rum; cover.

Makes about 1/3 cup

Variations

Cointreau, Cognac, Creme de Cacao, or Bourbon Syrup: Substitute Cointreau, Cognac, white creme de cacao liqueur or bourbon for rum.

Raspberry Brandy Syrup: Substitute 2 or 3 tablespoons clear raspberry brandy for rum.

Quick Coffee Sauce

Serve this creamy, easy-to-make sauce with Moist Mocha Squares, page 3.

3/4 cup whipping cream, well-chilled

2 tablespoons sugar

1-1/2 teaspoons instant coffee powder or freeze-dried coffee granules

Make this sauce a short time before serving it. In a large chilled bowl, combine cream, sugar and coffee powder. Whip at medium-high speed until slightly thickened; cream should be sauce-like and not stiff enough to form peaks. Cover and refrigerate until ready to serve.

Makes 8 to 9 servings (about 1-1/2 cups)

Variation

Hazelnut Liqueur Sauce: Use 1/2 cup whipping cream, 1 teaspoon sugar and 2 tablespoons plus 1 teaspoon hazelnut liqueur (Frangelico).

Almond Praline

Praline, or caramelized toasted nuts, is delicious as a flavoring for soufflés, ice creams, and fillings such as Praline Chocolate Whipped Cream, page 54.

1/3 cup whole blanched almonds

1/4 cup sugar

3 tablespoons water

Preheat oven to 350F (175C). Toast almonds in a shallow baking pan about 8 minutes. Remove from oven; leave in baking pan to keep warm. Lightly oil a baking sheet.

Combine sugar and water in a heavy, very small saucepan that does not have a black interior. Heat mixture over low heat until sugar dissolves, gently stirring occasionally. Increase heat to high and boil, brushing down any sugar crystals from side of pan with a brush dipped in water, until mixture begins to brown. Reduce heat to medium low. Continue cooking, swirling pan gently, until mixture is a rich brown and a trace of smoke begins to rise from pan. Do not let caramel get too dark or it will burn and praline will be bitter; if caramel is too light, praline will be too sweet.

Immediately remove caramel from heat; stir in warm nuts, being careful not to splash, until they are well-coated with caramel. Stir over low heat 1-1/2 minutes. Immediately transfer to oiled baking sheet.

Cool completely. Break praline into small chunks. Grind praline in food processor, scraping mixture occasionally, until as fine as possible. Immediately transfer praline to an airtight container. *Praline can be kept several months in an airtight container at room temperature or in freezer.*

Makes about 2/3 cup

Variation

Hazelnut Praline: Use 1/3 cup hazelnuts, 3 tablespoons sugar and 2 tablespoons water. Toast hazelnuts in a 350F (175C) oven and remove skins, page 179. Leave in baking pan to keep warm. Continue as in recipe.

CHOCOLATE TECHNIQUES

Keeping Chocolate

Keep chocolate in a dry, airy place, not hot or humid, preferably at about 65 to 70F (20C). If the temperature of the room becomes hot, the chocolate may get white streaks but is still suitable for all dessert-making purposes except tempering. Dark chocolate keeps for years, but milk and white chocolates are best if used within a year. In very warm weather, keep white and milk chocolate pieces in the refrigerator.

Chopping Chocolate

Chopping chocolate by hand is quite easy. The chocolate can be chopped most evenly in this way. Always use a dry board and a heavy dry knife. If chopping a large piece of chocolate, it is easiest to begin chopping at a corner.

If you prefer to use a food processor, cut chocolate first in small chunks. On a hot day, chill the processor container and blade and the chocolate about 10 minutes. Chop chocolate with on/off turns just until it forms small pieces.

For some recipes, chocolate is ground in a food processor until very fine. Do not overprocess or the chocolate may begin to melt or stick together, especially on a hot day. If some large chunks remain, remove the remaining chocolate and grind the chunks alone.

Grating Chocolate

Use either the fine or the large holes of a grater. Hold the chocolate with waxed paper so it will not melt from the warmth of your hands. On a hot day, chill the chocolate and the grater 10 minutes before grating.

Melting Chocolate

Chocolate should be chopped so it will melt evenly. It can be melted in the top of a double boiler or in a heat-proof bowl. For delicate work, such as dipping candies, the container of chocolate should be set above a pan of hot water over low heat and the water should not touch the bottom of the container of chocolate; for other purposes, the container of chocolate can be set in the hot water over low heat.

Stir slightly when the chocolate begins to melt to evenly distribute the heat. Then stir occasionally as it melts. Stirring also gives a feel as to whether the chocolate is completely melted.

Chocolate can also be melted in a microwave. It should be chopped, put in a dry bowl and melted uncovered at medium power, until it is very shiny and soft but still keeps its shape. Remove and stir until smooth.

Depending on the recipe, the chocolate may be used immediately or may be cooled before being mixed with other ingredients. If letting it cool first, cool it until it no longer feels warm to the touch, but do not let it harden or it will not mix with other ingredients.

White and milk chocolate sometimes do not melt as smoothly as dark chocolate. Usually they will smooth out when stirred with a whisk.

Chocolate can be melted on its own or with liquid. If it is melted on its own, the bowl must be completely dry. If a very small amount of liquid is added, the chocolate can harden instead of melting smoothly; to correct, gradually add more liquid.

QUICK CHOCOLATE CURLS

1. Use a bar or large piece of dark or white chocolate at warm room temperature, not a small square. On a cold day, let chocolate soften slightly in a warm place in kitchen.

2. Using a swivel-type vegetable peeler, peel curls from smooth side of bar, pressing firmly. Let curls fall directly onto cake or onto waxed paper. Refrigerate until ready to use.

3. Do not touch curls; they will melt from warmth of your hands. If curls are on waxed paper, use a fork or wooden pick to carefully transfer them to dessert; or let them fall from waxed paper onto dessert. Some of chocolate will come off in thin straight pieces or "shaved chocolate," instead of curls. Use them also.

Shaved Chocolate

Prepare as above, but use short quick strokes of the vegetable peeler on a piece of cool chocolate.

Use this technique for making chocolate butterflies, simple flowers, hearts, fruits or any shape you like. Use it also for writing with chocolate. Writing in script is easier than in separate letters.

1. Choose a simple drawing. Trace the drawing from a book or magazine onto a piece of thin paper. If tracing butterflies, trace each half separately so it can be made in 2 pieces. Very simple flowers, hearts and chocolate writing can be done without a pattern.

2. Tape a sheet of waxed paper to a work surface in 2 places so it will be steady. If using a pattern, slide it under sheet of waxed paper.

3. Make 2 parchment paper piping cones, or have ready a small pastry bag with a very fine piping tip.

4. Melt 3 ounces fine quality bittersweet or semisweet chocolate (preferably "couverture") in a small bowl set above a saucepan of hot, not simmering, water over low heat, stirring often. Remove from heat. Pour about 1/2 of chocolate into another bowl and cool to 88F (30C) or slightly less than body temperature, leaving rest of chocolate above water. (If you have already tempered chocolate for dipping, use it.)

5. Spoon cooled chocolate into piping cone or bag and fold or twist top to close it.

6. Pipe melted chocolate onto waxed paper in words, in a free-form shape or following outline of drawing. If desired, pipe a few lines inside drawing to give some detail. Continue piping shapes until chocolate in piping cone becomes too firm to pipe.

7. Move waxed paper to a tray and refrigerate until chocolate sets. Cool remaining chocolate, spoon into second piping cone and make more decorations.

8. Remove decorations very carefully by peeling off parchment. Transfer to a tray, cover and keep in refrigerator or freezer. To use, set on a dessert. Handle as little as possible to avoid melting the decorations; the thin chocolate melts easily.

TEMPERING CHOCOLATE

An instant-read thermometer can be used but for very serious candymakers, there is a special thermometer available through cookware catalogs and specialty stores.

Professional Method

1. Melt chopped bittersweet or semisweet chocolate in a double boiler or medium bowl over hot, not simmering, water over low heat, stirring very often with a rubber spatula, until it reaches about 115F (45C). Stir until smooth. Remove from pan of water.

2. Dry base of container of chocolate. Pour about 1/2 the chocolate onto a marble slab. Spread it and scrape it back and forth with a scraper or metal spatula until it begins to set and is about 80F (25C).

3. Scrape chocolate from marble and return it immediately to remaining chocolate. Mix thoroughly. Set above hot water and heat it, stirring constantly, until it reaches 88F (30C).

Short Method

1. Melt chopped bittersweet or semisweet chocolate in a double boiler or heatproof medium bowl over hot, not simmering, water over low heat, stirring very often with a rubber spatula. Stir until smooth. Remove from pan of water.

2. Transfer container of chocolate to a bowl of cold, not iced, water and cool chocolate, stirring often, until it reaches 80F (25C) on an instant-read thermometer.

3. Set container of chocolate above hot, not simmering, water and heat, stirring very often, until it reaches 88F (30C).

Tempering Milk Chocolate or White Chocolate

In either tempering method, after cooling chocolate, reheat it to 84F (29C).

Tempering is a special procedure for melting and cooling chocolate. It basically involves melting chocolate, letting it cool completely and then heating it very slightly until it reaches the ideal temperature for dipping.

Tempered chocolate gives a crisper, shinier shell to truffles and other dipped candies, helps the chocolate set faster and helps prevent streaks. It is also the best procedure for preparing chocolate leaves, scrolls and other decorations.

Professional chocolatiers always have tempered chocolate ready. It is prepared and kept at the proper temperature by special machines. For home cooking, tempering helps give shiny decorations and truffle coatings but is not absolutely necessary.

Several methods are used to temper chocolate. Following are a short method and the longer professional method.

For either method, work in a cool room. Use the finest quality fresh "couverture" chocolate. Do not use chocolate that you have already melted for previous dipping or chocolate that is old, streaked or unevenly colored.

Chocolate Cutouts

1. Melt 2 or 3 ounces fine quality bittersweet or semi-sweet chocolate in a small bowl set above a saucepan of hot, not simmering, water over low heat, stirring often. Remove from water and cool to 88F (30C) or slightly less than body temperature. Cool to 84F (29C) if using white chocolate. (Previously tempered chocolate can be used.)

2. Set a sheet of waxed paper on a tray. Pour chocolate onto waxed paper and spread it to a fairly thin layer (about 1/8 inch thick). Refrigerate briefly until chocolate begins to set but is not firm.

3. Cut shapes in chocolate but leave in place (see suggestions below). Refrigerate again until set. Do not refrigerate for too long because cutouts may become brittle. Carefully peel paper from cutouts. If not using immediately, transfer carefully to a plate, cover with plastic wrap and keep in freezer. Any chocolate scraps can be remelted and used in desserts.

Substituting Regular Chocolate for "Couverture"

When "couverture" chocolate is not available, use this recipe with ordinary chocolate. The addition of oil, cocoa butter or shortening makes the chocolate more fluid and easier to use for dipping.

6 oz. semisweet or bittersweet chocolate, chopped

1 tablespoon vegetable oil, cocoa butter or vegetable shortening

Combine chocolate with oil in a double boiler or medium bowl set above a saucepan of hot, not simmering, water over low heat. Leave until melted, stirring often. Remove from water.

Circles/Crescents

Use a small round 2-1/2-inch cutter. To make crescents: After cutting a circle, use edge of same cutter to cut a crescent from about 1/4 of the circle.

Rings

After cutting a circle, cut a smaller circle inside it, using a 3/4-inch cutter or the wide end of a piping tip. When set, carefully peel off paper. Both a ring and circle can be be used for garnish.

Ovals

After cutting a circle, use edge of same cutter to cut about 1/2 of the circle to form a leaf shape or pointed oval.

CHOCOLATE SCROLLS OR CIGARETTES

CHOCOLATE WRAPPING

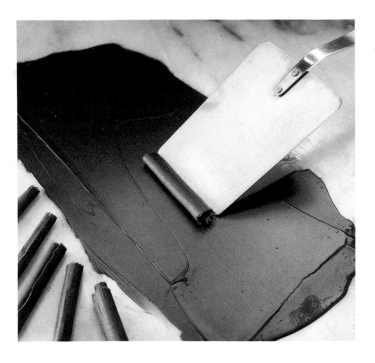

1. Melt and cool 2 or 3 ounces fine quality bittersweet or semisweet chocolate (preferably "couverture") as directed in Chocolate Cutouts, Step 1, page 175. If using white chocolate, cool to 84F (29C).

2. Pour chocolate onto a cool marble slab or the clean underside of a baking sheet. Using a long metal spatula, spread chocolate in as thin a layer as possible without leaving any holes. If chocolate is too thick, it will not roll. Holding spatula flat, move it back and forth lightly over chocolate to cool it.

3. When chocolate changes color and is nearly set, begin making scrolls: Holding a knife, a metal pastry scraper or a sharp pancake turner at approximately a 45 degree angle, with blade resting on chocolate, draw it across chocolate sideways, pushing gently on chocolate to form long scrolls.

4. Using a fork or wooden picks, transfer chocolate scrolls delicately to a plate.

A band of chocolate wrapped around a cake makes a beautiful presentation. The cake should first be frosted with buttercream so the chocolate wrapping will stick to the frosting. For an 8-inch 2-layer cake, use 4 ounces fine-quality bittersweet chocolate.

1. Cut a 28" x 6" piece of waxed paper; fold in half lengthwise. Set it on a tray. Melt chocolate in a medium bowl over nearly simmering water. Stir until smooth. Remove from pan of water; cool slightly. Spread a very even layer of chocolate on waxed paper, covering paper entirely except for 1 inch on each short end. Do not leave any holes.

2. Let stand until chocolate is slightly firm, about 10 minutes. On a hot day, refrigerate briefly. Do not let chocolate set or it will be brittle.

3. Leaving waxed paper attached, wrap chocolate band around cake so chocolate adheres to frosting. Chocolate band should meet at both ends but not overlap. It should be a bit higher than top of cake. Refrigerate until chocolate sets. Carefully peel off waxed paper from chocolate.

CHOCOLATE LEAVES

Use stiff, non-poisonous leaves such as rose leaves, lemon leaves and gardenia leaves. Choose leaves with well-defined veins.

1. Wash leaves and thoroughly pat dry with paper towels. Line a tray with waxed paper or foil.

2. Melt and cool 4 ounces fine quality bittersweet or semisweet chocolate (preferably "couverture") as directed in Chocolate Cutouts, Step 1, page 175. If using white chocolate or milk chocolate, cool to about 84F (29C).

3. Spread chocolate on underside of leaf, using a small spatula or knife, so it is about 1/8 inch thick; do not spread it too thin or chocolate leaf will break. Leave a little of leaf next to stem uncoated so it will be easy to remove chocolate. Wipe off any drips of chocolate from other side of leaf.

4. Set leaves on lined tray and refrigerate about 10 minutes or until chocolate is just set.

5. Gently peel off leaf from chocolate. If not using immediately, gently transfer leaves to a container, cover and keep in refrigerator or freezer. Makes about 20 leaves.

Chocolate Mint Leaves

These are unlike other chocolate leaves because here the leaf is eaten with its coating. The mint has a refreshing flavor that complements the rich chocolate. Use these leaves to decorate chocolate-mint desserts, such as Chocolate-Mint Ice Cream, page 99.

1. Melt and cool 4 ounces fine quality bittersweet or semisweet chocolate (preferably "couverture") as directed in Chocolate Cutouts, Step 1, page 175.

2. Rinse about 20 large very fresh mint leaves and thoroughly pat dry with paper towels. Line a tray with waxed paper or foil.

3. Dip leaf entirely in bowl of chocolate so that both sides of leaf are coated. Let excess chocolate drip into bowl. Set on lined tray. Refrigerate until set. There is nothing to peel off; you eat the mint leaf with the chocolate. These keep in refrigerator up to 2 days.

Half-Dipped Chocolate Mint Leaves

Dip 1/2 of each mint leaf, either lengthwise or crosswise, in chocolate and set on a tray. Refrigerate until set. Cover if not using immediately. These keep 1 day.

USING EGG WHITES

Eggs can be separated most easily when they are cold but egg whites whip up best at room temperature.

Egg whites freeze very well. They can be defrosted and measured and substituted for fresh egg whites.

Although whites of large eggs vary somewhat in size, following are convenient measures to use. Measures are "generous"; measure them slightly above the line on the measuring cup.

2 egg whites = generous 1/4 cup
4 egg whites = generous 1/2 cup
6 egg whites = generous 3/4 cup
8 egg whites = generous 1 cup.

Whipping Egg Whites

Begin beating whites at low or medium speed of mixer. When they become very foamy and begin to turn white, gradually increase speed. Finish whipping them at high speed. If adding sugar, add it gradually while beating at high speed.

After the sugar is added, it usually takes only about 15 to 30 seconds of beating until the whites are shiny. Do not overbeat egg whites; those with a large amount of sugar become watery and lose their stiffness, while those with little sugar become dry and lumpy.

FOLDING INGREDIENTS INTO MIXTURES

Proper folding of whipped cream, egg whites or flour into batters and other mixtures helps ensure their lightness. A flexible rubber spatula is a good tool to use for folding because it unsticks the mixture from the edge of the bowl. Always fold lightly but quickly.

To fold quickly and efficiently, fold clockwise while turning the bowl counterclockwise: With your right hand, pull the spatula down through the center of the mixture to the bottom of the bowl. Move the spatula under the mixture towards the left side of the bowl, scraping the bottom and side of the bowl. At the same time, with your left hand, turn the bowl counterclockwise. Repeat the motion several times, just until the ingredients are blended. Reverse the directions if you are left-handed.

USING NUTS

The fresher the nuts, the better the desserts will taste. Do not keep nuts for too long. Walnuts turn rancid easily and are best kept in the refrigerator or freezer.

Chopping Nuts

To chop nuts coarsely, it is better to use a knife than a food processor because the pieces will be more even in size.

Grinding Nuts

When sugar is ground with the nuts in a food processor, the sugar helps prevent their oil from coming out so the ground nuts are light and not pasty.

Grind nuts using an on/off motion of the food processor. Be careful not to grind them for too long because they will start to cake and lose their light texture. If using a large quantity of nuts, it is best to grind them in batches. Scrape them inward toward the blade occasionally to further ensure even grinding.

To grind nuts without a food processor, use a hand rotary grater or an electric nut grinder and add the nuts in batches. In this case, do not add sugar to the nuts during grinding; instead, stir it into the ground nuts.

Blanching Almonds

Bring to a boil enough water to generously cover almonds. Add almonds and return to a boil. Boil about 10 seconds.

Remove 1 almond with a slotted spoon. Press on 1 end of almond with your thumb and index finger; almond will come out of its skin. If it does not, boil them a few more seconds and try again. When almonds can be peeled easily, drain them and peel the rest.

Spread blanched almonds in a layer on shallow trays or dishes lined with paper towels; put paper towels on top of almonds as well. Pat almonds dry. They should be thoroughly dried before they are ground.

Desalting Macadamia Nuts

Unsalted macadamia nuts are available in health food stores, specialty shops and some supermarkets. Salted nuts give an equally good result, however, and require only a brief extra step.

Preheat oven to 250F (120C). Put nuts in a large strainer and rinse them with warm water for about 10 seconds, tossing them often. Drain them for 5 minutes in strainer, tossing them occasionally.

Transfer them to a baking sheet. Dry them in oven 5 minutes, stirring occasionally. Transfer them to a plate and cool them completely.

Toasting Hazelnuts

Preheat oven to 350F (175C). Toast hazelnuts in a shallow baking pan in oven about 8 minutes or until skins begin to split. Transfer to a strainer. Rub hot nuts against strainer with a terrycloth towel to remove most of skins. Cool nuts completely.

Toasting Brazil Nuts

Preheat oven to 350F (175C). Toast nuts in a shallow baking pan in oven 10 minutes. Transfer half of nuts to a large strainer. Turn off oven; leave in remaining nuts. Rub nuts against strainer with a terrycloth towel to remove most of skins. Lift nuts from strainer and transfer to a large bowl. Tap strainer on surface to remove skins. Repeat with remaining nuts. Cool completely.

Toasting Walnuts or Slivered Almonds

Preheat oven to 350F (175C). Toast walnuts or almonds in a shallow baking pan in oven, stirring often, about 5 minutes or until very lightly browned. Transfer to a plate; cool completely.

USEFUL EQUIPMENT

A scale: A scale is important for weighing chocolate, especially if you buy it in large blocks.

Thermometers: An instant-read thermometer or special chocolate thermometer is useful for measuring relatively low temperatures, such as those used in melting and cooling chocolate, cooking custards and heating egg yolk mixtures by the "sabayon method." A candy thermometer is needed for measuring higher temperatures, such as those used in cooking sugar syrup, but can be used for any temperature above 100F (40C). When checking the temperature of a small amount of mixture, tilt the mixture so the thermometer tip is well immersed in it, ideally by 2 inches, but does not touch the bottom of the bowl or pan.

Pastry bag and tips: The most useful are a 1/2-inch plain tip and small, medium and large star tips.

Pastry brushes: Pastry brushes are useful for moistening cakes with liqueur or syrup and for brushing pastries and cakes with glaze.

Mixer: It is best to use a heavy-duty mixer, preferably one with three types of beaters: a flat beater, a whip and a dough hook. The countertop mixer is especially convenient for those recipes requiring lengthy beating or whipping. Use the flat beater for creaming and the whip for beating egg whites or cream. If your mixer has only one type of beater, use it for both purposes. For preparing yeast doughs in a mixer, a dough hook is needed.

Food Processor: A relatively large powerful one is best. It is useful not only for chopping and pureeing, but also for making a variety of doughs.

MAIL-ORDER SOURCES

Brands of Fine Chocolate

* *Callebaut (Belgian)
* *Droste (Dutch)
* Feodora (German)
* *Lindt (Swiss)
* Tobler (Swiss)
* *Valrhona (French)
* Ghirardelli (American)
* Guittard (American)
* Nestle "Peter" (American)
* Van Leer American Chocolate (American)
* World's Finest (American)

* *available as couverture*

Fine Chocolate & Special Equipment

Here are the addresses of some companies which specialize in fine chocolate and/or special equipment for working with chocolate. Write or telephone to inquire about specific products.

Williams-Sonoma
Mail-Order Department
P.O. Box 7456
San Francisco, CA 94120
(800) 541-2233 or (415) 421-4242

Maid of Scandinavia
3244 Raleigh Avenue
Minneapolis, MN 55416
(800) 328-6722 or (612) 927-7966

S. E. Rykoff & Company
P.O. Box 21467
Los Angeles, CA 90021
(800) 421-9873 or (213) 624-6094

Paprikas Weiss Importers
1572 Second Avenue
New York, NY 10028
212-288-6117

The Chef's Catalogue
3215 Commercial Avenue
Northbrook, IL 60062
(800) 338-3232 or (312) 480-9400

Comparison to Metric Measure

When You Know	Symbol	Multiply By	To Find	Symbol
teaspoons	tsp	5.0	milliliters	ml
tablespoons	tbsp	15.0	milliliters	ml
fluid ounces	fl. oz.	30.0	milliliters	ml
cups	c	0.24	liters	l
pints	pt.	0.47	liters	l
quarts	qt.	0.95	liters	l
ounces	oz.	28.0	grams	g
pounds	lb.	0.45	kilograms	kg
Fahrenheit	F	5/9 (after subtracting 32)	Celsius	C

Fahrenheit to Celsius

F	C
200–205	95
220–225	105
245–250	120
275	135
300–305	150
325–330	165
345–350	175
370–375	190
400–405	205
425–430	220
445–450	230
470–475	245
500	260

Liquid Measure to Milliliters

1/4 teaspoon	=	1.25 milliliters
1/2 teaspoon	=	2.5 milliliters
3/4 teaspoon	=	3.75 milliliters
1 teaspoon	=	5.0 milliliters
1-1/4 teaspoons	=	6.25 milliliters
1-1/2 teaspoons	=	7.5 milliliters
1-3/4 teaspoons	=	8.75 milliliters
2 teaspoons	=	10.0 milliliters
1 tablespoon	=	15.0 milliliters
2 tablespoons	=	30.0 milliliters

Liquid Measure to Liters

1/4 cup	=	0.06 liters
1/2 cup	=	0.12 liters
3/4 cup	=	0.18 liters
1 cup	=	0.24 liters
1-1/4 cups	=	0.3 liters
1-1/2 cups	=	0.36 liters
2 cups	=	0.48 liters
2-1/2 cups	=	0.6 liters
3 cups	=	0.72 liters
3-1/2 cups	=	0.84 liters
4 cups	=	0.96 liters
4-1/2 cups	=	1.08 liters
5 cups	=	1.2 liters
5-1/2 cups	=	1.32 liters

Index

A

Almond & Cream Topping 43
Almond Cake, Light 131
Almond Cookies, Cocoa- 120
Almond Fudge Tart, Chocolate- 43
Almond Pastry Shell 43
Almond Praline 171
Almond Sandwiches, Chocolate- 120
Almond-Cinnamon Dough with Chocolate Chips 130
Almond-Ginger Cake, Chocolate- 32
Almond-Truffle Petits Fours 131
Almonds, Chocolate-Dipped 151
American Chocolate Ice Cream 98
Angel Food Cake, Chocolate 25
Angelina's Hot Chocolate 155
Apricot Glaze 95
Apricot Terrine, Chocolate 86

Baked Alaska, Chocolate 111
Baked Mocha Custards 67
Baked White & Cocoa Meringues 113
Banana Crepes, Chocolate- 73
Bars, Golden Pine Nut-Chocolate Chip 125
Bavarian Cream 88
Bavarian Cream, Bourbon 91
Bavarian Cream, Chocolate 45, 95
Bavarian Cream, Chocolate-Flecked 90
Bavarian Cream, Chocolate-Rum 88
Bavarian Cream, Truffled 90
Bavarian Pie, Chocolate 45
Bavarian Squares, White Chocolate 89
Berries & Cream 106
Berries & Cream, Chocolate Swiss Roll with 37
Berries, Chocolate & Cream Tart 41
Berries, Frozen Chocolate Mousse Ring with Fresh 106
Berry & Chocolate Cream Filling 41
Berry & Cream Filling 37

Biarritz Pistachio-Chocolate Cake 23
Bittersweet Belgian Truffles 141
Bittersweet Brownies 122
Bittersweet Brownies, Ganache-Frosted 122
Bittersweet Chocolate Cake 34
Bittersweet Chocolate Sponge Cake 29
Bittersweet Chocolate-Chestnut Soufflé 65
Bittersweet Ganache Centers 141
Black Forest Cherry Torte 31
Black Forest Trifle 72
Blackberry Loaf, Chocolate 110
Blackberry Mousse, Chocolate- 110
Blackberry Sauce 168
Bombe, Chocolate-Strawberry 108
Bombe, Rum-Raisin-Chocolate 104
Bourbon Balls, Chocolate-Walnut 153
Bourbon Bavarian Cream 91
Bourbon Sauce 164
Bourbon Soufflé, Dark Chocolate 62
Brandied Brownies 123
Brandied Chocolate-Pecan Brownies 123
Brandy Butter Frosting 123
Brandy Sauce, Flourless Fudge Cake with Raspberry- 12
Brandy Sauce, Raspberry- 168
Brazil Nut Brownies, Fudgy 124
Brazil Nut Cake, Chocolate- 9
Brazil Nuts, Chocolate Crepe Gâteau with 75
Bread Pudding, Chocolate 71
Brioche Dough, Easy 55
Brown-Bottom Charlotte 91
Brownie Ice Cream Cake 116
Brownies
   Bittersweet Brownies 122
   Brandied Brownies 123
   Fudgy Brazil Nut Brownies 124
   Ganache-Frosted Bittersweet Brownies 122
   Hazelnut Fudge Brownies 124
   Thin Fudge Brownies 116

Butter Cake, Chocolate-Wine 11
Butter Frosting, Brandy 123
Butter Sponge Cake, Chocolate 5
Buttercream, Chocolate Meringue 161
Buttercream, Classic 160

C

Café au Lait Truffles 145
Cappuccino-Chocolate Ice Cream 100
Caramel Fudge Sauce, Hot 166
Caramel-Chocolate Swirl Ice Cream 101
Caramel-Fudge Sauce, Individual Chocolate Parfaits with 109
Cashew Cake, Chocolate 28
Cashew Custard Pie, Chocolate- 44
Cashew-Maple Cake, Chocolate- 28
Chantilly Cream 162
Checkerboard Cake 21
Cheesecake, White Chocolate 16
Chef Chambrette's Chocolate Macaroon Cake 17
Cherries, Poached 31
Cherry Torte, Black Forest 31
Chestnut Log, Chocolate 96
Chestnut Soufflé, Bittersweet Chocolate- 65
Chiffon Cake, Chocolate-Coconut 7
Chiffon Pie, Chocolate-Marbled 48
Chocolate & Cream Tart, Berries 41
Chocolate & Hazelnut Cake Layers 32
Chocolate & Macadamia Liqueur Whipped Cream 163
Chocolate & Vanilla Buttercreams, Pistachio 23
Chocolate & Vanilla Cream Fillings 30
Chocolate Angel Food Cake 25
Chocolate Baked Alaska 111
Chocolate Bavarian Cream 45, 95
Chocolate Bavarian Pie 45
Chocolate Bombe Mousse 104
Chocolate Bread Pudding 71
Chocolate Butter Sponge Cake 6
Chocolate Cake à l'Orientale 2

Chocolate Charlotte with Raspberries 92
Chocolate Crème Brûlèe with Raspberries 68
Chocolate Crepe Gâteau with Brazil Nuts 75
Chocolate Crown 5
Chocolate Cups 148
Chocolate Cutouts 175
Chocolate Dacquoise 36
Chocolate Designs & Writing 173
Chocolate Dream 20
Chocolate Egg Nog 156
Chocolate Gâteau Paris Brest 54
Chocolate Glaze 160
Chocolate Ladyfingers 136
Chocolate Leaves 177
Chocolate Macaroons 135
Chocolate Marzipan Filo Triangles 57
Chocolate Meringue Buttercream 161
Chocolate Meringue Fingers 129
Chocolate Mint Leaves 177
Chocolate Mousse 83, 87, 106
Chocolate Mousse Supreme 79
Chocolate Mousse with Grand Marnier 81
Chocolate Mousseline Filling 51
Chocolate Napoleon 51
Chocolate Pecan Sundae Pie 112
Chocolate Sauce 75, 112
Chocolate Scrolls or Cigarettes 176
Chocolate Sponge Cake 37
Chocolate Swiss Roll with Berries & Cream 37
Chocolate Symphony 36
Chocolate Techniques 172-177
Chocolate Truffle Frosting 158
Chocolate Velvet Frosting 159
Chocolate Whipped Cream 164
Chocolate Whipped Cream, Praline 54
Chocolate Wrapping 176
Chocolate Yule Log 24
Chocolate-Almond Filling 43
Chocolate-Almond Fudge Tart 43

Chocolate-Almond Sandwiches 120
Chocolate-Almond-Ginger Cake 2
Chocolate-Apricot Terrine 86
Chocolate-Banana Crepes 73
Chocolate-Banana Filling 73
Chocolate-Blackberry Loaf 110
Chocolate-Blackberry Mousse 110
Chocolate-Brazil Nut Cake 9
Chocolate-Cashew Cake 28
Chocolate-Cashew Custard Pie 44
Chocolate-Cashew-Maple Cake 28
Chocolate-Cinnamon Frosting 33
Chocolate-Cinnamon Raisin Rolls 55
Chocolate-Cinnamon Squares 130
Chocolate-Coated Coconut Kisses 132
Chocolate-Coconut Chiffon Cake 7
Chocolate-Coffee Centers 145
Chocolate-Cognac Marquise 94
Chocolate-Dipped Almonds 151
Chocolate-Dipped Orange
    Sections 151
Chocolate-Flecked Bavarian Cream 90
Chocolate-Hazelnut Cake with Fudge
    Frosting 14
Chocolate-Honey Frosting 158
Chocolate-Macadamia Nut
    Pudding 70
Chocolate-Macadamia Pudding 70
Chocolate-Macadamia Triangles 152
Chocolate-Marbled Chiffon Pie 48
Chocolate-Marzipan Cookies 127
Chocolate-Marzipan Rosettes 127
Chocolate-Mint Cream Puffs 49
Chocolate-Mint Ice Cream 99
Chocolate-Orange Boule de Neige 69
Chocolate-Orange Centers 142
Chocolate-Orange Custard 69
Chocolate-Orange Mousseline
    Filling 50
Chocolate-Pear Pizza 56
Chocolate-Pear Topping 56
Chocolate-Pecan Gâteau 4
Chocolate-Pecan Sundae Pie 112
Chocolate-Pecan Torte 33
Chocolate-Pistachio Genoise 23
Chocolate-Raspberry Coupe 102
Chocolate-Raspberry Filling 126
Chocolate-Rum Bavarian Cream 88
Chocolate-Strawberry Bombe 108
Chocolate-Studded Kugelhopf 8
Chocolate-Wafer Crust 45
Chocolate-Walnut Bars 126
Chocolate-Walnut Bourbon Balls 153
Chocolate-Walnut Crust 48
Chocolate-Wine Cake 10
Chopping chocolate 172
Choux Pastry 60
Cinnamon Dough with Chocolate
    Chips, Almond- 130
Cinnamon Frosting Chocolate- 33
Cinnamon Pastry Cream 55
Cinnamon Raisin Rolls, Chocolate- 55
Cinnamon Squares, Chocolate 130
Cinnamon Topping, Light
    Chocolate- 130
Classic Buttercream 160
Classic Chocolate Gâteau 27
Coating, White Chocolate 143
Cocoa Cake, Light 111
Cocoa Cake, Pecan- 33
Cocoa Crumb Crust, Pecan- 16
Cocoa Cupcakes 134
Cocoa Genoise 27
Cocoa Meringues, Baked
    White & 113
Cocoa Sponge Cake, Rich 31
Cocoa, Spiced Mexican Hot 155
Cocoa-Almond Cookies 120
Cocoa-Pecan Crust 112

Coconut Chiffon Cake, Chocolate- 6
Coconut Kisses, Chocolate-
    Coated 132
Coconut-Coated Chocolate Balls 153
Coffee Centers, Chocolate- 145
Coffee Sauce, Quick 170
Coffee-Chocolate Sauce 103
Coffee-Flavored Ganache 131
Coffeecake, Marbled Chocolate 7
Cognac Marquise, Chocolate- 94
Cognac Truffles, Quick 146
Cold Chocolate-Raspberry Soufflé 87
Cooked Chocolate Custard 72
Cooked Meringue 113
Cookie Dough, Walnut 126
**Cookies, Brownies & Petits Fours
117-137**
Cream Puffs, Chocolate-Mint 49
Cream Puffs, Sultan's 50
Cream Tart, Berries, Chocolate & 41
Cream Topping, Almond & 43
Cream, Berries & 106
Cream, Chantilly 162
Cream, Chocolate Bavarian 45
Cream, Cinnamon Pastry 55
Cream, Macadamia 70
Cream, Mint Pastry 49
Cream, Parisian 32
Cream, White Chocolate Pastry 47
Creamy Chocolate Mousse with
    Grand Marnier 81
Crème Brûlée with Raspberries,
    Chocolate 68
Crepe Gâteau 75
Crepes 77
Crepes Belle Hélène 76
Crepes, Chocolate-Banana 73
Crisp Chocolate Chip-Macadamia Nut
    Cookies 121
Crumb Crust, Pecan-Cocoa 16
Crumble Topping, Nutty 126
Crust, Chocolate-Wafer 45
Crust, Chocolate-Walnut 48
Crust, Cocoa-Pecan 112
Crust, Pecan-Cocoa Crumb 16
Cupcakes, Cocoa 134
Cupcakes, Devil's Food 134
Cups, Meringue 82
Custard Pie, Chocolate-Cashew 44
Custard Sauce, Vanilla Bean 169
Custard, Chocolate-Orange 69
Custard, Cooked Chocolate 72
Custard, Rich Chocolate 68
Custards, Baked Mocha 67
Custards, Gingered Chocolate 66

D
Dacquoise, Chocolate 36
Dark Chocolate Mousse 82
Dark Chocolate Mousse in Meringue
    Cups 82
Dark Chocolate Sauce 165
Dark Chocolate-Bourbon Soufflé 62
Devil's Food Cupcakes 134
Double Chocolate Cream Filling 38
Double-Chocolate Pecan Pie 42
Double-Dipped Strawberries 150
Dried Fruit Chocolate Medallions 149

E
Easy Brioche Dough 55
Egg Nog, Chocolate 156
Extra-Creamy Truffles 142

F
Filled Chocolates, Molded
    Gianduja 147
Fillings
    Berry & Chocolate Cream
        Filling 41

Berry &Cream Filling 37
Chocolate & Vanilla Cream
    Fillings 30
Chocolate-Almond Filling 43
Chocolate-Banana Filling 73
Chocolate Mousseline Filling 51
Chocolate-Orange Mousseline
    Filling 50
Chocolate-Raspberry Filling 126
Double Chocolate Cream
    Filling 38
Ice Cream Filling 113, 116
Pear Filling 76
White Chocolate-Cheese Filling 17
White & Dark Chocolate Chiffon
    Filling 48
Filo Triangles, Chocolate Marzipan 57
Florentines 136
Flourless Fudge Cake with Raspberry-
    Brandy Sauce 12
Folding Ingredients Into
    Mixtures 178
French-Italian Chocolate Ice
    Cream 98
Frosting, Sauces & Basics 157-179
Frostings
    Brandy Butter Frosting 123
    Chocolate-Cinnamon Frosting 33
    Chocolate-Honey Frosting 158
    Chocolate Meringue Butter-
        cream 161
    Chocolate Truffle Frosting 158
    Chocolate Velvet Frosting 159
    Classic Buttercream 160
    Fudge Frosting 159
    Maple Frosting 162
    Pistachio, Chocolate & Vanilla
        Buttercreams 23
    Rich Chocolate Frosting 134
Frozen Chocolate Mousse Ring with
    Fresh Berries 106
Frozen Chocolate Soufflé 105
Frozen Chocolate Soufflé with
    Candied Ginger 105
Fruit & Topping 68
Fruit Chocolate Medallions,
    Dried 149
Fruit Layers, Ladyfinger & 72
Fudge Brownies, Hazelnut 124
Fudge Brownies, Thin 116
Fudge Cake with Raspberry-Brandy
    Sauce, Flourless 15
Fudge Frosting 159
Fudge Frosting, Chocolate-Hazelnut
    Cake with 13
Fudge Sauce, Hot Caramel 166
Fudge Sauce, Individual Chocolate
    Parfaits with Caramel- 109
Fudge Tart, Chocolate-Almond 43
Fudgy Brazil Nut Brownies 124

G
Ganache 36
Ganache Centers 140
Ganache Centers, Bittersweet 141
Ganache Centers, White 143
Ganache, Coffee-Flavored 131
Ganache, Semisweet 122
Ganache, White Chocolate 120
Ganache-Frosted Bittersweet
    Brownies 122
Genoise, Chocolate Rich 20
Genoise, Chocolate-Pistachio 23
Genoise, Cocoa 27
Ginger Cake, Chocolate-Almond 3
Ginger, Frozen Chocolate Soufflé with
    Candied 105
Gingered Chocolate Custards 66
Glazes

Apricot Glaze 95
Chocolate Glaze 6, 20, 160
Cocoa-Wine Glaze 11
Powdered Sugar 51
Quick Glaze 127
Shiny Chocolate Glaze 30
Sweet Chocolate Glaze 34
Golden Pine Nut-Chocolate Chip
    Bars 125
Grand Marnier Chocolate Cups 148
Grand Marnier Soufflés in Orange
    Cups, Individual Chocolate- 63
Grand Marnier Whipped Cream 69
Grand Marnier, Creamy Chocolate
    Mousse with 81
Grating chocolate 172

H
Hawaiian Chocolate-Flecked
    Macadamia Nut Cake 1
Hazelnut Cake 26
Hazelnut Cake Layers,
    Chocolate & 32
Hazelnut Cake with Fudge Frosting,
    Chocolate- 14
Hazelnut Cream, Profiteroles with 53
Hazelnut Fudge Brownies 124
Hazelnut Praline-Chocolate Soufflé 64
Hazelnut Whipped Cream 53
Hazelnut-Truffle Cake 26
Honey Frosting, Chocolate- 158
Hot Caramel Fudge Sauce 166
Hot Chocolate, Angelina's 155

I
Ice Cream Cake, Brownie 116
Ice Cream Filling 113, 116
**Ice Creams, Frozen Desserts & Ice
    Cream Cakes 97-116**
American Chocolate Ice Cream 98
Cappuccino-Chocolate Ice
    Cream 100
Caramel-Chocolate Swirl Ice
    Cream 101
Chocolate-Mint Ice Cream 99
French-Italian Chocolate Ice
    Cream 98
Italian Chocolate Chip Ice
    Cream 99
Individual Chocolate Parfaits with
    Caramel-Fudge Sauce 109
Individual Chocolate-Grand Marnier
    Soufflés in Orange Cups 63
Introduction viii-ix
Italian Chocolate Chip Ice Cream 99

K
Kahlua Whipped Cream 67
Keeping chocolate 172
Kirsch Syrup 23
Kirsch Whipped Cream 163
Kugelhopf, Chocolate-Studded 8

L
Ladyfinger & Fruit Layers 72
Ladyfingers, Chocolate 136
**Layer Cakes, Tortes & Mousse
    Cakes 19-39**
Light Almond Cake 131
**Light Cakes, Butter Cakes & Fudge
    Cakes x**
Light Chocolate-Cinnamon
    Topping 130
Light Cocoa Cake 111

M
Macadamia Cream 70
Macadamia Liqueur Whipped Cream,
    Chocolate & 163
Macadamia Nut Cake, Hawaiian
    Chocolate-Flecked 1

Macadamia Nut Cookies, Crisp
    Chocolate Chip 121
Macadamia Nut Pudding,
    Chocolate- 70
Macadamia Pudding, Chocolate- 70
Macadamia Triangles, Chocolate 152
Macaroon Cake, Chef Chambrette's
    Chocolate 17
Macaroons, Chocolate 135
Mail-Order Sources 179
Maple Cake, Chocolate-Cashew- 28
Maple Frosting 162
Marbled Chiffon Pie, Chocolate- 48
Marbled Chocolate Coffeecake 7
Marzipan Cookies, Chocolate- 127
Marzipan Filo Triangles, Chocolate 57
Marzipan Rosettes, Chocolate 127
Melting chocolate 172
Meringata 103
Meringue Buttercream, Chocolate 161
Meringue Cups 82
Meringue Cups, Dark Chocolate
    Mousse in 82
Meringue Fingers, Chocolate 129
Meringue Kisses 103
Meringue Mushrooms 128
Meringue Topping 111
Meringue, Cooked 113
Meringues, Baked White &
    Cocoa 113
Mint Cream Puffs, Chocolate- 49
Mint Ice Cream, Chocolate 99
Mint Pastry Cream 49
Mocha Custards, Baked 67
Mocha Petits Pots de Crème 67
Moist Chocolate Cake 39
Moist Mocha Squares 3
Molded Chocolate Mousse 83
Molded Gianduja Filled
    Chocolates 142
Mousse Cake with Dark Chocolate
    Chips, White Chocolate 39
Mousse in Meringue Cups, Dark
    Chocolate 82
Mousse Parfait, Triple-Chocolate 85
Mousse Supreme, Chocolate 79
Mousse with Grand Marnier, Creamy
    Chocolate 81
Mousse with Strawberry Sauce, White
    Chocolate 80
Mousse, Chocolate 83, 87, 106
Mousse, Chocolate Bombe 104
Mousse, Chocolate-Blackberry 110
Mousse, Dark Chocolate 82, 83
Mousse, Raspberry 87
Mousse, White Chocolate 39, 80
**Mousses, Bavarian Creams &
    Charlottes 78-96**
Mushrooms, Meringue 128

N
Napoleon, Chocolate 51
Nut Torte, Viennese Chocolate- 32
Nuts, Using 178
Nutty Crumble Topping 126

O
Orange Boule de Neige,
    Chocolate- 69
Orange Centers, Chocolate- 142
Orange Cups, Individual Chocolate-
    Grand Marnier Soufflés in 63
Orange Custard, Chocolate- 69
Orange Mousseline Filling,
    Chocolate- 50
Orange Sections, Chocolate-
    Dipped 151
Orange Sponge Cake 24

P
Parfait, Triple-Chocolate Mousse 85
Parfaits with Caramel-Fudge Sauce,
    Individual Chocolate 109
Parisian Cream 32
Pastry Cream, Cinnamon 55
Pastry Cream, Mint 49
Pastry Cream, White Chocolate 47
Pastry Shell, Almond 43
Pastry Shell, Sweet 59
Pastry, Choux 60
Pear Filling 76
Pear Pizza, Chocolate- 56
Pear Topping, Chocolate- 56
Pecan Brownies, Brandied
    Chocolate- 123
Pecan Crust, Cocoa- 112
Pecan Gâteau, chocolate- 5
Pecan Pie, Double-Chocolate 42
Pecan Torte, Chocolate- 33
Pecan-Cocoa Cake 33
Pecan-Cocoa Crumb Crust 17
Pecan Sundae Pie, Chocolate- 112
Petits Fours, Almond-Truffle 131
Pie Shell 58
Pies & Pastries 40-60
Pine Nut-Chocolate Chip Bars,
    Golden 125
Pistachio Genoise, Chocolate- 23
Pistachio, Chocolate & Vanilla
    Buttercreams 23
Pistachio-Chocolate Cake, Biarritz 23
Pizza, Chocolate-Pear 56
Poached Cherries 31
Powdered Sugar Glaze 51
Praline Chocolate Whipped Cream 54
Praline, Almond 171
Praline-Chocolate Soufflé,
    Hazelnut 64
Profiteroles with Hazelnut Cream 53
Pudding, Chocolate-Macadamia 70
Pudding, Steamed Chocolate-
    Macadamia Nut 70

Q
Queen of Sheba Cake 11
Quick Chocolate Curls 172
Quick Coffee Sauce 170
Quick Cognac Truffles 146
Quick Glaze 127

R
Raisin Rolls, Chocolate-Cinnamon 55
Raisin-Chocolate Bombe, Rum- 104
Raspberries, Chocolate Charlotte
    with 92
Raspberries, Chocolate Crème Brûlèe
    with 68
Raspberry Cake, Two-Tone
    Chocolate- 29
Raspberry Coupe, Chocolate- 102
Raspberry Filling, Chocolate- 126
Raspberry Mousse 87
Raspberry Sauce 102
Raspberry Soufflé, Cold
    Chocolate- 87
Raspberry-Brandy Sauce 168
Raspberry-Brandy Sauce, Flourless
    Fudge Cake with 12
Rich Chocolate Custard 68
Rich Chocolate Frosting 134
Rich Chocolate Genoise 20
Rich Chocolate Sauce 53
Rich Chocolate Sponge Cake 30
Rich Cocoa Sponge Cake 31
Rigo Jancsi 30
Rolls, Chocolate-Cinnamon Raisin 55
Rosettes, Chocolate-Marzipan 127
Royal Chocolate Charlotte 95
Rum Bavarian Cream, Chocolate- 88
Rum Syrup 170

Rum-Raisin-Chocolate Bombe 104
S
Sabra Sundae 102
Sachertorte 34
Sauces
    Blackberry Sauce 168
    Bourbon Sauce 164
    Chocolate Sauce 112
    Coffee-Chocolate Sauce 103
    Dark Chocolate Sauce 165
    Hot Caramel Fudge Sauce 166
    Quick Coffee Sauce 170
    Raspberry Sauce 102
    Raspberry-Brandy Sauce 168
    Spirited Cold Chocolate Sauce 165
    Strawberry Sauce 80
    Vanilla Bean Custard Sauce 169
Self-Frosted Chocolate Cake 16
Semisweet Ganache 122
Shaved chocolate 172
Shell, Almond Pastry 43
Soft Truffles 90
Soufflé with Candied Ginger, Frozen
    Chocolate 105
Soufflé, Bittersweet Chocolate-
    Chestnut 65
Soufflé, Cold Chocolate-Raspberry 87
Soufflé, Dark Chocolate-Bourbon 62
Soufflé, Frozen Chocolate 105
Soufflé, Hazelnut Praline-
    Chocolate 64
Soufflés in Orange Cups, Individual
    Chocolate-Grand Marnier 63
**Soufflés, Baked Custards, Puddings
    & Crepes 61-77**
Spiced Mexican Hot Cocoa 155
Spirited Cold Chocolate Sauce 165
Spirited White Chocolate Truffles 143
Sponge Cake 38
Sponge Cake, Bittersweet
    Chocolate 29
Sponge Cake, Chocolate 37
Sponge Cake, Chocolate Butter 5
Sponge Cake, Orange 24
Sponge Cake, Rich Chocolate 30
Sponge Cake, Rich Cocoa 31
Steamed Chocolate-Macadamia Nut
    Pudding 70
Strawberries, Double-Dipped 150
Strawberry Bombe, Chocolate- 108
Strawberry Sauce 80
Strawberry Sauce, White Chocolate
    Mousse with 80
Strawberry Topping 47
Strawberry-White Chocolate Tart 47
Substituting Regular Chocolate for
    "Couverture" 175
Sultan's Cream Puffs 50
Sundae Pie, Chocolate-Pecan 112
Sundae, Sabra 102
Sweet Pastry Shell 59
Sweet Yeast Dough 56
Swiss Roll with Berries & Cream,
    Chocolate 37
Syrup, Rum 170
Syrup, Kirsch 23

T
Tempering Chocolate 174
Terrine, Chocolate-Apricot 86
Thin Fudge Brownies 116
Topping, Chocolate-Pear 56
Topping, Light Chocolate-
    Cinnamon 130
Topping, Meringue 111
Traditional Truffles 140
Trifle, Black Forest 72
Triple Chocolate Chip Cookies 118
Triple-Chocolate Mousse Parfait 85

Truffle Cake, Hazelnut- 26
Truffle Petits Fours, Almond 131
Truffled Bavarian Cream, 90
Truffles, Bittersweet Belgian 141
Truffles, Café au Lait 145
**Truffles, Candies & Drinks
    138-156**
Truffles, Extra-Creamy 142
Truffles, Quick Cognac 146
Truffles, Soft 90
Truffles, Spirited White
    Chocolate 143
Truffles, Traditional 140
Two-Tone Chocolate-Raspberry
    Cake 29
Two-Toned Vacherin 114
Types of Chocolate viii

U
Useful Equipment 179
Using Egg Whites 178
Using Nuts 178

V
Vacherin, Two-Toned 114
Vanilla Bean Custard Sauce 169
Vanilla Buttercreams, Pistachio,
    Chocolate & 23
Vanilla Cream Fillings,
    Chocolate & 30
Viennese Chocolate-Nut Torte 32

W
Wafer Crust, Chocolate- 45
Walnut Bars, Chocolate 126
Walnut Bourbon Balls,
    Chocolate- 153
Walnut Cookie Dough 126
Walnut Crust, Chocolate- 48
Whipped Cream 2
Whipped Cream, Chocolate &
    Macadamia Liqueur 163
Whipped Cream, Chocolate 164
Whipped Cream, Grand Marnier 69
Whipped Cream, Hazelnut 53
Whipped Cream, Kahlua 67
Whipped Cream, Kirsch 163
Whipped Cream, Praline
    Chocolate 54
White & Cocoa Meringues,
    Baked 113
White & Dark Chocolate Chiffon
    Filling 48
White Chocolate Bavarian Squares 89
White Chocolate Cheesecake 16
White Chocolate Coating 143
White Chocolate Ganache 120
White Chocolate Mousse 39, 80
White Chocolate Mousse Cake with
    Dark Chocolate Chips 39
White Chocolate Mousse with
    Strawberry Sauce 80
White Chocolate Pastry Cream 47
White Chocolate Tart, Strawberry- 47
White Chocolate Truffles,
    Spirited 143
White Ganache Centers 143
Wine Cake, Chocolate 11

Y
Yeast Dough, Sweet 56
Yule Log, Chocolate 24

Z
Zuccotto 38